Study Guide

for use with
PRODUCTION/OPERATIONS MANAGEMENT

Sixth Edition

William J. Stevenson
Rochester Institute of Technology

Prepared by
William J. Stevenson
Paul Van Ness
Rochester Institute of Technology

**Irwin
McGraw-Hill**

Boston   Burr Ridge, IL   Dubuque, IA   Madison, WI   New York   San Francisco   St. Louis
Bangkok   Bogotá   Caracas   Lisbon   London   Madrid
Mexico City   Milan   New Delhi   Seoul   Singapore   Sydney   Taipei   Toronto

Irwin/McGraw-Hill

*A Division of The **McGraw·Hill** Companies*

Study Guide for use with
PRODUCTION/OPERATIONS MANAGEMENT

2 3 4 5 6 7 8 9 0 EDW/EDW 9 3 2 1 0 9 8

ISBN 0-07-290664-2

http://www.mhhe.com

PREFACE

This study guide is intended to provide you with supplemental material that can be used to enhance your understanding of the material presented in the textbook.

Among the important features of the study guide are:

1. Each chapter begins with a set of key ideas. These help to identify the most important elements of the chapter.
2. Many chapters have a section called "study tips" or "tips for solving problems." The first of these gives suggestions for approaching the material, which is important for very long chapters or for chapters having numerous models and/or formulas. The problem-solving tips are more specific to setting up problems, interpreting what a problem is asking for, and similar items. These are based on questions frequently asked by students such as yourself.
3. Each chapter has a sample test containing true/false and multiple-choice questions and a test key.
4. Most chapters have problems similar to those in the textbook. Solutions are provided for all problems.
5. The answers to the questions and the solutions to the problems immediately follow the chapter so as to minimize the chore of flipping through pages to find the answers. We recommend that you cover the answers while you are attempting the questions and the problems.

We, the authors, have found Production/Operations Management to be a challenging and rewarding field of study. We hope that you will, too.

TABLE OF CONTENTS

CHAPTER 1
PRODUCTION AND OPERATIONS MANAGEMENT

KEY IDEAS

1. Society provides goods and services to satisfy individual or collective needs and wants. Production uses capital and human knowledge to transform materials and services into products; these products can either be tangible (goods) or intangible (services). The essence of production/ operations management is managing the conversion of inputs outputs.

2. By systematizing operations, and by conducting training in the use of equipment, management makes it possible for employees to become skilled in their jobs; the productivity and efficiency of the system, and the quality and reliability of products are enhanced by supplementing training with incentives for doing good work.

3. Production/operations management designs the system and controls it; this include arranging facilities, scheduling tasks, developing procedures for inventory acquisition and turnover, as well as providing corrective actions to insure that changes are made whenever it is necessary to do so.

4. Production and operations systems can be classified in a variety of ways: degree of standardization, from highly standardized, such as an automobile assembly plant, to highly customized, such as a job shop; type, such as physical, storage, transportation exchange, entertainment or communication, and manufacturing vs service. In general manufacturing produces material goods that require a distribution system to get them into the hands of consumers, while service industries tend to deal directly with consumers.

5. Studying the historical evolution of production/operations management gives us an appreciation of how the current state of operations management developed, and some of the key elements of that development, such as *interchangeable parts* and the *division of labor*. it may also provide insight into future developments in the field.

6. An important new approach to production of manufactured goods is lean production. It gets its name from the fact that it requires less inventory, time, and other resources than mass production. The evolution of manufacturing began with craft production, where skilled workers using general purpose tools produced custom-made goods. This was supplanted by mass production in the early 1900s. In contrast to craft production, production workers were generally low-skill, machines were specialized, and jobs became narrow. Specialization and division of labor were key concepts. Costs decreased while quality and productivity increased. Mass production is starting to give way in some industries to lean production. Lean production has the advantage of greater flexibility than mass production, and can usually achieve higher quality than mass production.

7. There are quite a few current issues that have an impact on operations management, and hence, issues that operations managers (and other managers) must contend with. These issues include global competition, new emphasis on operations strategy, the advantages of flexibility, emphasis on time reduction, emphasis of quality, technology, involving workers in decision making and problem solving, and environmental issues.

8. The central purpose of this book is to provide an understanding of the theory and practice of operations management and the role of the operations manager, and of some of the quantitative techniques used to support good managerial practices at the operating level.

GLOSSARY

degree of standardization

> *customized output:* products or services designed to meet the specifications of a customer.

> *standardized output:* products or services designed to appeal to a broad set of customers.

craft production: one person (or perhaps a small crew) would be responsible for making the product from start to finish.

division of labor: an operation, such as assembling an automobile, is broken up into a series of small tasks

> and one of those tasks is assigned to a worker who repeats it on each individual product.

interchangeable parts: standardized parts, so that any part in a batch of identical parts would fit any individual product coming down the assembly line.

lead time: length of time needed to fill an order or to receive an order from a supplier.

lean production: a production system which emphasizes quality, flexibility, time reduction and teamwork.

> It has led to a *flattening* of the organizational structure with fewer levels of management.

mass production: large volumes of standardized goods are produced by low-skilled or semi-skilled workers using highly specialized, and often costly, equipment.

operations function: along with marketing and finance, one of the three primary functions in most business organizations. Operations consists of all activities related to producing goods or providing services.

operations management: responsible for systems that create goods or provide services. Includes both design and operation of production systems.

Pareto Principle: a relatively small percentage of items or factors are very important in achieving an objective or solving a problem.

production: the creation of goods or services.

re-engineering: a radical approach that involves "starting from scratch" by asking basic questions about processes such as how and why they are done the way they are, in order to significantly improve them.

transformation process: conversion of inputs into outputs.

type of operation

> *manufacturing:* production of a tangible output such as a toaster, a stereo.

> *service:* implies an act rather than a tangible output (e.g.. wash a car).

valued-added: the amount by which the price or value of an output is increased due to the addition of material, labor, or other resource.

TRUE/FALSE QUESTIONS

1. The three primary functions of a firm are financial management, operations management, and accounting.

2. Frederick W. Taylor is generally credited with introducing the moving assembly line.

3. The principal activity in all production operations is to convert inputs into outputs that satisfy consumer wants.

4. Human effort, technology, raw materials, information and time are all examples of the necessary inputs to operations.

5. The elements of the transformation process include the production system, equipment, facilities, and employee motivation and skill.

6. Outputs of operations may be classified as goods, raw materials and profits.

7. It is easier to measure productivity for an operation that provides services than for one that produces goods.

8. Both inputs and outputs are more uniform for an operation that provides services than for one that produces goods.

9. System design includes managing personnel, inventory management, scheduling, project management and quality assurance.

10. Craft production involves the use of interchangeable parts.

11. The operation of the production system includes capacity, location, layout and equipment-acquisition decisions.

12. According to the Pareto principle, a relatively few factors are very important in achieving an objective or solving a problem.

13. Two recent trends in P/OM are flexibility and specialization.

14. Mass production is based on the division of labor.

MULTIPLE-CHOICE QUESTIONS

1. Which one of the following would not generally be considered an aspect of operations management?
    a. Schedule work
    b. Secure financial resources
    c. Maintain quality
    d. Oversee the transformation process
    e. Manage inventories

2. Which one of the following is not a typical question dealt with by an operations managers?
    a. How much capacity will be needed in the months ahead?
    b. What is a satisfactory location for a new facility?
    c. Which products/services should be offered?
    d. How to motivate employees?
    e. All are typical of operations decisions.

3. Which one of these people was not involved in the Scientific Management movement?
    a. Henry Ford
    b. F. W. Taylor
    c. John D. Rockefeller
    d. Frank Gilbreth
    e. Lillian Gilbreth

4.   Which one of these was not mentioned in the list of recent trends in P/ OM?

a. Total quality management

b. Worker involvement

c. Global competition.

d. Automation.

e. Environmental issues.

5.   Which came *last* in the development of manufacturing techniques?

a. Lean production.

b. Division of labor.

c. Mass production.

d. Craft production.

e. Interchangeable parts.

6.   Match this list of contributions with the originator:

a. moving assembly line   1. F. W. Taylor

b. motion study principles   2. Henry Ford

c. principles of scientific management   3. Japanese manufacturers

d. interchangeable parts   4. Adam Smith

c. emphasis on quality and time reduction   5. Frank Gilbreth

f. division of labor   6. Eli Whitney

g. emphasis on manufacturing strategy   7. W. Skinner

CHAPTER 1 INTRODUCTION

True/False

Question	Answer	Glossary/ Key Idea	Textbook ref. Page
1	F		6
2	F		21
3	T	1	6-7
4	T	1	8
5	T	2, 3	8
6	F	1	8
7	F		13-14
8	F		13-14
9	F		12
10	F		18,21
11	F		12
12	T	G	17
13	F	6	24-27
14	T		21

Multiple-Choice

Question	Answer	Glossary/ Key Idea	Textbook ref. page
1	b		8-9,12
2	e		12
3	c		19-21
4	d	6	24-27
5	a		27
6	a-2		20
	b-5		
	c-1		
	d-6		
	e-3		
	f-4		
	g-7		

CHAPTER 2
PRODUCTIVITY, COMPETITIVENESS, AND STRATEGY

KEY IDEAS

1. The operations manager makes both strategic broad-scope decisions, and tactical moderate-scope decisions, as well as running the day-to-day operations of the production system. Strategic planning includes selecting products, choosing locations and technology, and overseeing new construction. Tactical decisions include setting employment and output levels, selecting equipment and controlling the flow of funds.

2. A key responsibility of the production manager is to achieve productive use of an organization's resources. This is often measured as the ratio of outputs to inputs which is called a productivity ratio. The closer the ratio is to 1.0, the higher the productivity; the closer the ratio is to 0.0, the lower the productivity. U.S. productivity is high, but many other nations are close behind, and gaining at a rapid pace. Productivity is important because it relates to an organization's ability to compete, and to the overall wealth and standard of living of a nation. Productivity is affected by work methods, capital, quality, technology, and management. A list of ways that productivity can be improved is given in the textbook.

3. The postwar experience of Japanese industry has provided lessons in management effectiveness, quality low-cost production, and employee motivation; it has also enabled Japan to overcome a prewar reputation for low quality, and to become a leading industrial power, even though the country has limited natural resources.

4. Business organizations compete with each other in a variety of ways, such as price, quality, product or service features, flexibility, and delivery time. Operations and marketing functions must decide on an approach to competition, and work together to achieve success, capitalizing on strengths and exploiting competition weaknesses.

5. The most successful business organizations have carefully thought out strategies for accomplishing the mission and the goals of the organization. Corporate strategy is the overall strategy of the organization. It is affected by both Internal and external factors. These are listed and described in your textbook. Operations strategy should support the corporate strategy. It has a narrower focus; it pertains to the transformation aspect of the organization's activities. Operations strategy often relates to cost, quality, flexibility, and availability of products or services.

GLOSSARY

competition: the efforts of two or more parties to secure the business of another party by offering the most favorable terms.

competitiveness: how successful one party is in offering favorable terms and securing the business. More favorable terms may involve a lower price, higher quality, a faster delivery time, and other aspects of the product.

hierarchy of decisions: strategic decisions (broad scope) establish the framework for tactical decisions (moderate scope) which in turn establish the framework for operating decisions (narrow scope).

mission: the basis for an organization; its reason or purpose.

operations strategy: the management of processes, methods, resources, quality, costs, lead time, and scheduling in order to produce a product or a service.

productivity: a measure of output relative to input; the ratio of output to input.

strategy: a general plan for achieving a goal.

tactic: a method or action intended to accomplish a strategy.

TRUE/FALSE QUESTIONS

1. The mission of a firm should be designed to support the firm's overall strategy.

2. Operations managers measure productivity as the ratio of input to output.

3. Productivity can be measured only on workers.

4. Value is the ratio of the performance of the product to its cost.

5. A company can compete with other companies manufacturing a similar product only by reducing its price.

6. Much of the responsibility for improving productivity rests with management.

MULTIPLE-CHOICE QUESTIONS

1. Which of the following can have a positive impact on productivity?
   a. Low propensity of consumers to save.
   b. Use of robots.
   c. Government regulations.
   d. Increasing demand for services.
   e. Emphasis on long-run performance.

2. Which one of the following is not generally cited as a negative impact on productivity?
   a. Government regulations
   b. Liability claims
   c. Increased emphasis on services
   d. Emphasis on short-term performance
   e. All are reasons.

3. Which is the correct hierarchy of operations management decisions (highest first)?
   a. Operating, tactical, strategic
   b. Operating, strategic, tactical
   c. Tactical, strategic, operating
   d. Strategic, operating, tactical
   e. Strategic, tactical, operating

4. Which formula correctly describes productivity?

   a. $\dfrac{Output - Input}{Output}$ c. $\dfrac{Output}{Input}$

   b. $\dfrac{Input - Output}{Input}$ d. $\dfrac{Input}{Output}$

5.   Operations strategy is affected by both internal and external factors. Which one of the following would come under both headings (internal and external)?

    a. Competition

    b. Technology

    c. Suppliers

    d. Markets

    e. Facilities and equipment

6.   Which of these is not usually a basis for competition?

    a. Flexibility

    b. Price

    c. Quality

    d. Strategy

    e. Product differentiation

7.   Order qualifiers refer to:

    a. distinctive competencies.

    b. minimum standards of acceptability.

    c. value added in manufacturing.

    d. environmental scanning.

    e. price competition.

PROBLEMS

1.   The Cool-Tech Company produces various types of fans. In May, the company produced 1,728 window fans at a standard price of $40.00. The company has 12 direct labor employees whose compensation (including wages and fringe benefits) amounts to $21.00 per hour. During May, window fans were produced on 9 working days (of 8 hours each), and other products were produced on other days. Determine the labor productivity of the window fans.

2.   The Cool-Tech Company (see # 1) also produces desk fans at a standard price of $25.00. During May, 1,872 desk fans were produced on 11 working days (of 8 hours each). On one day, two employees called in sick.

    a. Determine the labor productivity of the desk fans.

    b. Was productivity higher for the window fans or for the desk fans in May?

3.   Here is additional information about the Cool-Tech Company (see #1 & #2). There were 20 working days in May. The direct material cost of window fans is $7.00; the direct material cost of desk fans is $5.00. The annual overhead expense incurred in operating the factory is $144,000.

    a. Determine the multi-factor productivity of the Cool-Tech Company in May.

    b. What is the interpretation of the multi-factor productivity?

CHAPTER 2 PRODUCTIVITY, COMPETITION, AND STRATEGY

True/False

Question	Answer	Glossary/ Key Idea	Textbook ref. page
1	F	G	45
2	F	G, 3	38-40
3	F		40
4	T		44
5	F		43-44
6	T	2	38

Multiple-Choice

Question	Answer	Glossary/ Key Idea	Textbook ref. page
1	e		40-42
2	b		40-41
3	e	1	47
4	c	G, 2	38
5	b		51-52
6	d		43-44
7	b		48

SOLUTIONS TO PROBLEMS

1. P = Productivity

   W = Number of window fans = 1728

   H = Number of direct labor hours = 8 hours per day

   E = Number of employees = 12

   D = Number of working days = 9

   $$P = \frac{W}{E*D*H} = \frac{1728}{12*9*8} = 2 \text{ fans per hour.}$$

2. P = Productivity

   F = Number of desk fans = 1,872

   H = Number of direct labor hours = 8 hours per day

   E_1 = Number of employees = 12; E_2 = Number of employees = 12 - 2 = 10

   D_1 = Number of days = 11 - 1 = 10 D_2 = Number of days = 1

   a. $P = \dfrac{F}{(E_1*D_1*H)+(E_2*D_2*H)} = \dfrac{1872}{(12*10*8)+(10*1*8)} = 1.8 \text{ fans per hour.}$

   b. The productivity of the window fans is higher.

3. P = Multi-factor productivity

   W_S = Standard price of window fans = $40

   F_S = Standard price of desk fans = $25

   L = Labor cost per hour = $21

   M_W = Direct material cost of window fans = $7

   M_F = Direct material cost of desk fans = $5

   H = Total direct labor hours = 864 + 1040 = 1904

   a. $P = \dfrac{(W*W_S)+(F*F_S)}{(H*L)+(W*M_W)+(F*M_F)} = \dfrac{(1728*40)+(1872*25)}{(1904*21)+(1728*7)+(1872*5)} = 1.89$

   b. A dollar's worth of inputs produces $1.89 worth of outputs.

CHAPTER 2S
DECISION MAKING

KEY IDEAS

1. Managers are decision makers. By making decisions, they exert an influence over the resources of the organization. Hence, decision making is a fundamental part of management. decision making consists of these steps:

    (1) Specify objectives and decision criteria

    (2) Develop a list of alternatives

    (3) Analyze alternatives

    (4) Select the best alternative

    (5) Implement the alternative

    (6) Monitor results

2. A key tool in decision making is the use of models, which are abstractions of reality. Models are valuable to decision makers because they enable decision makers to focus on a relatively few important aspects of a decision, they provide the ability to manipulate variables, and they increase understanding of a problem.

3. Poor decisions can occur for a variety of reasons, including faulty or inadequate information, failure to consider key alternatives, and skipping or rushing through some of the steps listed above.

4. Decision theory is a general approach to decision making that can be used for decisions that involve a set of possible future conditions (states of natures) that will affect the payoff to the organization, a list of alternatives from which to choose, and an estimated payoff for each alternative under each possible future condition. It can be very helpful to organize this information-nation into a payoff table, listing the alternatives down the left side of the table, the possible future conditions across the top of the table, and the payoffs in the body of the table.

5. If estimated probabilities for events are available, the environment is one of risk. A typical approach in such cases is the following:

    a. Compute the expected payoff for each alternative using the probabilities.

    b. The alternative with the best expected payoff is the optimal decision.

    c. Additional information over and above that specified can sometimes be obtained. The *expected value of perfect information (EVPI)* is the difference between the *expected value of the best payoff each* event and the *expected value of the payoffs for the best* (single) alternative; an alternative definition of EVPI is expected regret.

6. If probabilities for events are unknown, the environment is one of uncertainty, and one or more of four decision criteria can help us decide which alternative is best:

    maximin (pessimistic): the alternative with the best value of the worst payoffs.

    maximax (optimistic): the alternative with the best payoff.

    Laplace (equal weights): since the actual probabilities for events are unknown, for each alternative compute the expected value of the payoff, assuming every event has the same probability weight; the event with the highest expected payoff is the one selected.

minimax regret (cautious):. the terms "regret" and "opportunity loss" mean the same thing: given an event E, for every alternative A. compute the difference between each payoff and the best payoff obtainable for any alternative with E, that difference is called regret. Calculate the regrets for every (A, E) pair and organize them into a matrix having the same dimensions as the payoff matrix. Select the alternative with the lowest value of the highest regrets, the minimax regret.

7. Because the four uncertainty criteria all have different psychological bases, varying from extreme pessimism about the outcome to extreme outcomes, it would be most unusual if all of them agreed on what the right decision Is. As a test for the reasonableness of the results obtained from this analysis, the decision maker should select the criterion that comes closest to representing the decision maker's own psychological makeup, and compare results with one or more of the other four criteria.

8. In this discussion, payoff is considered to be "positive" profit or revenue. The same decision process can be applied to costs, which are considered to be negative, including events, alternatives and payoffs.

9. In the special case that there are just two states of nature, say El and E2,. sensitivity studies can be performed graphically to find ranges of probability values for optimal decision making, without assuming that the probability distribution is known. The type of graph is shown in Example 8 of Chapter 2S. The horizontal axis is p, the probability of event E2, and (1 - p) is the probability of El; the vertical axes show the payoffs. At the lefthand edge p = 0.0, denoting that the probability of E2 is 0.0 and the probability of El is 1.0; at the right-hand edge, the probabilities are reversed, 1.0 for E2 and 0.0 for E1. For each decision alternative draw a straight line from the point representing the of (A, El) at p = 0.0 to the point denoting the payoff of (A, E2) at p = 1.0. Every point on that line payoff is the expected value of alternative A for the respective p. The solid line at the top of the graph shows the highest expected payoff for every value of p, and the decision alternative associated with that payoff.

GLOSSARY

alternative: one of the choices available to the decision maker.

certainty: the event that will occur is known beforehand.

event: see state of nature.

expected value: for an alternative, obtained by multiplying each payoff by the column probability and summing the results; the mean.

expected value of perfect information (EVPI): the expected payoff assuming certainty minus the optimal payoff under risk; also the expected value of the regret for the alternative that has the best expected value.

Laplace criterion: assign equal probabilities to all events, and choose the alternative with the highest expected value.

maximax criterion: an optimistic approach to decision making under uncertainty; select the alternative with the best single payoff.

maximin criterion: a pessimistic view of the possible outcomes of the decision process under uncertainty; select the alternative with the best of the worst payoffs.

minimax regret criterion: a cautious approach to decision making under uncertainty; the absolute value of the difference between the payoff associated with an alternative-event pair (A, E) and the highest payoff for any decision in the E column of the matrix.

model: a simplified version of something; an abstraction of reality.

payoff: for every alternative/state of nature combination, the associated profit, cost, etc.

payoff matrix: a two-way layout, the rows representing the decision-maker's alternatives and the columns nature's events; an entry in a cell of the matrix is the payoff associated with the corresponding event and alternative.

probability: see probability distribution.

probability distribution: a set of nonnegative numbers called probabilities, each probability represents the chance that its corresponding event will occur; the sum of the probabilities for all events is 1.00.

regret: the difference between the payoff associated with an alternative-event pair (A,E) and the highest payoff for any alternative in the E column of the matrix; also known as the opportunity loss.

risk: there is a known probability distribution for the events.

sensitivity: the extent to which the results of modeling are influenced by changes in the probabilities or the probability distribution.

state of nature: an event that could occur, that would not be under the control of the decision maker.

uncertainty: the possible events that could occur are known, but the probability distribution is unknown.

TRUE/FALSE QUESTIONS

1. States of nature are alternatives available to a decision maker.

2. Certainty is a situation that exists when it is known which state of nature will occur.

3. The expected value of perfect information (EVPI) is the expected value of the difference between the payoff of a decision under certainty and the optimal decision under risk.

4. EVPI is the expected value of the regret for the optimal decision under risk.

5. Minimax opportunity loss and minimax regret are actually the same thing.

6. With both risk and uncertainty the probabilities for events are known.

7. A decision tree branches out all of the possible decisions and all of the possible events.

8. The expected value of the payoff for the optimal decision under risk is the best payoff that can be had without acquiring additional information.

9. An example of maximax decision making is when people buy lottery tickets hoping for a very big payoff.

MULTIPLE CHOICE QUESTIONS

1. Which of the following is not a criterion for decision making under uncertainty?
   a. EVPI
   b. Maximin
   c. Maximax
   d. Laplace method
   e. Minimax regret

2. Which one of the following statements is not correct relative to decision making under risk?
   a. The sum of the state-of-nature probabilities must be 1.00.
   b. Every probability must be greater than or equal to zero.
   c. All probabilities are assumed to be equal.
   d. Probabilities are used to compute expected values.
   e. Perfect information assumes that the state of nature that will actually occur is known.

The next three questions are based on the following payoff table of the present values:

Alternative	High	Low
buy	90	-10
rent	70	40
lease	60	55

3. The maximax strategy is:
    a. buy   b. lease   c. rent   d. high   e. low

4. The maximin strategy is:
    a. buy   b. lease   c. rent   d. high   e. low

5. If the probability of the state of nature "high" is 0.7, the decision with the highest expected value is:
    a. buy   b. lease   c. rent   d. high   e. low

6. Which one of the following is not a step in the decision-making process?
    a. Identifying the problem.
    b. Specifying objectives
    c. Developing alternatives
    d. Analyzing alternatives
    e. Selecting the best alternative

7. Which one of the following would not generally be given as a reason for poor decisions?
    a. Unforeseeable circumstances
    b. Bounded rationality
    c. Suboptimization
    d. Mistakes in the decision process
    e. All are reasons

PROBLEMS

1. Here is a payoff matrix; parentheses designate a loss, The probabilities of the states of nature, $p(1)$ and $p(2)$, are unknown.

Alternatives	States of Nature 1	2
A	$500	$300
B	700	100
C	(300)	600

a. Which alternative should be selected under the maximax criterion?
    b. Which alternative should be selected under the maximin criterion?
    c. Which alternative should be selected under the Laplace criterion?
    d. What is the opportunity loss table?
    e. Which alternative should be selected under the minimax regret criterion?

2. Refer to Problem 1. Construct the sensitivity graph, as shown on p. 80 of your textbook.
    a. For what range of values of $p(2)$ is alternative A preferred?
    b. For what range of values of $p(2)$ is alternative B preferred?
    c. For what range of values of $p(2)$ is alternative C preferred?

3. Fall has come, and the department manager of the Purple Pentagon Discount Store must decide how many snow blowers to order for the winter season. He believes there is an association between the weather and the demand for snow blowers: a winter with heavy snow should produce a high demand, and a winter with light snow should produce a low demand. However, if he guesses wrong and orders a large number of snow blowers when the weather turns out to have light snow, he will suffer a loss. Here is his payoff matrix.

	States of Nature		
Alternatives	Heavy snow	Medium snow	Light snow
Large Order	$5,000	$1,000	$(4,000)
Medium Order	2,000	3,000	(2,000)
Small Order	500	500	1,000

    a.   Which alternative should be selected under the maximax criterion?

    b.   Which alternative should be selected under the maximin criterion?

    c.   Which alternative should be selected under the Laplace criterion?

    d.   What is the opportunity loss table?

    e.   Which alternative should be selected under the minimax regret criterion?

4. Refer to Problem 3. Suppose that the following probabilities are available regarding the snowfall next winter:

p(heavy snow) = .10

p(medium snow) = .50

p(light snow) = .40

    a.   Which alternative should be selected under the expected value criterion?

    b.   Which alternative should be selected under the lowest expected loss criterion?

    c.   What is the value of the EVPI?

    d.   What is the interpretation of the EVPI?

5. Solve problem #4 by using an EXCEL spreadsheet.

    a..   Find the expected monetary values. .

    b.   Find the largest expected monetary value.

    c.   Find the expected value of perfect information.

    d.   Compare the answers on your spreadsheet to the answers to problem #4.

6. (One step beyond) Here is a payoff matrix, in which the value of one payoff (X) is unknown.

	States of Nature	
	1 p = .20	2 p = .80
Alternative		
A	$500	$1,200
B	X	400

    a. Find the value of X for which the decision maker will be indifferent between alternatives A and B.

    b. Suppose X = $4,000. Will the decision maker prefer alternative A or alternative B?

CHAPTER 2S   DECISION MAKING

True/False

Question	Answer	Glossary/ Key Idea	Textbook ref. page
1	F	G, 4	66
2	T	G	67
3	T	G, 5c	71
4	T	G, 5c	71
5	T	G, 6	68
6	F	6	65
7	T		69-70
8	T	5b	69,71
9	T	6	67

Multiple-Choice

Question	Answer	Glossary/ Key Idea	Textbook ref. page
1	a	6	67,71
2	c		69
3	a		67-68
4	b		67-68
5	c		69
6	a	1	64
7	e	3	65

SOLUTIONS TO PROBLEMS

1.   a. The maximax criterion involves selecting the best payoff for each alternative and then selecting the best payoff in that set.

Alternative	Best Payoff
A	$500
B	700 (best)
C	600

Implement Alternative B.

b. The maximin criterion involves selecting the worst payoff for each alternative and then selecting the best payoff in that set.

Alternative	Worst Payoff
A	$300 (best)
B	100
C	(300)

Implement Alternative A.

c. The LaPlace criterion involves selecting the best mean payoff.

Alternative	Mean Payoff
A	$400* (tie)
B	400 (tie)
C	150

Implement Alternative A or Alternative B.

*Note: (500 + 300)/2 = 400.

d. Find the regret for each cell by subtracting each entry in the state of nature <u>column</u> from the maximum entry in the column.

State of Nature

Alternative	1	2
A	200	300
B	0	500
C	1,000	0

e. The minimax regret criterion involves selecting the worst regret for each alternative, and then selecting the best of that set.

Alternative	Worst Regret
A	$300 (best)
B	500
C	1,000

Implement Alternative A.

2.

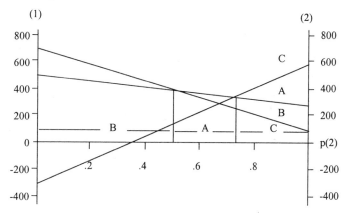

(1)   (2)

At the points where the lines in the diagram intersect the y coordinates are equal; $y = a + bx$, where a is the intercept on the (1) column and b = payoff #2 - payoff #1.

A line: $y = 500 + (300 - 500)x = 500 - 200x$.

B line: $y = 700 + (100 - 700)x = 700 - 600x$.

C line: $y = -300 + (600 - (-300))x = -300 + 900x$.

The A line and the B line intersect.

$$500 - 200p(2) = 700 - 600p(2)$$

$$-200 = -400p(2)$$

$$p(2) = 0.5$$

$$p(1) = 1 - p(2) = 1 - 0.5 = 0.5.$$

The A line and the C line intersect.

$$500 - 200p(2) = -300 + 900p(2)$$
$$800 = 1100p(2)$$
$$p(2) = 0.727$$
$$p(1) = 1 - p(2) = 1 - 0.727 = .273.$$

a. Choose A for $0.5 < p(2) < 0.727$.

b. Choose B for $0 < p(2) < 0.5$.

c. Choose C for $0.727 < p(2) < 1.0$.

3.   a.

Alternative	Best Payoff
Large Order	$5,000 (best)
Medium Order	3,000
Small Order	1,000

Place a large order.

b.

Alternative	Worst Payoff
Large Order	($5,000)
Medium Order	(2,000)
Small Order	500 (best)

Place a small order.

c.

Alternative	Mean Payoff
Large Order	$667*
Medium Order	1,000
Small Order	667

Place a medium order.

*Note: (5000 + 1000 - 4000)/3 = 667.

d. Find the regret for each cell in the payoff matrix by subtracting each entry in the state of nature <u>column</u> from the maximum payoff in the column. For the Heavy Snow column, the best payoff is $5,000, and the regrets are 0, $3,000, and $4,500.

State of Nature

Alternative	Heavy Snow	Medium Snow	Light Snow
Large Order	0	2,000	5,000
Medium Order	3,000	0	3,000
Small Order	4,500	2,500	0

e.

Alternative	Worst Regret
Large Order	$5,000
Medium Order	3,000 (best)
Small Order	4,500

Place a medium order.

4. a.

	State of Nature			
	Heavy Snow	Medium Snow	Light Snow	Expected
Alternative	.10	.50	.40	Value
Large Order	5,000	1,000	(4,000)	(600)*
Medium Order	2,000	3,000	(2,000)	900 (best)
Small Order	500	500	1,000	700

Place a medium order.

*Note: 5000(.10) + 1000(.50) - 4000(.40) = -600.

b.

	State of Nature			
	Heavy Snow	Medium Snow	Light Snow	Expected
Alternative	.10	.50	.40	Loss
Large Order	0	2,000	5,000	3,000*
Medium Order	3,000	0	3,000	1,500 (best
Small Order	4,500	2,500	0	1,700

*Note: 0(.10) + 2000(.50) + 5000(.40) = 3000.

Place a medium order. The strategy which is selected by the least expected loss criterion will always be the same as the one selected by the best expected value criterion.

c. EVPI = least expected loss = $1,500.

d. $1,500 is the absolute maximum which might be spent to obtain information about the states of nature. The manager might, for example, hire a weather forecaster to forecast next winter's snowfall.

	State of Nature		
	Heavy Snow	Medium Snow	Light Snow
Alternative	.10	.50	.40
Large Order	$5,000	$1,000	-$4,000
Medium Order	2,000	3,000	2,000
Small Order	500	500	1,000

a. In Cell H-8: =D6*D8+E6*E8+F6*F8

In Cell H-9: =D6*D9+E6*E9+F6*F9

In Cell H-10: =D6*D10+E6*E10+F6*F10

b. In Cell D-12: =MAX(H8:H10)

c. In Cell D-13: =MAX(D8:D10)*D6+MAX(E8:E10)*E6+MAX(F8:F10)*F6-D12

d. Did you get the same answers?

5.

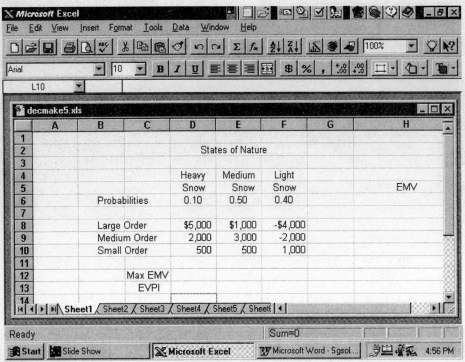

a. In Cell H-8: =D6*D8+E6*E8+F6*F8
    In Cell H-9: =D6*D9+E6*E9+F6*F9
    In Cell H-10: =D6*D10+E6*E10+F6*F10
b. In Cell D-12: =MAX(H8:H10)
c. In Cell D-13: =MAX(D8:D10)*D6+MAX(E8:E10)*E6+MAX(F8:F10)*F6-D12
d. Did you get the same answers?

6. a. Set E(A) = E(B); solve for X.
        .20(500) + .80(1200) = .20X + .80(400)
        X = $3,700.
    b. Since E(B) > E(A) at X = $4,000, the decision maker would prefer alternative B.

CHAPTER 3
FORECASTING

KEY IDEAS

1.   Successful operations planning requires good forecasts.

2.   Forecasting is imprecise, but the errors in prior forecasts are measurable.

3.   There are both qualitative and quantitative forecast systems.

    a.   The qualitative systems include expert or executive opinions, sales force composites, opinion surveys and the Delphi technique. The Delphi method includes a sequence of questionnaires administered to a select group of qualified experts; the design of each questionnaire is based upon the results of the previous questionnaire.

    b.   Quantitative forecasting methods include exponential smoothing, moving averages, and associative (regression-based) systems. A forecast system may be a combination of several of these.

    c.   The "naive" model is a simple special case: the value for the next period is predicted to be the same as it was in the previous period. An alternative version of a naive model is that the difference between the value for this period and the value for the next period will be the same as the difference between the last period and this one.

4.   The accuracy of a forecast system depends upon:

    a.   accuracy of the historical time series data

    b.   similarity of patterns between the past and the future

    c.   grouping or aggregation of the data series

    d.   time lapse between the historical periods and the period for which the prediction is being made

    e.   choice of a model.

5.   Exponential smoothing is an of adaptive forecasting technique with some advantages over other types of moving averages and other statistically based measures. These advantages include:

    a.   the calculations are simple.

    b.   the weighting pattern can be changed simply by changing the smoothing constant.

    Both exponential smoothing and simple moving averages smooth the data and lag changes in a time series.

6.   If there is trend in the historical data, single exponentially smoothed forecasts tend to lag behind the actual values. Therefore, it is necessary to incorporate trend adjustments, with double smoothing.

7.   Associative techniques involve the use of predictor (independent) variables in equation form to estimate values of the variable of interest (dependent variable). Least squares analysis is used to obtain the coefficients of the regression equation. [Note the comments on the use of linear regression analysis in your textbook.]

8.   Moving averages and trend lines can be used to compute monthly, weekly or daily indexes that show how one part of a "season" compares to the average value of a time series. These indexes are used in conjunction with trend calculations to generate spot predictions that take account of the cycle of demand or economic activity within a period of a year, as well as of the long-run changes over a period of several years.

9.   This chapter shows how to continuously monitor and control the accuracy of ES forecasts. The mean absolute deviation (MAD) is a measure of how far the actual values were from the predictions for previous periods, on the average. The tracking signal (TS) is a measure of the bias of the differences between the actual values and the predictions.

TIPS FOR SOLVING PROBLEMS

Many of the end-of-chapter problems are fairly specific in terms of what you are required to do. However, two frequently encountered questions are (1) Which technique should I use? and (2) How can I tell if the forecast is working properly?

In terms of which technique to use, begin by plotting the data. Does the plot reveal a trend? If so, either a trend line or trend-adjusted exponential smoothing should be used. A linear trend line requires less effort than trend-adjusted smoothing requires. If no trend is present, select one of the averaging techniques, such as moving average or exponential smoothing. Whether trend or averaging is used, you may also want to consider whether seasonal variations are a factor. Again, examine the plot to determine if major ups and downs occur periodically. Note that when annual data are plotted, seasonality cannot be discerned because these values have been aggregated into annual amounts, thereby concealing any possible seasonal variation.

In terms of the forecast working properly, the preferred approach is to use a control chart to analyze forecast errors. A forecast can be said to be working properly if (a) all errors are within the control limits, and (b) a plot of errors does not reveal any patterns such as trends, cycling, etc.

GLOSSARY

action limits: for a tracking signal, the "tracks" or outer limits of the value of the TS; a tendency to go outside the action limits is an indication that some feature of the forecasting model, such as the value of one of the smoothing constants, might be changed so as to keep the TS inside the limits.

alpha (α): *see* single exponential smoothing.

associative forecasting: forecasting such as regression that estimates the effects of a causal variable or variables upon a dependent variable.

autoregressive series: a set of time series data that shows a great deal of dependence of the results for one period on the results of previous periods.

bias: The tendency of forecast errors to be successively positive or negative.

causal variable: a variable whose changes in value cause fluctuations in other variables; for example, the duty on imported steel affects the price of steel in the USA.

centered moving average: a moving average that is positioned at the middle of the group of numbers it represents.

composite: a forecast taken by averaging the results of opinion surveys of employees or specialists in the field, such as, for example, salesmen.

control chart: a technique that shows the extent to which the differences between forecasted and actual values stay within predefined statistically computed ranges; control charts are used extensively in quality control and are discussed at greater length in Chapter 10.

correlation: the degree to which the values of two variables have a tendency to change in the same (or opposite) directions.

decomposition: isolating seasonal cyclical, trend and random effects in a time-series data.

Delphi technique: forecasting that forms a consensus of qualified experts, in a series of stages; the results of the questionnaire at one stage are used to redesign the questionnaire at the next stage, and, if necessary, to redefine the problem for which the predictions are being made.

double exponential smoothing: removing the lag inherent in single exponential smoothing, by a model that combines single exponential smoothing of the raw data with secondary exponential smoothing of the predictions.

judgmental forecast: a forecast based entirely upon the experience and personal opinions of a qualified expert.

lag: a specified difference between actual and forecasted values, expressed in time units (e.g., years), rather than in customary physical or monetary units.

linear regression: see regression.

mean absolute deviation (MAD): the average of the absolute differences between the actual values and the predictions.

mean square error (MSE): the variance computed by averaging the squared differences between the predicted and the actual values.

moving average: a sequence of averages, derived from a set of time-series data, for a period of time, such as a season, week, month or day; each average covers n such periods and is computed by deleting the first period from the previous MA, and adding in the most recent period.

naive model: a prediction that the value in the next period will be the same as what it is in the current period, or *else* that the difference between the current period and the next one will be the same as the difference between the current period and the most recent one.

regression: a technique for generating forecasts by computing a linear (straight-line) equation that shows the influence of time or some other causal variable upon the dependent variable whose values are being forecasted.

seasonal relative: an index that expresses the degree to which the value of a series in a particular season tends to vary from the "average" if there were no seasonal variations.

simple (unweighted) average: an average that assigns equal weight to every member of a data series included in the average.

single exponential smoothing: smoothing by computing the weighted average of the most recent value and the most recent prediction; the most recent actual value has a weight of $0 < \alpha < 1$ and the most recent predicted value has a weight of $1 - \alpha$.

smoothing constant: see single exponential smoothing.

technological forecasting: forecasting that takes account of future anticipated technological changes.

time series: a time-ordered sequence of observations, made at regular intervals.

tracking signal (TS): a measure of the difference between the forecasted and the actual values; a good forecast will always have a TS within a range centering on zero, for example ±4, and there would be about the same number of values above zero as below zero.

trend: a long-term tendency of a time series to increase or decrease.

trend-adjusted smoothing: see double exponential smoothing.

TRUE/FALSE QUESTIONS

1. Accurate forecasting can be done with inaccurate historical data, providing the forecasting model is a good one.

2. Aggregated (grouped) data frequently generate better forecasts than non-aggregated data.

3. Simple exponential smoothing is a type of forecasting for which the forecasted values tend to lag behind the actual values.

4. Forecast accuracy decreases as the time horizon increases.

5.   If a particular season of the year shows greater than average sales, the seasonal relative for that season is greater than 1.00.

6.   The Delphi technique is a forecasting model that incorporates the use of multiple regression.

7.   A double exponentially smoothed model is more responsive to trend in the data series than a single smoothed model.

8.   The MAD is the average of the squared differences between the actual and the forecasted values.

9.   The tracking signal is supposed to run between the action limits,

10.   The tracking signal is computing using MAD.

11.   The MSE is the average of the squared differences between the actual and the forecasted values.

12.   In a good forecast, about half of the errors, e_i , should be randomly scattered above zero and half below zero.

13.   Single exponential smoothing should not be used where the data have a trend..

14.   A control chart is preferable to a tracking signal for monitoring forecast errors.

15.   Seasonality refers to data patterns that recur every year (or every week, or every month, etc.) at about the same time.

16.   Associative forecasting techniques are used to obtain seasonal indexes.

MULTIPLE-CHOICE QUESTIONS

1.   Which of the following forecasting techniques generates trend forecasts?
   a.   Delphi method
   b.   Sales force composites
   c.   Moving averages
   d.   Single exponential smoothing
   e.   None of the above

2.   For this set of errors: - 1, + 4, 0, + 2, + 3, MAD is:
   a.   1.0
   b.   1. 6
   c.   2.0
   d.   2.5

3.   Which probability distribution is used most extensively in dealing with forecasting errors?
   a.   Normal
   b.   Poisson
   c.   Exponential
   d.   Beta
   e.   Pareto

4.　Select the statement about moving averages and exponential smoothing that is not true.
　　a.　Both tend to lag changes in a series.
　　b.　Both smooth data.
　　c.　Both involve fairly simple calculations.
　　d.　Both can be used obtain seasonal index numbers.

5.　Demand data with relatively little variation about the mean value will tend to have a:
　　a.　low cumulative forecast error and a high MAD.
　　b.　high cumulative forecast error and a low MAD.
　　c.　low cumulative forecast error and a low MAD.
　　d.　high cumulative forecast error and a high MAD.

6.　The cumulative forecast error is important for determining the:
　　a.　Mean squared error.
　　b.　Bias in forecast error.
　　c.　Mean absolute deviation.
　　d.　Control limits.

7.　Of these values, the value of α that would track the data most closely is:
　　a.　0
　　b.　.01
　　c.　.10
　　d.　.20
　　e.　.30

PROBLEMS

1.　The data below consist of the closing price of the common stock of the American Telephone and Telegraph Corporation on some recent Fridays. Common stock prices are quoted in sixteenths of a dollar (1/16 = $.0625).

Time(t)	Price	Time(t)	Price
1	$45.2500	5	$48.0000
2	50.3125	6	55.6875
3	48.8750	7	55.8750
4	48.0000	8	57.3750

　　a.　Using a five-period moving average, forecast the price of the stock for period 9.
　　b.　In period 9. the actual price was $57.6250. What is the error of the forecast?
　　c.　Using a five-period moving average, forecast the price of the stock for period 10.

2. A product is manufactured in distinct batches of various sizes. The cost accountant wished to obtain an equation to use for estimating the cost of a batch. He obtained data on a number of batches, consisting of the size of the batch, measured in number of pieces, and the total cost of the batch, consisting of the setup cost and the variable costs of labor, material, etc. The total cost is stated in thousands of dollars. Here is the data.

Size of Batch	Cost of Batch
20	$1.4
30	3.4
40	4.1
50	3.8
70	6.7
80	6.6
100	7.8
120	10.4
150	11.7
650	$55.9

   a. Which is the dependent variable? The independent variable?

   b. Draw the scatterplot of this data. Does a straight line look like a reasonable fit?

   c. Obtain the x^2, xy, and y^2 columns.

   d. What is the value of the slope?

   e. What is the interpretation of the slope?

   f. What is the value of the y intercept?

   g. What is the interpretation of the y intercept?

   h. Estimate the cost of a batch of 125 pieces.

   i. What is the value of the coefficient of correlation? Does it appear to indicate a high degree of association between the size of the batch and the cost?

   j. What is the value of r^2?

3. The president of the Rich and Greene College of Business Administration wishes to forecast the enrollment for next fall. The enrollment is measured in Full Time Equivalents (FTE) which represent the number of full-time students which is equivalent to the existing mixture of full-time and part-time students. Data representing the fall enrollment for the past ten years is given below:

time(t)	Enrollment
1	907
2	981
3	1014
4	1015
5	1050
6	1071
7	1123
8	1118
9	1175
10	1216

   a. Draw a scatterplot. Does the data appear to contain a linear trend?

   b. Obtain the t, y, and ty columns.

   c. What is the value of the slope?

    d.   What is the interpretation of the slope?

    e.   What is the value of the y intercept?

    f.   What is the interpretation of the y intercept?

    g.   Forecast the enrollment for next fall.

4.   The table below contains data on the monthly amount, in millions of dollars, which was spent by "leading national advertisers" for advertising apparel and accessories in magazines, in four recent years.

Month		Year		
	1	2	3	4
January	$6.7	$7.9	$ 8.8	$ 7.4
February	6.2	8.4	10..3	17.4
March	12.1	15.1	20. 4	26.1
April	14.4	15.9	17.3	26.6
May	11.1	11.8	15.7	17.0
June	7.4	5.5	9.0	10.4
July	6.4	7.6	8.9	7.9
August	12.9	13.0	20.0	24.7
September	21.1	23.2	32.6	35.6
October	15.4	17.2	24.2	24.8
November	16.5	16.7	22.0	22.2
December	11.6	11.9	16.9	19.8

Source: Survey of Current Business, U.S. Department of Commerce, Washington, D.C., various dates.

Use this data to obtain a set of 12 monthly seasonal indexes.

    a.   Obtain the set of 37 12-month moving averages. The first value will fall between June and July of Year 1, and the last value will fall between June and July of Year 4.

    b.   Obtain the set of 36 centered 12 -month moving averages. The first value will fall in July of Year 1, and the last value in June of Year 4.

    c.   Obtain the 36 ratios of the observed values to the centered moving averages. Group them by months.

    d.   Find the mean of the ratios for each month.

    e.   Adjust the means to add to 12. These are the monthly seasonal indexes.

    f.   Describe the seasonal pattern in magazine advertising for apparel and accessories which is revealed by the monthly seasonal indexes.

5.   This problem utilizes the data in Problem #4 to make forecasts using the naive methods in your textbook.

    a.   Use the actual value in the previous period to forecast the amount which will be spent on advertising apparel and accessories for year 5.

    b.   Use the actual value in the same month of the previous year to forecast the amount which will be spent on advertising apparel and accessories for January of year 5.

6. Use the data for year 1 in Problem #4 for this problem. Calculate the single-factor exponential smoothing forecasts for advertising for the last 11 months of Year 1. Use the first actual value as the starting forecast, and $\alpha = 0.20$.

    a. Construct the worksheet for single-factor smoothing and obtain the forecasts for the months of February through December.

    b. Draw the graph of the actual values and the forecasted values.

7. Use your work in Problem #6 in this problem, which involves the mean squared error (MSE), the mean absolute deviation (MAD), and the tracking signal. Use the tracking signal to estimate when a change occurs in the rate of spending on advertising apparel and accessories.

    a. Obtain the actual column, the forecasted column, and the error column for single-factor smoothing of the data for year 1 in Problem #4. (The actual column will have 12 entries, and the forecasted column will have 11 entries.)

    b. Obtain squared error column.

    c. Obtain the MSE for year 1.

    d. Obtain the absolute error column.

    e. Obtain the MAD for year 1.

    f. Beginning with the absolute error of 0.50 for February of year 1, obtain updated estimates of MAD for the months of February through December. Use $\alpha = .20$.

    g. Obtain the tracking signal column.

    h. Plot the tracking signals on a control chart with limits of ± 4.

    i. What conclusion can be drawn from the tracking signal?

8. Solve problem #7-a, on an EXCEL spreadsheet.

    a. Obtain the cumulative (A - F) column on the same spreadsheet.

    b. Obtain the |A-F| column.

    c. Obtain the cumulative |A - F| column.

    d. Obtain the MAD column.

    e. Obtain the tracking signal column.

    f. Did you get the same answers?

9. Use the data for Year I in Problem 4 for this problem. Calculate the trend-adjusted exponential smoothing forecasts for advertising for the last 8 months of Year 1. Use $\alpha = \beta = .20$ and use the first four actual values to obtain the starting values.

    a. What is the starting estimate of the trend, T_4?

    b. What is the initial forecast, TAF_5?

    c. Construct the worksheet for trend-adjusted smoothing and obtain the forecasts for the months of May through December.

    d. Draw the graph of the actual values and the forecasted values.

CHAPTER 3 FORECASTING

True/False

Question	Answer	Glossary/ Key Idea	Textbook ref. page
1	F	4	
2	T	4	89
3	T	5	
4	F	4	89
5	T		106
6	F	G, 3	92-93
7	T	G, 5	104
8	F	G	116
9	T		117-118
10	T		118
11	T	G	116
12	T		120
13	T	6	104
14	T		122
15	T		94,106
16	F	9	108-109

Multiple-Choice

Question	Answer	Glossary/ Key Idea	Textbook ref. page
1	e		92, 95-100
2	c		116
3	a		118
4	d	5	95-100
5	c		116-117
6	b		119
7	e		99

SOLUTIONS TO PROBLEMS

1.   a.   A forecast for $t = 9$ will require the last five prices.

   $MA_5 = (48.0000 + 48.0000 + 55.6875 + 55.8750 + 57.3750)/5 = \$52.9875$.

   b.   Error = Actual - Forecast = 57.6250 - 52.9875 = \$4.6375.

   c. $MA_5 = (48.0000 + 55.6875 + 55.8750 + 57.3750 + 57.6250)/5 = \$54.9125$.

2.   a.   The size will be the independent variable (X) and the cost will be the dependent variable (Y).

   b.

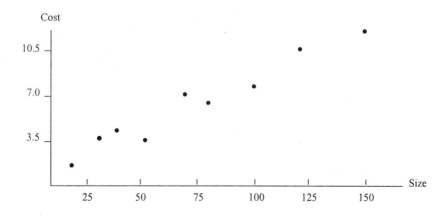

c. $\sum x = 660$; $\sum y = 55.9$; $\sum x^2 = 63,600$; $\sum y^2 = 439.11$; $\sum xy = 5,264$

d. $b = \dfrac{n(\sum xy) - (\sum x)(\sum y)}{n(\sum x^2) - (\sum x)^2} = \dfrac{9(5264) - (660)(55.9)}{9(63600) - (660)^2} = 0.0766$

e. It is estimated that each additional piece in a batch costs $.0766(10^3) = \$76.60$.

f. $a = \bar{y} - b\bar{x} = 6.211 - .0766(73.333) = 0.5937$.

g. It is estimated that the cost of setting up to produce a batch is $0.5937(10^3) = \$593.70$.

h. $y_0 = a + bx = 593.70 + 76.60(125) = \$10,168.70$.

i. $r = \dfrac{n(\sum xy) - (\sum x \sum y)}{\sqrt{n(\sum x^2) - (\sum x)^2} \bullet \sqrt{n(\sum y^2) - (\sum y)^2}}$

$= \dfrac{9(5264) - (660)(55.9)}{\sqrt{9(63600) - (660)^2} \bullet \sqrt{9(439.11) - (55.9)^2}} = 0.9854$.

This high value confirms the impression given by the scatterplot and indicates a strong linear relationship.

j. $r^2 = (.9854)^2 = .9710$.

3. a.

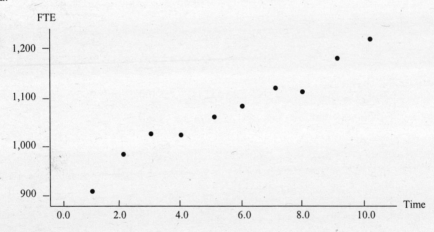

b. $\sum t = 55$; $\sum t^2 = 385$; $\sum y = 10,670$; $\sum ty = 61,187$

c. $b = \dfrac{n \sum ty - (\sum t)(\sum y)}{n \sum t^2 - (\sum t)^2} = \dfrac{10(61187) - 55(10670)}{10(385) - (55)^2} = 30.33$.

d. It is estimated that the enrollment increases by 30.33 FTE per year, on the average.

e. $a = \bar{y} - b\bar{t} = 1067 - 30.33(5.5) = 900.20$.

f. It is estimated that the enrollment at $t = 0$ was 900.2 FTE.

g. $y_0 = a + bt = 900.2 + 30.33(11) = 1233.83$ FTE.

4.   a.   The first 12-month total is: $6.7 + 6.2 + \ldots + 11.6 = 141.8$ and the average is 11.82.   The
second total is 143.0 and the average is 11.92. The last 12-month total is 239.9 and the average
is 19.99.

   b.   The first centered 12-month moving average is $(11.82 + 12.01)/2 = 11.87$. Here is the
complete set:

	Years			
	1	2	3	4
January		12.43	14.32	19.09
February		12.48	14.66	19.24
March		12.57	15.34	19.56
April		12.74	16.03	19.71
May		12.82	16.54	19.74
June		12.84	16.97	19.87
July	11.87	12.89	17.12	
August	12.00	13.01	17.36	
September	12.23	13.31	17.89	
October	12.42	13.59	18.52	
November	12.51	13.81	18.96	
December	12.46	14.12	19.07	

   c.   The first ratio is $6.4/11.87 = .5392$. The last ratio is $10.4/19.87 = .5234$. Each month has
three ratios.

   d, e.   Here are the totals of each month's ratios and the seasonal indexes:

	Total	Mean	Index
January	1.6377	.5459	.5459
February	2.2801	.7600	.7600
March	3.8656	1.2885	1.2886
April	3.6768	1.2256	1.2257
May	2.7308	.9103	.9103
June	1.4820	.4940	.4940
July	1.6487	.5496	.5496
August	3.2254	1.0751	1.0752
September	5.2906	1.7635	1.7636
October	3.8122	1.2707	1.2708
November	3.6886	1.2295	1.2296
December	2.6600	.8867	.8867
		11.9994	12.0000

   The adjustment factor = $12.0000/11.9994 = 1.00005$; multiply each mean by this factor.

   f.   Advertising for apparel and accessories is highest in the spring and fall months and lowest in
the winter and summer months. It is, perhaps, surprising that advertising is low in
December.

5.   a. $F_{Jan} = \$19,800,00.$

   b. $F_{Jan} = \$7,400,000.$

6.   a. $F_t = F_{t-1} + \alpha(A_{t-1} - F_{t-1})$

   $F_2 = A_1 = 6.7.$

   $F_3 = F_2 + \alpha(A_2 - F_2) = 6.7 + .20(6.2 - 6.7) = 6.60$

Here is the complete table:

Month	t	A_t	F_t	$(A_t–F_t)$
January	1	6.7	-	-
February	2	6.2	6.7	-5.5
March	3	12.1	6.6	5.5
April	4	14.4	7.7	6.7
May	5	11.1	9.04	2.06
June	6	7.4	9.45	-2.05
July	7	6.4	9.04	-2.64
August	8	12.9	8.51	4.39
September	9	21.1	9.39	11.71
October	10	15.4	11.73	3.67
November	11	16.5	12.46	4.04
December	12	11.6	13.27	1.67

b.

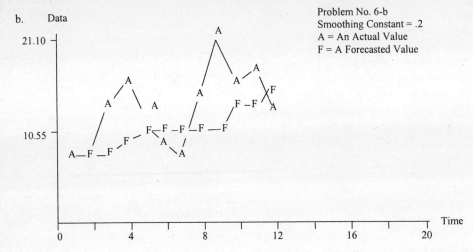

Problem No. 6-b
Smoothing Constant = .2
A = An Actual Value
F = A Forecasted Value

7.   a,b,d. Here is a portion of the table:

t	A	F	A - F	$(A-F)^2$	|A-F|
1	6.7				
2	6.2	6.70	-0.50	0.25	0.50
3	12.1	6.60	5.50	30.25	5.50
.	.	.	.	.	.
.	.	.	.	.	.
12	11.6	13.27	-1.67	2.79	1.67
				279.77	44.93

c. $MSE = \dfrac{\sum(A-F)^2}{(n-1)} = \dfrac{279.77}{(11-1)} = 27.98.$

e. $MAD = \dfrac{\sum|A - F|}{n} = \dfrac{44.93}{11} = 4.08.$

f,g. Here are the calculations for the first few rows.

$MAD_2 = 0.50$

$TS_2 = \dfrac{\sum(A - F)}{MAD_2} = \dfrac{-0.50}{0.50} = -1.00$

$MAD_3 = MAD_2 + \alpha(|A - F|_3 - MAD_2) = 0.50 + .20(5.50 - 0.50) = 1.50.$

$TS_3 = \dfrac{\sum(A - F)}{MAD_3} = \dfrac{5.00}{1.50} = 3.33.$

$MAD_4 = MAD_3 + \alpha(|A - F|_4 - MAD_3) = 1.50 + .20(6.70 - 1.50) = 2.54.$

$TS_4 = \dfrac{\sum(A - F)}{MAD_4} = \dfrac{11.70}{2.54} = 4.61.$

Here is the beginning and ending of the table.

t	A - F	Σ(A - F)	$|A - F|$	MAD	TS
2	-0.50	-.50	0.50	0.50	-1.00
3	5.50	5.00	5.50	1.50	3.33
4	6.70	11.70	6.70	2.54	4.61
.	.	.	.	.	.
.	.	.	.	.	.
12	-1.67	31.21	1.67	3.81	8.19

h.   Control Chart   Problem No. 7-h

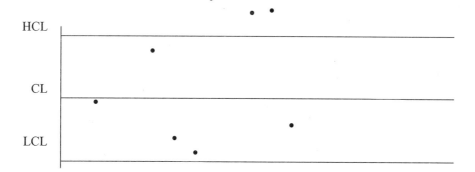

• = A Statistic

i. Since the tracking signal is seldom within the limits, the value of $\alpha = .20$ is a poor choice. In fact, the use of single-factor smoothing may be inappropriate with this time series. Two-factor smoothing may be preferable, since a trend appears to be present.

8.

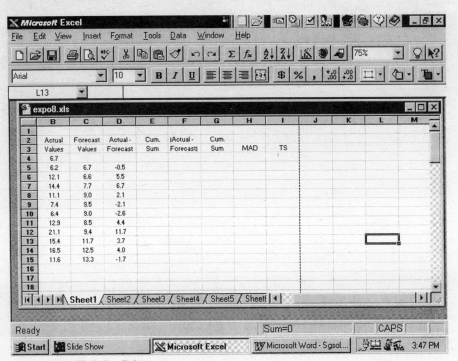

 In cell C-5: =B4

 In cell D-5:=B5-C5

 In cell C-6: =B5+0.20*D5

 In cell D-6: =B6-C6

 In cell C-7: =C6+0.20*D6

  etc.

a. In cell E-5: =D5

 In cell E-6: = SUM(D5:D6)

 In cell E-7: = SUM(D5:D7)

  etc.

b. In cell F5: =ABS(D5)

 In cell F6: =ABS(D6)

 In cell F7: =ABS(D7)

  etc.

c. In cell G5: =F5

In cell G6: =SUM(F5:F6)

In cell G7: =SUM(F5:F7)

etc.

d. In cell H5: =F5

In cell H6: =H5+0.20*(F6-H5)

In cell H7: = H6+0.20*(F7-H6)

etc.

e. In cell I-5: =E5/H5

In cell I-6: =E6/H6

In cell I-7: =E7/H7

etc.

f. Did you get the same answers?

9. a. $T_4 = \dfrac{(14.4 - 6.7)}{3} = 2.57.$

b. $TAF_5 = 14.4 + 2.57 = 16.97.$

c. Here are the calculations for the first two rows of the table.

$S_5 = TAF_5 + \alpha(A_5 - TAF_5) = 16.97+.20(11.1 - 16.97) = 15.80.$

$T_5 = T_4 + \beta(TAF_5 - TAF_4 - T_4) = 2.57+.20(0) = 2.57.$

$TAF_6 = S_5 + T_5 = 15.80 + 2.57 = 18.37..$

$S_6 = TAF_6 + \alpha(A_6 - TAF_6) = 18.37+.20(7.4 - 18.37) = 16.18.$

$T_6 = T_5 + \beta(TAF_6 - TAF_5 - T_5) = 2.57+.20(18.37 - 16.97 - 2.57) = 2.34.$

$TAF_7 = S_6 + T_6 = 16.18 + 2.34 = 18.52.$

Here is the complete table.

t	A	TAF	(A -TAF)
5	11.1	16.97	-5.87
6	7.4	18.37	-10.97
7	6.4	18.52	-12.12
8	12.9	18.00	-5.10
9	21.1	18.40	2.70
10	15.4	20.16	-4.76
11	16.5	20.97	-4.47
12	11.6	21.65	-10.05

d.

Advertising   Scatterplot

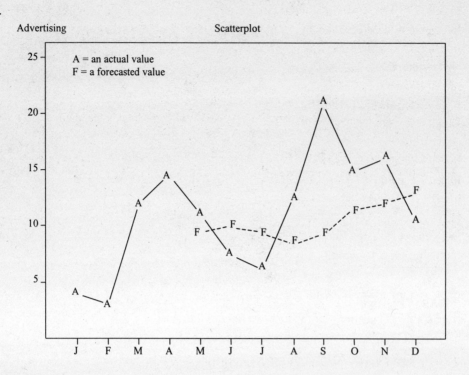

CHAPTER 4
PRODUCT AND SERVICE DESIGN

KEY IDEAS

1. Relevant considerations in planning a product or service system include: research, design, production, life cycle, safety in use, reliability, maintainability, regulatory and legal problems.

2. A marketable product is not always profitable. The reasons for this include:

    a. poor design that leads to an unsafe product may violate product codes or cause accidents that will result in future product liability lawsuits.

    b. the development may take so long that the product is being marketed past the time of peak demand.

    c. competition may result in obsolescence.

3. There are five stages to the product-demand life cycle: incubation, growth, maturity, saturation and decline. The production/operations system becomes an active participant early in the cycle, because of the need to plan production facilities.

4. Basic research is research that contributes knowledge but not products directly; applied research contributes knowledge about products; development contributes products; production/operations management delivers the products.

5. Computer-aided design and computer-aided manufacturing (CAD-CAM) enhance the productivity of both design and production personnel, because the computer can assimilate enormous quantities of information, display the consequences of a design or a course of action, and institute programmed controls of the manufacturing process.

6. Standardization of parts, components, and modularization, or standardizing larger components that might be used in several different products, has advantages for many reasons, including: reducing inventories; enhancing employee, customer and vendor familiarity; making it easier to purchase raw materials and component parts; and routinizing production and quality assurance activities. There are also some possible disadvantages in reduced consumer appeal and possible freezing of imperfect designs, with subsequent costly changeovers.

7. An important aspect of the design process is to design for manufacturability. This means avoiding designs that would require costly or time-consuming steps, or steps that would make it difficult to achieve desired quality levels. Instead, designers need to be aware of manufacturing capabilities, and create products that are easy to produce, and lend themselves to achieving desired quality levels.

8. The design of services differs in many respects from the design of products, because of certain basic differences that exist between products and services. For example, services tend to have higher customer contact than manufacturing, and services tend to be intangible. Also, services can't be inventoried. Because of these and other differences, the design of services requires attention to many different details than design of products.

9. Robust design refers to products or services that are relatively insensitive to some change in operating conditions. That is, products (or services) with robust design have a broader range of conditions under which they can function in an acceptable manner than products (or services) that do not have this feature. That can be a real advantage in terms of reliability and customer satisfaction.

10.   Reverse engineering refers to the dismantling of another firm's product to learn about any special features that can be adapted to one's own products.

11.   Quality function deployment (QFD) is a process for integrating the "voice of the customer" into the design of products and services. This intention is to achieve increased levels of customer satisfaction by incorporating customer requirements at the earliest possible stage in the production cycle.

GLOSSARY

applied research: research that is directed at the growth of scientific knowledge, with a specific commitment toward product development.

attribute: a characteristic that has only two possible states.

basic research: research that is directed at the growth of scientific knowledge, without any specific product orientation.

concurrent engineering: bringing engineering and manufacturing personnel together early in the design phase.

design for assembly: reducing the number of parts in an assembly as simplifying the assembly methods that will be employed in its manufacture.

design for dis-assembly: making it easier to take apart used products by using fewer parts and snap-fits where possible.

design for operations: taking into account the capabilities of the organization to deliver a particular product or service.

design for recycling: designing products to allow for dis-assembly in order to recover components and materials for reuse.

development: research and design activities that bring forth a serviceable and marketable product with a profit potential.

dimensions of quality: the many aspects of a product or service that affect the customer's satisfaction.

end item: a product sold or delivered to the ultimate user.

growth: the second stage of the product life cycle, representing growth in demand and marketability.

incubation: the first stage of the producer's product life cycle; usually it is an idea that is the result of either basic or applied research.

manufacturability: designing products with manufacturing capabilities in mind, and with an eye towards making products easy to produce, and easy to avoid mistakes.

maturity: the third or middle stage of the product life cycle, when the product reaches the peak of demand.

modularization: a high level of standardization, where the standardized components are assemblies or subassemblies of the end item product.

product liability: the legal responsibility of a manufacturer, in case there is a serious injury to a user because of a defect in the design or manufacture of a product.

product design: all activities connected with bringing forth a new product to market.

quality function deployment (QFD): integrating the "voice of the customer" into product and service design.

reliability: the ability of a product or system to perform its intended function under a prescribed set of conditions.

remanufacturing: removing some of the components of old products and using them in new products.

reverse engineering: dismantling another firm's product to learn about its special features.

robust design: design that results in products or services that can perform over a broad range of operating conditions.

saturation: the fourth stage of the product life cycle, when the demand for the product is just past its peak and *on the decline.*

standardization: the absence of variety in a product, process, or service. The extent to which all of the products are similar to each other , or the extent to which every customer receives the same service.

Uniform Commercial Code: in essence, the code specifies that every product must be usable for its intended purposes.

TRUE/FALSE QUESTIONS

1.   Basic research, applied research and development are all part of the product life cycle.

2.   Technological obsolescence can be prevented by designing a better product.

3.   Standardization of parts and components frequently leads to higher costs of production.

4.   The term *robust design* refers to particularly strong and durable products.

5.   The term *concurrent engineering* refers to bringing engineering and manufacturing personnel together early in the design phase.

6.   Modular design is a form of standardization.

7.   CAD uses computer graphics for product design.

8.   A service blueprint is typically used to guide construction of a service facility.

9.   Quality function deployment is a method of integrating the "voice of the customer" into the design process.

10.   Reverse engineering involves taking apart a product to see how it is designed.

11.   Standardized parts must be used in order to produce a high quality product.

12.   Designing for dis-assembly and designing for recycling are synonymous terms.

MULTIPLE-CHOICE QUESTIONS

1.   The advantages of standardization include:
    I.   early freezing of the design.
    II. fewer parts to deal with in inventory.
    III. reduced training cost and time.
    IV. more routine purchasing.
    a. I, II   b. I, IV   c. I, II, III   d. II, III, IV   e. I, II, III, IV

2. The term that pertains to incorporating customer ideas in product design is:
   a. TQM
   b. CAD
   c. QFD
   d. robust design.
   e. reverse engineering

3. Product design that uses computers is referred to as:
   a. QFD   b. CAM   c. RFD   d. CAD   e. TQM

4. Taking apart a competitor's product to better understand how it operates is:
   a. Service blueprint
   b. Concurrent engineering
   c. Robust design
   d. Illegal
   e. None of these

5. Which one of these is a tool used for service blueprinting?
   a. Flowchart.
   b. QFD.
   c. CAD.
   d. CAM.
   e. Reverse engineering.

6. The term "House of Quality" is associated with:
   a. Service blueprinting.
   b. The Taguchi approach.
   c. Quality function deployment.
   d. Robust design.
   e. Concurrent engineering.

7. Which of the following may be a dimension of quality?
   a. Performance.
   b. Conformance.
   c. Reliability.
   d. Durability.
   e. All may be dimensions of quality.

8. Remanufacturing means:
   a. Reassembling a defective product.
   b. Redesigning the layout of the factory.
   c. Reusing components of old products.
   d. Redesigning the product.
   e. Retraining the workers.

CHAPTER 4 PRODUCT AND SERVICE DESIGN

True/False

Question	Answer	Glossary/ Key Idea	Textbook ref. page
1	F	3, 4	156-157
2	T	G	157-159
3	F	6	154-156
4	F	G	160-161
5	T	G, 3	161-162
6	T		164
7	T	5	162-164
8	F		167
9	T	G	168
10	T	G, 10	151
11	T		157

Multiple-Choice

Question	Answer	Glossary/ Key Idea	Textbook ref. page
1	d	6	156
2	c	11	168
3	d	5	162
4	e		151
5	a		167
6	c		168-171
7	c		157

CHAPTER 4S
RELIABILITY

KEY IDEAS

1. Product descriptions and specifications frequently require that a product have a minimum specified reliability. Reliability has both qualitative or descriptive aspects, the ability of the product to perform its intended function, and quantitative aspects, as a measure of the probability of success.

2. The probability of success is measured in one of two ways:

    a. attributes, success or failure: the probability of a success on a single usage or trial; for example, the opening or closing of a switch.

    b. time-to-failure analysis, the probability that the product will perform its intended function for a specified period of time such as, for example, a warranty period for an automobile.

3. If we assume that components succeed or fail independently, the reliability of a serial system is the product of the reliabilities of the components. There is a dual relationship between serial and parallel, redundant or standby systems; for a parallel system the unreliability, or probability of failure, is the product of the unreliabilities of the components.

4. For time-to-failure components or systems, the failure rate tends to follow the bathtub curve:

    a high but declining failure rate when the product is new, constant failure rate during the normal service period, followed by increasing failure rate, or wearout. The following diagram is typical:

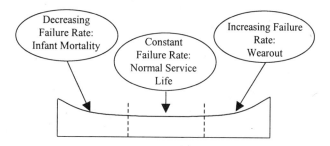

The central period of constant failure rate is characterized by the exponential distribution; it represents the majority of the service lifetime of the product. Manufacturers try to reduce or eliminate the defects that cause early failures through quality assurance activities and employee motivation, in order to increase customer satisfaction and reduce complaints or the possibility of lawsuits. The wearout period is the time that one might expect the customer to strongly consider purchasing a replacement, because of the difficulty in getting satisfactory service. Warranties usually cover early failures and the beginning of non-normal service life, but not wearout.

5. The interpretation of the reliability-MTBF relationship is that during the normal service-life period, if T is a specified lifetime, such as a warranty period, the reliability R is

$$R = e^{(-T/MTBF)}$$

where $e = 2.71828$ is the base of natural (Naperian) logarithms, and T is frequently called the "mission time" of the system.

Elaboration:

In both cases (attributes and time-to-failure), note that the concern is with failures. Thus, an alternate definition is that the reliability is the probability that a failure will not occur before it is supposed to occur, if ever. Estimating the reliability of a product or system is a statistical problem based upon lifetime and failure data obtained either with laboratory testing or the failure reports of equipment in the field.

The reliability may be estimated for a component, a module, a system or an assembly. The distinctions between the three types is arbitrary. Since the advent of microminiaturization, tiny chips which are a fraction of the size of a fingernail can contain several thousand transistors and diodes, and perform complex electronic logic at amazingly low cost. A convenient distinction is that a component is an element that is tested as a unit. A module is a collection of components; an assembly is a finished product or end item; and a system is a collection of end items intended to perform a specific function.

A system or subsystem for reliability purposes is organized according to a specific logic. If there are n components and all of them must work in order for the system to work properly, it is called a serial system. If all components succeed or fail independently, the reliability of the system is the product of the reliabilities of all n components. If every component is protected by a standby or parallel element that can perform its function, the system is parallel or redundant, and the unreliability or probability of failure is the product of the unreliabilities of the parallel elements.

6.   Some companies have found that by reducing the number of components in a product, the reliability of those products has increased. With fewer parts, fewer processes are required (less chance for mistakes), there are fewer interfaces to deal with (so designers can be more focused), and less time is required (less time for mistakes to occur). An alternate approach is to use backup, or redundant, components to increase reliability.

GLOSSARY

bathtub curve: a description of the changing failure rate of a product over its lifetime decline: the fifth or final stage of the product life cycle, when the demand for the product has just about phased out and it is the time to find new products to produce and market.

exponential functions: mathematical functions that incorporate the constant *e*, the base of natural logarithms.

infant mortality: the first stage of the product life cycle in use, characterized by high but declining failure rate.

MTBF: the mean time between failures, the inverse of the failure rate.

parallel system: a system for which only one of several alternative components is needed for success.

redundancy: a situation where if a specific component fails, a substitute component is available to take over the specified function.

reliability: the probability that a product, or component, or system will perform its intended function under a prescribed set of conditions..

series system: a system for which all components are needed for success.

time-to-failure analysis: for a product or system that is supposed to have a specified lifetime or period of service, time-to-failure analysis measures the length of life, the failure rate or MTBF, and any characteristic changes that may occur over the lifetime of the product in use.

TRUE/FALSE QUESTIONS

1. Reliabilities are typically specified with respect to normal operating conditions.

2. Redundancy is sometimes used in product design to increase reliability.

3. The typical service life of a product usually consists mainly of a period of constant failure rate.

4. If a system is made up of two components that are in series, and both have failure rates of 50%, the probability that the system will fail is 75%.

5. It is theoretically possible that the service life of a component or element can be described by the normal distribution.

6. The probability that a serial system will work is the sum of the probabilities that each component will work.

7. A redundant system is a parallel system.

MULTIPLE-CHOICE QUESTIONS

1. A system is composed of three components, I. II, III. All three of these components must function in order for the system to work. Their reliabilities are respectively: I. 0.4; II, 0.5; III, 0.5. The overall system reliability is:

    a. 0.70
    b. 0.99
    c. 0.10
    d. 0.18
    e. 0.97

2. A system is composed of three components, I, II, III. The reliabilities of the three components are respectively 0.5, 0.4, and 0.9. II is a standby for I that switches on only if I fails, and III is a standby for II. The overall system reliability is:

    a. 0.70
    b. 0.99
    c. 0.10
    d. 0.18
    e. 0.97

3. A life test has shown that coffeemakers fail in use at the rate of 0.04257 per month. The manufacturer warranties that a coffeemaker will last for 12 months of ordinary usage. What is the reliability of a coffeemaker?

    a. 0.4   b. 0.5   c. 0.6   d.   0.7   e.   0.8.

4. In Problem #3, assume that lifetime failures have a negative exponential distribution. What is the MTBF in months?

    a. 1.00.   b. 23.50   c. 1.67   d.   12.00   e.   1.04

5. Assume that the distribution of lifetime failures of coffeemakers is normal with a mean equal to the answer you obtained in #4, and a standard deviation of 10 months. What is the reliability of the coffeemaker in this case?

    a. 0.8749   b. 0.1251   c. 1.15   d.   0.5000   e.   0.9574

PROBLEMS

1. A system has four components, A, B, C, D. The probability that each component will work is p(A) =.90, p(B) = .70, p(C) =.95, and p(D) = .60; all components must operate in order for the system to work. Since the probabilities associated with components B and D are low, backup components, B-B and D-D, with the same probabilities are provided:

    a. Draw the box and line diagram for this system.

    b. What is the probability that each component will not work?

    c. What is the probability that the system will work without the backup components?

    d. List the ways in which the system can work with the backup components.

    e. What is the probability that the system will work with the backup components?

    f. How much improvement in reliability do the backup components provide?

2. (One step beyond) A simple system consists of three components, A. B, C, as shown below, with the probability that each component will work. Component A costs $20,000 each, B costs $10,000 each, and C costs $6,000 each.

    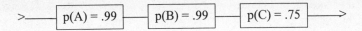

    a. Is this a serial or a parallel system?

    b. What is the probability that the system will work?

    c. Management wishes to have at least a .95 probability that the system will work, and proposes to achieve this goal by adding redundant component C's to the system, which are identical to the existing component C. Each new C would switch on if the preceding C's failed. How many C's will be required?

    d. Draw the diagram of the new system.

    e. Is this a serial or a parallel system?

    f. How much will it cost to achieve a .95 probability by adding C's?

3. The mean operating life (MTBF) of TV picture tubes is 4,000 hours, and the failure rate of the tubes can be modeled by a negative exponential distribution. Use Table 4S-2 in your textbook, or use the e^x or In x keys on your pocket calculator to solve these problems.

    a. Determine the probability that a picture tube will fail within 3,200 hours.

    b. Determine the probability that a picture tube will last at least 6,400 hours.

    c. The manufacturer wishes to provide a warranty on which he will be obligated to make a replacement of only 2% of the picture tubes sold. For how many hours should the picture tubes be warranted?

    d. Does the MTBF come in the middle of this distribution?

4.   The service life of automobile tires is modeled by a normal curve; the Mean Time Between Failures (MTBF) is 20,000 miles and the standard deviation is 800 miles. Use Table A in the Appendix to solve these problems.

   a.   Determine the probability that a tire will fail before 22,000 miles.

   b.   Determine the probability that a tire will last at least 19,000 miles.

   c.   The manufacturer wishes to provide a warranty on which he will be obligated to make a replacement of only 1% of the tires sold. For how many miles should he warrant the tires?

   d.   Does the MTBF come in the middle of this distribution?

   e.   What is the difference between modeling the service life with the negative exponential distribution or with the normal curve?

CHAPTER 4S RELIABILITY

Chapter 4S

True/False

Question	Answer	Glossary/ Key Idea	Textbook ref. page
1	T		172
2	T	6	180
3	T	4	181-182
4	T		179-180
5	T		183
6	F		179-180
7	T		180

Multiple-Choice

Question	Answer	Glossary/ Key Idea	Textbook ref. page
1	c	3	179-180
2	e		179-180
3	c		179
4	b		181
5	a		183-184

SOLUTIONS TO PROBLEMS

1.   a.

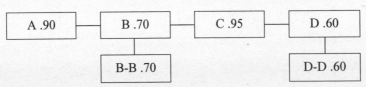

    b.   Let p($\overline{A}$) be the probability that component A does not work.

       p($\overline{A}$) = 1 - p(A) = 1 - .90 = .10.

       p($\overline{B}$) = 1 - p(B) = 1 - .70 = .30.

       p($\overline{C}$) = 1 - p(C) = 1 - .95 = .05.

       p($\overline{D}$) = 1 - p(D) = 1 - .60 = .40.

    c.   p(system works) = p(A)p(B)p(C)p(D) = (.90)(.70)(.95)(.60) = .3591.

    d.   1)   A works; B works; C works; D works.

       2)   A works; B fails; B-B works; C works; D works.

       3)   A works; B works; C works; D fails; D-D works.

       4)   A works; B fails; B-B works; C works; D fails; D-D works.

    e.   The probability will be the sum of the probabilities for each of the four cases above.

       1)   p(A)p(B)p(C)p(D) = .3591.

       2)   p(A)p($\overline{B}$)p(B-B)p(C)p(D) = .1077.

       3)   p(A)p(B)p(C)p($\overline{D}$)p(D-D) = .1436.

       4)   p(A)p($\overline{B}$)p(B-B)p(C)p($\overline{D}$)p(D-D) = .0431.

       The probability that the system will work is .6535.

    f.   The improvement is .6535 - .3591 = .2944. The backups have nearly doubled the reliability of the system, but it is still very low. Even with the backups, the system can be expected to fail about 1 time in 3.

2. a. A serial system.

    b   (system works) = p p(A)p(B)p(C) = .7351.

    c.. For one additional C:

    p(works)   .7351

    p(A)p(B)p($\overline{C}$)p(C) =   .1838

    p(works)   .9189

    For 2 additional C's:

    p(works) =   .9189

    p(A)p(B)p($\overline{C}$)p($\overline{C}$)p(C) =   .0460

    p(works)   .9649   (> .95; stop)

    Two additional C's will be required.

    d.

    $p(A) = .99$ — $p(B) = .99$ — $p(C_1) = .75$

    $p(C_2) = .75$

    $p(C_3) = .75$

    e. A parallel system.

    f. Two C's will cost $12,000.

3. a. $p(T < 3200) = 1 - e^{-T/MTBF} = 1 - e^{-3200/4000} = 1 - .4493 = .5507.$

    b. $p(T > 6400) = e^{-T/MTBF} = e^{-6400/4000} = .2019.$

    c. p(failure before time, T) = .02.

    $1 - e^{-T/4000} = 0.02.$

    $e^{-T/4000} = 0.98.$

    $\ln(e^{-T/4000}) = -T/4000;\ \ln(0.98) = -0.02.$

    $T/4000 = 0.02.$

    T = 80 hours.

    d. No; over half of the area falls to the left of the MTBF.

4. a. Convert from the T scale to the z scale.

    z = (T - MTBF)/s = (22000 - 20000)/800 = 2.50.

    p(T < 22000) = p(z < 0) + p(0 < z < 2.50) = .5000 + .4938 = .9938.

    b. Convert from the T scale to the z scale.

    z = (T - MTBF)/s = (19000 - 20000)/800 = -1.25.

    p(T > 19000) = p(-1.25 < z < 0) + p(z > 0) = .3944 + .5000 = .8944.

c. Let T' = the warranted service life. Then,

p(T < T') = .01; p(T' < T < MTBF) = .5000 - .0100 = .4900. Find the area of .4900 in the table of the standardized normal curve, read the z value, and convert to the T scale.

p(T' < T < MTBF) = p(z' < z < 0); z' = -2.33.

T' = MTBF - z' = 20000 - 2.33(800) = 18,100 miles.

d. Yes; half of the area is on each side of the MTBF.

e. The negative exponential distribution is skew positive, and the normal model is symmetrical. The normal model indicates that half of the items will fail before the MTBF, while the exponential model indicates that over half of the items will fail before the MTBF.

CHAPTER 5
PROCESS SELECTION AND CAPACITY PLANNING

KEY IDEAS

1. Process selection involves making choices concerning the way an organization will produce its products or provide services to its customers. It has major implications for capacity planning, layout and work methods.

2. Organizations which make rather than buy products, or provide rather than subcontract for services, naturally become more involved in process selection than those who buy or subcontract. [See the list of factors relating to make vs. buy in the text, page 182.]

3. Organizations can select from three types of processing: continuous, intermittent, and project. Note that many organizations use all three, but for different aspects of their operations. However, many other organizations rely primarily on one type of processing. Essentially, continuous processing is used for high-volume operations that have Standardized output, intermittent processing is used for lower-volume, customized operations, and projects are used for limited-time, unique sets of tasks.

4. Process selection may lead to automation or computer-aided manufacturing. [You should find it helpful to list the different types of computer-aided manufacturing, along with a brief description and advantages and limitations of each type.]

5. A key issue in process selection is the management of technology. See the discussion under the Operations Strategy section. Another key issue in process selection is flexibility.

6. Production-system design and capacity planning are twin concepts: the system is designed for a stated capacity.

7. Strategically, capacity and financial decisions are made first, followed by decisions on location of the facility, design of the product, layout and work systems.

8. Capacity is the maximum rate of output for the system under normal operating conditions.

9. If products are similar enough, capacity is measured in common units or rates of output; when products are dissimilar, for example, as in a job shop, capacity is in units of resources used: machine time, labor hours, etc. Capacity is not measured in dollar units, because there can be substantial changes in prices over the life cycle of the product.

10. The capacity decision is often difficult and/or costly to modify.

11. Effective capacity is less than the design capacity, because the system may have alternative product-mix strategies, because of changes in design of the product and quality specifications, job requirements or work rules. Actual output would usually be less than effective capacity, because of shortages, delays, bottlenecks or changes in demand. Efficiency and utilization are ratios, expressed as percentages, that show the relationships between actual output and measures of capacity: efficiency is the ratio of actual output to effective capacity; utilization is the ratio of actual output to design capacity.

12. Planning considerations involve long-run trends. seasonal shifts in demand, and joint and competing products and services.

13. Cost-volume (breakeven analysis, supplemented by marginal analysis on the optimum size of a plant, helps in determining the optimum design capacity, for a variety of output rates.

14. The linear breakeven model discussed in this chapter assumes that there is only one product, all production is sold, variable cost per unit of output is constant, and that there is no change in fixed costs or in per unit revenues, regardless of volume. If there are major deviations from these assumptions, a nonlinear model should be used instead of a linear one.

GLOSSARY

automation: the substitution of machinery for human labor, including sensing and control devices that enable it to operate automatically.

batch processing: producing moderate volumes of similar products.

breakeven analysis: see cost-volume analysis.

breakeven point: the output level at which total cost = total revenue.

capacity: the upper limit on the planned rate of output.

capacity alternatives: different levels of planned output having different cost structures for a range of outputs.

continuous processing: producing a highly uniform product in large quantities, or providing a continuous service.

cost-volume analysis: focuses on relationships between cost, revenue, and volume of output. *cyclical factors:* factors that affect the rate of output, based on the business cycle. *design capacity:* a specified rate of output that the plant is theoretically capable of producing.

effective capacity: an achievable rate of output that is usually less than the design capacity because of operational difficulties.

efficiency: the ratio of actual output to effective capacity, expressed as a percentage.

external factors: circumstances that affect the plant capacity and the rate of output, which are either externally imposed, such as health and safety regulations, or else negotiated, such as by union work rules.

facilities factors: environmental factors that affect the rate of output, based on the design or the location of the plant.

financial analysis: planning for receipt and payout of funds and maintaining cash flow, taking into account the present value of funds to be received or paid out in the future.

fixed cost: those expenses which do not increase (or decrease) when the volume of output increases (or decreases).

human factors: psychological and physical aspects of the layout of the facility and work spaces that affect employee morale, performance and output.

job shop: has the capability to perform certain operations; generally it produces a product or a service to meet the specifications of the customers.

operational factors: scheduling problems, bottlenecks, equipment failures, or breakdowns in communication between different sections of the plant that affect performance and output.

process factors: technology, specifications or special customer requirements that affect performance and output.

product/service factors: factors that affect the rate of output, based on the degree of specialization in the product or service, or in the design of the production system.

project: a set of activities directed towards a unique goal.

repetitive production: producing one or a small number of similar products or services.

utilization: the ratio of actual output to design capacity, expressed as a percentage.

variable cost: the total of per-unit material, labor and operational cost, assumed to be constant per unit of product in a linear breakeven model.

TRUE/FALSE QUESTIONS

1. Short-run variations in demand can influence design capacity.

2. Intermittent systems are designed for high volume output.

3. Flexible manufacturing systems can handle a variety of dissimilar products.

4. Systems that produce highly standardized items are sometimes called continuous systems.

5. A project approach is often the best choice when a complex set of tasks has a limited life span.

6. Design capacity is not the same as effective capacity.

7. Peak loads and seasonal requirements affect design capacity planning, as well as effective capacity and actual output.

8. Linear breakeven analysis does not consider when in time the breakeven point is achieved.

9. A capacity decision is irrevocable.

10. Plant efficiency increases as the ratio of design capacity to actual output increases.

11. A job shop is similar to a batch production plant in that both may produce products or services to meet the customers' specifications.

12. The capacity of the plant is determined by the machinery and equipment installed therein.

MULTIPLE-CHOICE QUESTIONS

1. Efficiency, in capacity terms, is the ratio of.
   a. actual output to effective capacity.
   b. actual output to design capacity.
   c. effective capacity to actual output.
   d. design capacity to effective capacity.
   e. design capacity to actual capacity

2. Which one of the following statements is incorrect?
   a. Short-term capacity is less concerned with trends or cycles than with deviations from the average.
   b. Long-term capacity needs are obtained by converting trend forecasts into capacity requirements.
   c. Product standards and specifications do not restrict management's options of increasing capacity or using existing capacity.
   d. Human factors that influence capacity are more subtle than quantifiable factors, such as the rate of output.
   e. Employee motivation has an important connection with capacity, as do both absenteeism and labor turnover.

3. Seasonal variations are often easier to deal with in capacity planning than trend, because seasonal factors tend to be:

    a. predictable.

    b. smaller.

    c. larger.

    d. controllable.

    e. none of the above is correct.

4. The assumptions of the linear breakeven cost-volume model include:

    I. the variable cost per unit is the same regardless of volume.

    II. fixed costs do not change when the volume changes.

    III. revenue per unit is the same regardless of volume.

    a. I only.

    b. I and II only.

    c. II only.

    d. II and III only.

    e. I, II, and III.

5. What is the breakeven quantity of weekly production for this particular situation:

    fixed cost: $1,500 per week

    variable cost: $3 per unit

    revenue: $6 per unit

    a. 200   b. 500   c. 100   d. 600   e. 300

6. Product variety in a job shop tends to be:

    a. high.   b. moderate.   c. low.   d. very low.

7. The system that has the highest equipment flexibility is:

    a. Job shop.

    b. Batch.

    c. Repetitive production.

    d. Continuous processing.

8. The efficiency ratio must be larger than the utilization ratio because:

    a. Effective capacity is larger than design capacity.

    b. Actual output is larger than effective capacity.

    c. Design capacity is larger than effective capacity.

    d. Actual output is larger than design capacity.

9. Match the products in the first column with the manufacturing system which would probably be most appropriate for producing them.

Products	Systems
1. Gasoline	a. job shop
2. Bread	b. batch processing
3. Toothpaste	c. repetitive production
4. A muffler for a classic car	d. continuous processing
5. Dishwasher detergent	
6. Light bulbs	

PROBLEMS

1.   The Crystal Sparkle Co. produces glass tumblers. The plant Is designed to produce 400 tumblers per hour, and there is one eight-hour shift per working day. However, the plant does not operate for the full eight hours: the employees take two 15-minute breaks in each shift, one in the first four hours and one in the second four hours, the first thirty minutes of the shift are spent raising the kilns to the required temperature for firing glass. The plant usually produces about 10,000 tumblers per five-day workweek. Answer the following questions by adjusting the data to one eight-hour shift.

   a.   What is the design capacity in tumblers?

   b.   What is the effective capacity in tumblers? As a percent?

   c.   What is the actual output in tumblers?

   d.   What is the efficiency?

   e.   What is the utilization?

2.   The Goode and Cooke Company produces several models of frying pans. There is little difference in the production time required for the various models; the plant is designed to produce 160 frying pans per eight-hour shift, and there are two shifts per working day. However, the plant does not operate for the full eight hours: the employees take two 12-minute breaks in each shift, one in the first four hours and one in the second four hours; two hours per week are devoted to cleaning the factory and performing maintenance on the machines; one four-hour period every four weeks is devoted to the meeting of the quality circle. The plant usually produces about 3,500 frying pans per four-week period. You may ignore holidays in solving this problem. Answer the following questions by adjusting the data to a four-week time period.

   a.   What is the design capacity in frying pans?

   b.   What is the effective capacity in frying pans? As a percent?

   c.   What is the actual output?

   d.   What is the efficient?

   e.   What is the utilization?

   f.   Re-work the problem using a time period of one eight-hour shift.

3.   The selling price of the product is $199.95. The variable costs per unit are:

Labor	$60.25
Raw material	25.70
Purchased component	21.50
Variable overhead	17.50

The fixed costs total $300,000 per year. Perform a breakeven analysis of this company.

a. What is the total revenue function?

b. What is the total cost function?

c. What is the profit function?

d. What is the breakeven point in units of the product?

e. What is the revenue at the breakeven point?

f. What is the income at the breakeven point?

g. Estimate the profit when 9,000 units of the product are sold in a year.

h. How many units must be sold for the company to make $900,000?

4. The Lade & Bach Company produces office chairs. The price of the chairs is $99.75 and the variable cost per chair is $49.75. The following fixed costs are incurred:

Depreciation of plant and equipment per year	$20,000
Property taxes per year	12,000
Manager's salary and fringe benefits per month	5,200

Perform a breakeven analysis of this company:

a. What is the total revenue function?

b. What is the total cost function?

c. What is the profit function?

d. What is the breakeven point in number of chairs?

e. What is the revenue at the breakeven point?

f. What Is the income at the breakeven point?

g. Estimate the profit when 1,500 chairs are produced in a year.

h. How many chairs must be sold for the company to make $75,000 in a year?

5. The telephone company has three billing plans.

A: An unlimited number of local telephone calls per month for $20.00

B: Fifty (or fewer) local telephone calls per month for $16.00 plus $0.08 per call above 50 calls.

C: Twenty (or fewer) local telephone calls per month for $12.00 plus $0. 10 per call above 20 calls.

The subscriber is uncertain as to whether the number of local telephone calls will be about 60 per month, or about 90 per month, or about 120 per month, or about 160 per month. Use decision theory to determine which billing plan the subscriber should select:

a. What is the payoff table?

b. Which plan should be selected under the minimax regret criterion?

c. Why is it improper to use the maximax criteria here?

d. Suppose that the subscriber assesses probabilities as follows:

p(60 calls) = .40   p(120 calls) = .20

p(90 calls) = .30   p(160 calls) = .10

Which plan should be selected under the best expected value criterion?

e. Which plan should be selected under the least expected regret criterion?

6. (One step beyond) PC Fun & Games, Inc., produces a game for personal computers on a CD-ROM disk which is entitled: Armageddon, the Final Battle. The company sells the disk to software retailers for $20.00, each, with a 5% discount for orders of 100 copies or more. virtually every retailer takes the discount. The variable costs of producing the disks are low, totaling only $7.00 each for the blank disk onto which the game is copied, the wages of the machine operator, and the packaging.

    The game has become a best seller, and the production manager must plan to expand the capacity of the plant to turn out CD-ROM disks. CD-ROM disks are produced on a machine which makes copies of a master disk, one at a time. Each copy takes fifteen minutes, which includes inserting the blank disk, imprinting the game, and removing the finished disk.

    At present, the Company has four machines; each machine cost $80,000 and has a service life of five years. The Company operates two eight-hour shifts per day, 50 weeks per year, and the machines require servicing and adjustments for one hour every day.

    New machines can be purchased for $85,000. They also have a service life of five years and require one hour of servicing, but they can make copies in ten minutes. Because of the savings in copying time, the variable cost will drop to $6.00 per disk.

    a. What is the annual effective capacity of one present machine?

    b. What is the annual depreciation expense of one present machine? (Use straight line depreciation expense = cost/service life.)

    c. What is the present breakeven point?

    d. What is the annual effective capacity of one new machine?

    e. What will be the annual effective capacity of the plant if one new machine is purchased?

    f. What will be the new average variable cost per unit?

    g. What will be the new breakeven point?

    h. Suppose a second new machine is purchased. What will be the annual capacity of the plant?

    i. What will be the new average variable cost per unit?

    j. What will be the new breakeven point?

CHAPTER 5
PROCESS SELECTION AND CAPACITY PLANNING

True/False

Question	Answer	Glossary/ Key Idea	Textbook ref. page
1	T		211
2	F	3	198
3	F		197
4	T		197
5	T	3	201
6	T	G, 11	211
7	F		199
8	T	13	219-220
9	T		223
10	F		211
11	T		198-199
12	T		199

Multiple-Choice

Question	Answer	Glossary/ Key Idea	Textbook ref. page
1	a	G, 11	211
2	c	G	201
3	e		212-213
4	e	14	221-222
5	b		219-220
6	a		199
7	a		199
8	c		211
9	1-d		199
	2-b		
	3-c		
	4-a		
	5-d		
	6-c		

SOLUTIONS TO PROBLEMS

1. a. Design capacity = 8 hrs. x 400 tumblers = 3,200 tumblers per 8-hour shift.

    b. Effective capacity = Design capacity - Nonproductive activities.

        Design capacity   8.0 hrs.

        Less: Breaks   .5 hrs.

        Heat-up   .5 hrs.

        Net productive time   7.0 hrs.

        Effective capacity = 7 hrs. x 400 tumblers = 2,800 tumblers.

        Effective capacity percent = (100)(2800)/3200 = 87.5%.

    c. Actual output = 10,000/5 = 2,000 tumblers per 8-hour shift. (This is a mean output. In reality there will be variation; some shifts will exceed 2,000 tumblers and some will fall short.)

    d. Efficiency = Actual output/Effective capacity = (100)(2000)/2800 = 71.43%.

    e. Utilization = Actual output/Design capacity = (100)(2000)/3200 = 62.50%.

2. a. Design capacity = 160 frying pans x 2 shifts x 20 working days = 6,400 frying pans per four weeks.

    b. 160/8 = 20 frying pans per hour.

        8 hrs. x 2 shifts x 20 working days = 320 hrs. available.

        Less)

Breaks: (12 min. x 2 per shift x 2 shifts x 20 working days)/60 =	16 hrs.
Cleaning: 2 hrs. x 4 weeks	8 hrs.
Quality Circle	4 hrs.
Therefore, Net productive time is:	292 hrs.

        Effective capacity = 292 hrs. x 20 frying pans = 5,840 frying pans per four weeks.

        Effective capacity percent = (100)(5840)/6400 = 91.25%

    c. Actual output = 3,500 frying pans.

    d. Efficiency = Actual output/Effective Capacity = (100)(3500)/5840 = 59.93%.

    e. Utilization = Actual output/Design capacity = (100)(3500)/6400 = 54.69%.

    f. In terms of one 8-hour shift: Design capacity = 160 frying pans.

        Effective capacity = 5840/40 = 146 frying pans.

        The percentage answers will be the same as above.

3. a. Total Revenue = R x Q = 199.95Q.

    b. Total cost = FC + VC x Q = 300000 + (60.25 + 25.70 + 21.50 + 17.50)Q = 300000 + 124.95Q.

    c. Profit per year = R x Q - (VC x Q + FC) = 199.95Q - (124.95Q - 300000) = 75Q - 300000.

    d. Q_{BEP} = FC/(R - VC) = 300000/75 = 4,000 units.

    e. Revenue at the break-even point = 4000(199.95) = $799,800.

    f. Income at the break-even point = $0.

    g. Profit at 9,000 units = 75(9000) - 300000 = $375,000.

    h. Number of units = (SP + FC)/(R - VC) = (900000 + 300000)/75 = 16,000 units.

4. a. Total revenue = R x Q = 99.75Q.

    b. Total cost = FC + VC x Q = 94400 + 49.75Q.

    c. Profit per year = R x Q - (VC x Q + FC) = 99.75Q - (49.75Q + 94400) = 50Q - 94400.

    d. Q_{BEP} = FC/(R - VC) = 94400/50 = 1,888 chairs.

    e. Revenue at the break-even point = 99.75(1888) = $188,328.

    f. Income at the break-even point = $0.

    g. Profit at 1,500 chairs = 50(1500) - 94400 = -$19,400, which is a net loss.

    h. Number of chairs = (SP + FC)/(R - VC) = (94400 + 75000)/50 = 3,388 chairs.

5.   a.   It is necessary to estimate the total cost of each possible number of calls under each billing plan.

Plan a) The cost will be $20, regardless of the number of calls.

Plan b) The cost will be $16 + (number of calls - 50) x $0.08, when there are more than 50 calls.

Plan c) The cost will be $12 + (number of calls - 20) x $0.10, when there are more than 20 calls.

The payoff table will be:

| | State of Nature | | | |
Alternative	60 calls	90 calls	120 calls	160 calls
Plan a	20.00	20.00	20.00	20.00
Plan b	16.80	19.20	21.60	24.80
Plan c	16.00	19.00	22.00	26.00

b.   Select the best payoff for each state of nature; they are 16.00, 19.00, 20.00, and 20.00. Subtract every entry in the <u>column</u> from the best entry. The differences are the regrets.

| | State of Nature | | | |
Alternative	60 calls	90 calls	120 calls	160 calls
Plan a	4.00	1.00	0	0
Plan b	.80	.20	1.60	4.80
Plan c	0	0	2.00	6.00

Pick the worst regret for each alternative:

Alternative	*Worst Regret*
Plan a	4.00 (best)
Plan b	4.80
Plan c	6.00

The subscriber should select Plan a.

c.   It is improper to use the maximax criterion here because the payoffs are expenses rather than incomes.

d.   Incorporate the probabilities into the payoff table and calculate the expected value of each plan.

| | State of Nature | | | |
| Probability | .40 | .30 | .20 | .10 |
Alternative	60 calls	90 calls	120 calls	160 calls
Plan a	20.00	20.00	20.00	20.00
*Plan b	16.80	19.20	21.60	24.80
Plan c	16.00	19.00	22.00	26.00

The subscriber should select Plan c.

*Note: (16.80)(.40) + (19.20)(.30) + (21.60)(.20) + (24.80)(.10) = 19.28.

e.   The subscriber should select Plan c.

6. a. Capacity = 4 disks/hr. x 15 hrs./day x 250 days/yr. = 15,000 disks/yr.

    b. Depreciation = cost/service life = $80,000/5 yrs. = $16,000.

    c. Q_{BEP} = FC/(R - VC) = 4($16,000)/($19 - $7) = 5,333 disks.

    d. Capacity = 6 disks/hr. x 15 hrs./day x 250 days/yr. = 22,500 disks/yr.

    e. Capacity = 4(15,000) + 1(22,500) = 82,500 disks/yr.

    f. VC = [$7(60,000) + $6(22,500)]/82,500 = $6.727.

    g. Q_{BEP} = FC/(R - VC) = [4($16,000) + 1($17,000)]/($19 - $6.727) = 6,600 disks.

    h. Capacity = 4(15,000) + 2(22,500) = 105,000 disks/yr.

    i. VC = [$7(60,000) + $6(45,000)]/105,000 = $6.571.

    j. Q_{BEP} = FC/(R - VC) = [4($16,000) + 2($17,000)]/($19 - $6.571) = 7,885 disks.

CHAPTER 5S
LINEAR PROGRAMMING

KEY IDEAS

1. A linear programming (LP) model is a linearized mathematical representation of a system of relationships about a set of decision variables. The objective is to maximize or else to minimize a linear objective function, subject to a set of linear constraints and bounds for the variables.

2. The job of an analyst is to recognize the problem, formulate the model to solve the problem and supply the necessary input data. Because of the availability of computers and standardized LP codes, solving the model is now a fairly routine task.

3. An LP problem consists of an objective function, a set of constraints, plus a set of bounds for the decision variables, all linear functions. The objective function is a linear function with an unspecified value, Z. that is to be either maximized, if the problem deals with revenues or profits, or minimized, if it deals with costs. Because Z is not a specified constant, in graphical LP the objective function is represented by a family of parallel straight lines.

   The feasible space is the area of the first quadrant bounded both by the axes and by all of the constraints. A solution is a point in two-dimensional space, whether it satisfies the model or not. A feasible solution is a solution inside the feasible space. The optimal solution is the feasible solution that either maximizes or minimizes the objective function.

   The optimal solution is always a corner point of the feasible space. In order to find the exact values of x and y for a corner point, two constraint-boundary equations are solved simultaneously.

4. Small problems with just two decision variables, are usually solved graphically. The text includes detailed step-by-step procedures for: (1) plotting the constraint boundaries that enclose the space of feasible solutions; (2) drawing the *isoprofit (or isocost)* lines that are parallel to the objective function; and (3) identifying the corner point of the feasible space at the intersection of two constraint boundaries, representing the optimum solution.

   Two-variable maximizations with all less-than-or-equal-to ($\leq$) constraints have feasible spaces that are entirely enclosed inside upper-limit boundaries; if both variables are also nonnegative (>0), the (0,0) origin is feasible. Minimizations with all greater-than-or-equal to ($\geq$) constraints have feasible spaces that are entirely enclosed by the x- and y-axes, unbounded from above and bounded from below by lower-limit boundaries.

5. After the optimum is attained, sensitivity analysis can determine;

   a. The range of feasibility, which is the range of values of the RHS quantities of a constraint for which the shadow prices and the variables in solution remain the same.

   b. The range of optimality, which is the range of values over which the objective function coefficient of a decision variable can change without changing either the list of variables in solution or their optimal quantities, although the value of the objective function will change.

   c. The range of insignificance, which is the range of values over which the objective function coefficient of a variable that is not in solution can change and still not cause it to come into solution.

GLOSSARY

algorithm: a procedure that always results in an optimum solution if the input data conform to the requirements for a mathematical model of this class.

constraint: a linear function of the decision variables that defines boundaries for the feasible space; a constraint could be an inequality of either the less-than-or-equal-to ($\leq$) or the greater-than-or-equal-to ($\geq$) type, or else an equality (=).

continuous variable: a variable that is not restricted to integer or discrete values.

corner point: a corner point of the feasible space could occur whenever two linear constraint boundaries intersect; the optimum solution of an LP problem is at a comer point.

decision variable: a variable whose value can be set by a decision maker.

feasible solution: a solution that satisfies all constraints and boundary conditions, with all decision variables and all slack variables nonnegative ($\geq$ O).

graphical linear programming: an LP problem with two decision variables, x and y, where the solution is obtained on a two-dimensional grid that displays the constraint boundaries, the feasible space and the comer points of the feasible space.

heuristic: a procedure for solving a mathematical model that is not always guaranteed to result in the best possible solution.

linear programming (LP): an procedure for finding the values of decision variables, that results in the best solution of an optimization problem with linear constraints and a linear objective function.

linear function: a mathematical function of the form $m = ax + by + cz + ...$, where a, b, c, etc. are constants, $x, y. z$, etc. are variables; and m could be either a constant or a variable. maximization: a requirement that at the optimum, the objective function shall be at its highest possible value, within the feasible space.

maximization: a requirement that at the optimum, the objective function shall be at its highest value, within the feasible space.

minimization: a requirement that at the optimum, the objective function shall be at its lowest possible value, within the feasible space.

nonnegativity: all decision variables and all slack variables are required to be ≥ 0.

objective function: a linear function of the decision variables, that is either maximized or minimized by the LP solution.

optimal solution: the best feasible solution, i. e., the values of the decision (and slack or surplus) variables that either maximize or minimize the value of the objective function.

range of feasibility: the range over which the righthand side value of a constraint can change without changing its shadow price.

range of optimality: the range over which the value of an objective function coefficient can change and not change the optimal solution.

sensitivity analysis: an extension of simplex used to assess the impact of a change in the value of an objective function coefficient or a change in the right-hand-side value of a constraint.

shadow price: for a constraint, the amount that the value of the objective function would change if the RHS value of the constraint was changed by one unit.

simplex method: the algorithmic procedure for finding the optimal solution of an LP problem.

simultaneous solution: finding the coordinates of the point at which two straight lines intersect.

slack variable: a variable whose value is zero if the corresponding ≤ constraint is at its boundary, or > 0 if the lefthand side of the constraint is less than the righthand side.

solution: a set of decision variables, and their respective values.

suboptimization: in LP, suboptimization implies that the proposed solution attained is not actually the overall optimum; it can be a comer point of the feasible space other than the optimum, or else any point in the feasible space, even if it isn't a corner.

surplus variable: a variable whose value is zero is the corresponding ≥ constraint is at its boundary or > 0 if the lefthand side of the constraint is greater than the righthand side.

TRUE/FALSE QUESTIONS

1. LP operations are performed in an environment of certainty.

2. LP always involves either maximizing or minimizing an objective function.

3. The optimum solution of a graphical LP includes at least one corner point of the feasible set.

4. A circle would be an example of a feasible solution space for an LP problem.

5. Without exception, all of the functions in graphical LP are either straight lines. or families of straight lines.

6. It is possible to have more than one corner point of the feasible set as an optimum solution to an LP problem.

7. All constraints are either ≤ or ≥ inequalities.

8. Sensitivity analysis must be performed before an optimal solution can be found.

9. The range of feasibility is the range of values of the decision variables for which the solution is optimal..

10. A shadow price tells how much a decision variable can be increased or decreased without changing the value of the solution.

11. The range of optimality gives ranges of values for the objective-function coefficients within which the values of the decision variables are optimal.

12. In a binding constraint, the value of the slack variable is zero.

MULTIPLE-CHOICE QUESTIONS

1. Which objective function is parallel to the line 4x + 2y = 200?
   a. 2x + 4y
   b. 2x + y
   c. 2x + 2y
   d. 2x - y
   e. 2x - 4y

2.   Which of the choices below is a simultaneous solution of these two equations: $3x + 4y = 10$ and $5x + 4y = 14$?

    a. $x = 2, y = 0.5$

    b. $x = 49, y = -0.5$

    c. $x = 2, y = 1$

    d. $x = y$

    e. $y = 2x$

3.   Choose the best answer: In an LP problem

    a. two-variable problems cannot be handled by simplex.

    b. calculus is used to achieve the optimum solution.

    c. both maximization and minimization can be achieved in the same problem.

    d. an optimum solution has to include a corner point.

    e. all of the above statements are correct.

    f. none of the above statements is correct.

4.   Which of the statements below about shadow prices is correct?

    a. A shadow price refers to the objective function.

    b. A shadow price refers to the RHS of a constraint.

    c. A shadow price refers to the LHS of a constraint.

    d. a and b above.

    e. a and c above.

    f. b and c above.

5.   A constraint that forms the optimal corner point of the feasible solution space is called

    a. redundant.

    b. slack.

    c. surplus.

    d. binding.

    e. optimal.

6.   Which of these is not an assumption of linear programming models?

    a. Divisibility

    b. Certainty

    c. Negativity

    d. Linearity.

7. Which one of these would not be considered as a component of an LP model?
    a. Shadow price
    b. Decision variable
    c. Constraint
    d. Parameter
    e. All are components

8   If a constraint has non-zero slack in the solution, then:
    a. The constraint is not redundant.
    b. The constraint is a $\leq$ constraint.
    c. The constraint is binding.
    d. The constraint is non-linear.
    e. The constraint is incorrect.

PROBLEMS

1. Given this LP problem:

    Maximize $4x_1 + 3x_2$

    s.t.:   A) $14x_1 + 6x_2 \leq 84$

    B) $7x_1 + 12x_2 \leq 84$

    C) $x_1, x_2 \geq 0$

    Solve the problem using the graphical method:
    a. Plot and label the constraints.
    b. Indicate the feasible solution space.
    c. Plot the objective function and use it to identify the optimum point of the graph.
    d. Use simultaneous equations to determine the optimal values of x_1, and x_2
    e. Compute the optimum value of the objective function.

2. Solve problem #1 by using an EXCEL spreadsheet.
    a. How do you enter the objective function?
    b. How do you enter the constraints?
    c. What are the optimal values of x_1 and x_2?
    d. What is the value of the objective function?
    e. How much slack does each constraint, A and B, have?

3.   Given this LP problem:

Minimize $5x_1 + 8x_2$

s.t.:   A) $2x_1 + 2x_2 \geq 100$

       B) $10x_1 + 35x_2 \geq 700$

       C) $x_2 \geq 15$

       D) $x_1, x_2 \geq 0$

Solve this problem using the graphical method.

a.   Plot and label the constraints.

b.   Indicate the feasible solution space.

c.   Plot the objective function and use it to identify the optimum vertex.

d.   Use simultaneous equations to determine the optimal values of x_1 and x_2.

e.   Compute the optimal value of the objective function.

4.   Solve Problem #3 by using an EXCEL spreadsheet.

a.   How do you enter the objective function?

b.   How do you enter the constraints?

c.   What are the optimal values of x_1 and x_2?

d.   What is the value of the objective function?

e.   How much surplus does each constraint, A , B, and C have?

5.   A dietitian in a hospital is required to devise a recipe for a food which will provide at least the following amounts of vitamins: 500 units of vitamin A. 500 units of vitamin B. and 700 units of vitamin C. The dietitian may use three ingredients, P, Q, and R in the recipe which are described below. At least one ounce of ingredient R must be used in the recipe.

Units per Ounce:

Ingredient	A	B	C	Cost per Ounce
P	20	30	60	$0.30
Q	60	30	0	$0.20
R	10	50	30	$0.15

a.   Is this a problem in maximization or minimization?

b.   What are the decision variables?

c.   What is the objective function?

d.   What are the constraints?

6. Solve problem #6 on an EXCEL spreadsheet.

   a. How do you enter the objective function?

   b. How do you enter the constraints?

   c. How much of each ingredient should be used in the recipe?

   d. How large is one serving of this food, in kilograms? In ounces? (I kg. = 2.2 lbs., or 35.2 oz.)

   e. What is the cost of one serving?

   f. How much extra of each vitamin does this recipe provide?

7. Refer to your EXCEL spreadsheet for Problem #6.

   a. What is the shadow prices for each constraint?

   b. If it is necessary to economize on the recipe, which should be reduced: the requirements for vitamin A. or for vitamin B. or for vitamin C?

   c. Find the range of feasibility for each constraint.

   d. What is the interpretation of the range of feasibility?

   e. Find the range of optimality for each coefficient in the objective function.

   f. What is the interpretation of the range of optimality?

8. The Fairley and Winn Company produces hockey sticks, hockey pucks, and baseball bats; it is necessary to plan the production schedule for next week. The hockey sticks, hockey pucks, and baseball bats are made of oak, of which the company has 600 board feet. A hockey stick requires 4 board feet, a puck requires 2 board feet, and a baseball bat requires 3 board feet. The company has a power saw for cutting the oak boards into the appropriate pieces; a hockey stick requires 3.0 minutes, a puck requires 1.5 minutes, and a baseball bat requires 1.5 minutes. The power saw is expected to be available for 3.6 hours next week. After cutting, the pieces of work in process are hand finished in the finishing department, which consists of 4 skilled and experienced craftsmen, each of whom can complete any of the products. A hockey stick requires 60 minutes of finishing, a puck requires 30 minutes, and a baseball bat requires 90 minutes. The finishing department is expected to operate for 40 hours next week. Hockey sticks sell for $29.95 and have a unit variable cost of $17.95; a puck sells for $11.95 and has a unit variable cost of $4.95; a baseball bat sells for $16.95 and has a unit variable cost of $8.95. The company has an order for two dozen hockey sticks which must be filled. It wishes to produce no more than 50 hockey pucks. Determine the linear programming form of this problem.

   a. Is this a problem in maximization or minimization?

   b. What are the decision variables? Suggest symbols for them.

   c. What is the objective function?

   d. What are the constraints?

9.   Solve Problem #8 on an EXCEL spreadsheet.
    a.   How do you enter the objective function?
    b.   How do you enter the constraints?
    c.   How much of each product should be produced?
    d.   How much profit will be generated by selling all of the output?
    e.   How much oak will be unused?
    f.   How much idle time will there be in the finishing department?
    g.   How much idle time will there be in the finishing department?

10.   Use your EXCEL spreadsheet in Problem #9 to solve this problem.
    a.   What is the shadow price of each constraint?
    b.   If it is necessary to produce more baseball bats, would more oak, more saw time, or more finishing time be required?
    c.   What is the range of feasibility of each constraint?
    d.   What are the interpretations of the ranges of feasibility?
    e.   What is the range of optimality of each objective function coefficient?
    f.   What are the interpretations of the ranges of optimality?

CHAPTER 5S   LINEAR PROGRAMMING

True/False

True/False

Question	Answer	Glossary/ Key Idea	Textbook ref. page
1	T		235
2	T	1	234
3	T	3	246
4	F	1, 3	246
5	T	1, 3	235
6	T		247
7	F	5	235
8	F	5	254
9	F	G, 5	255
10	F	G	255
11	T	G, 6	254
12	T		249

Multiple-Choice

Question	Answer	Glossary/ Key Idea	Textbook ref. page
1	b		242-244
2	c		245
3	d		246
4	d	3	255
5	d		249
6	c		235
7	a		234
8	b		249

SOLUTIONS TO PROBLEMS

1.   a,b,c.

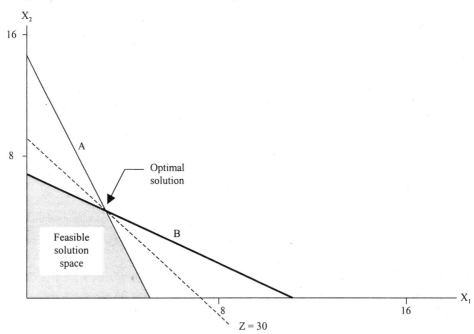

d. $x_1 = 4$; $x_2 = 4.67$.

e. $Z = 4(4) + 3(4.67) = \$30.00$.

2.

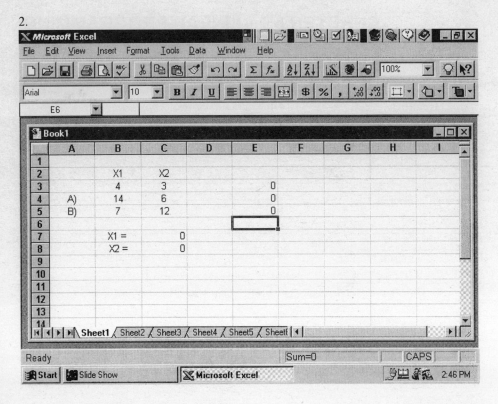

a. In cell E3: =B3*C7+C3*C8.

b. In cell E4: =B4*C7+C4*C8.

In cell E5: =B5*C7+C5*C8.

(It is not necessary to enter the non-negativity constraints.)

Hint: Format your answer cells. Click on Format; Click on Cells; Select Number and 3 or 4 decimal places.

c. Click on Tools; Click on Solver. Set Target Cell E3. Maximize. By Changing Cells C7,C8.

Click on Add. Cell Reference E4, <=, 84 (for constraint A). Click on OK.

Click on Add. Cell Reference E5, <=, 84 (for constraint B). Click on OK

Click on Solve. $x_1 = 4.00$; $x_2 = 4.67$.

d. In the SOLVER box, click on the answer report. Did you get the same answer as in Problem #1?

e. Both constraints equal their RHS and have no slack.

3.   a,b,c.

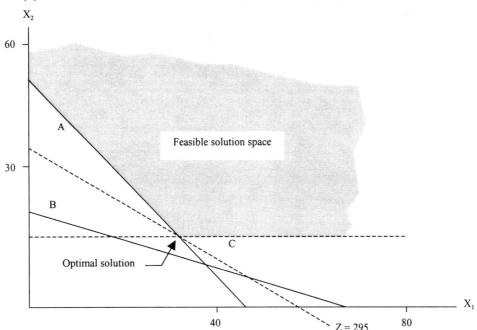

d. $x_1 = 35$; $x_2 = 15$.

e. $Z = 5(35) + 8(15) = \$295.00$.

4.

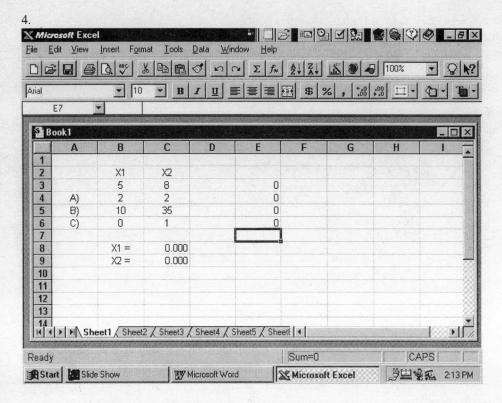

a. In cell E3: =B3*C8+C3*C9.

b. In cell E4: =B4*C8+C4*C9 for constraint A

In cell E5: =B5*C8+C5*C9 for constraint B

In cell E6: =B6*C8+C6*C9 for constraint C.

(It is not necessary to enter the non-negativity constraints.)

Hint: Format your answer cells. Click on Format; Click on Cells; Select Number and 3 or 4 decimal places.

c. Click on Tools; Click on Solver. Set Target Cell E3. Minimize. By Changing Cells C8,C9.

Click on Add. Cell Reference E4, >=, 100 (for constraint A). Click on OK.

Click on Add. Cell Reference E5, >=, 700 (for constraint B). Click on OK

Click on Add. Cell Reference E6, >=, 15 (for constraint C). Click on OK

Click on Solve. $x_1 = 35$; $x_2 = 15$.

d. In the SOLVER box click on the answer report Did you get the same answer as in Problem #3?

e. Constraints A and C equal their RHS and have no surplus; constraint B has a surplus of 175.

Note: EXCEL calls this "slack," but since this is a <u>minimization</u> problem you must interpret it as a surplus.

5.
   a. Since the problem contains information about the cost of the ingredients, it will involve minimization.
   b. The dietician can decide how much of each ingredient to use in the recipe. Use P ,Q and R as symbols.
   c. Minimize $Z = .30P + .20Q + .15R$.
   d. The food must provide certain quantities of vitamins.
      A) $20P + 60Q + 10R \geq 500$ units
      B) $30P + 30Q + 50R \geq 500$ units
      C) $60P + 0Q + 30R \geq 700$ units
      D) $R \geq 1$

6.

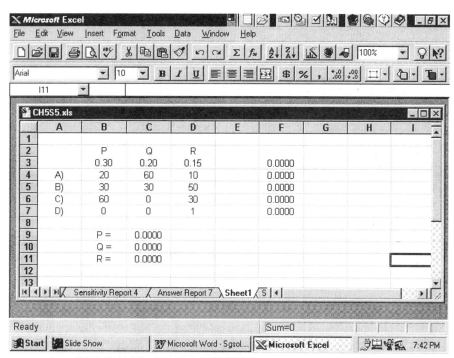

   a. In cell F3: B3*C9+C3*C10+D3*C11.
   b. In Cell F4: B4*C9+C4*C10+D4*C11
         etc.
   c. Click on Tools; click on Solver; click on options; select assume linear model; click on OK. Set Target Cell F3. Minimize. By Changing Cells C9,C10,C11.
      Click on Add. Cell Reference F4, >=, 500 (for constraint A). Click on OK.
      Click on Add. Cell Reference F5, >=, 500 (for constraint B). Click on OK
      Click on Add. Cell Reference F6, >=, 700 (for constraint C). Click on OK
      Click on Add. Cell Reference F7, >=, 1 (for constraint D). Click on OK.
      Click on Solve.   P = 11.17, Q = 4.44, R = 1.

    d.   In the SOLVER RESULTS box, select the ANSWER report. Use 11.17 oz. of P, 4.44 oz. of Q, and 1 oz. of R. The recipe will make 16.61 oz.

    e.   One batch costs $4.39.

    f.   The recipe provides no extra vitamin A or vitamin C, but 18.33 extra units of vitamin B.

        Note: EXCEL calls this "slack," but since this is a <u>minimization</u> problem you must interpret it as a surplus.

7.   a.   In the SOLVER RESULTS box, select the SENSITIVITY report.

    b.   Vitamin C has the largest shadow price ($.0039). If the RHS of the C constraint could reduced by one unit, to 699, the value of the objective function (and the cost of the recipe) would be reduced by almost 4 cents.

    c.   On the SENSITIVITY report: the allowable increase and decrease for the RHS of each constraint is given. The RHS of vitamin A may increase by 1E+30; read this as infinity; it may increase without limit. It may decrease by 36.67 to 463.33. Obtain the other ranges in the same manner.

    d.   Within the range of feasibility, the shadow price indicates the effect on the value of the objective function of a one unit change in the RHS of the constraint.

        (The shadow price of vitamin B is zero. An increase in the RHS up to 18.33 or any decrease will have no effect on the value of the objective function. You may use the SOLVER facility to test this result by changing the RHS of the B constraint.)

    e.   For the coefficient of ingredient P, the allowable increase is 0 and the allowable decrease is .23 to .07. Handle the rest of the coefficients in the same manner.

    f.   Within the range of optimality, the values of the decision variables in the solution will not change.

8.   a.   Since selling prices are given, it is a problem in maximization.

    b.   The management can decide how many hockey sticks, hockey pucks, and baseball bats to produce next week. We suggest using H = Hockey sticks, P = Hockey pucks, B = baseball bats. You may have thought of others.

    c.   Maximize $Z = 12H + 7P + 8B$.

    d.   Oak: $4H + 2P + 3B \leq 600$ board feet

        Saw: $.05H + .025P + .025B \leq 3.6$ hours

        Finishing: $H + .5P + 1.5B \leq 160$ hours

        Sticks: $H \geq 24$

        Pucks: $P \leq 50$.

9.

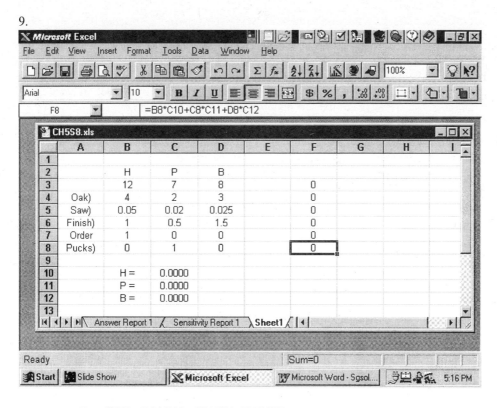

a. In cell F3: B3*C10+C3*C11+D3*C12.

b. In cell F4: B4*C10+C4*C11+D4*C12

   etc.

c. Click on Tools; click on Solver; click on options; select assume linear model; click on OK. Set Target Cell F3. Maximize. By Changing Cells C10,C11,C12.

   Click on Add. Cell Reference F4, >=, 600 (for oak). Click on OK.

   Click on Add. Cell Reference F5, >=, 3.6 (for the saw). Click on OK

   Click on Add. Cell Reference F6, >=, 160 (forfinishing). Click on OK

   Click on Add. Cell Reference F7, >=, 24 (for hockey sticks). Click on OK.

   Click on Add. Cell Reference F8, $\leq$, 50 (for hockey pucks). Click on OK

   Click on Solve. Produce 24 hockey sticks, 50 hockey pucks, and 56 baseball bats.

d. In the SOLVER RESULTS box, select the ANSWER report. The profit will be $1,086.00.

e. There will be 236 board feet of oak left over.

f. There will be no free time on the saw.

g. There will be 27 unused hours of finishing time.

10 a. In the SOLVER RESULTS box, select the SENSITIVITY report.

b. The saw has the largest shadow price ($320). If the RHS of the saw constraint could be increased, the value of the objective function (and the profits) would be increased by $320.per hour.

c. On the SENSITIVITY report: the allowable increase and decrease for the RHS of each constraint is given. The RHS of the saw may increase up to .45 of and hour (27 minutes) and may decrease infinitely. Obtain the other ranges in the same manner.

d. Within the range of feasibility, the shadow price indicates the effect on the value of the objective function of a one unit change in the RHS of the constraint.

   (The shadow price of oak is zero. Any increase in the RHS or a decrease of 236 board feetwill have no effect on the value of the objective function. You may use the SOLVER facility to test this result by changing the RHS of the B constraint.)

e. For the coefficient of hockey pucks, the allowable increase is $0.75 to $8.75 and the allowable decrease is $200 to $6.00. Obtain the other ranges in the same manner.

f. Within the range of optimality, the values of the decision variables in the solution will not change.

CHAPTER 6
FACILITIES LAYOUT

KEY IDEAS

1. Production/operations systems are classified into three fundamental types, according to the way the service is performed or the end item is put together: continuous flow, for example, an assembly line; intermittent or batch-flow processing as in computer jobs; and project, as in the building of a house. In some cases, there can be mixtures of the three types, for example, putting up a cement mixer at a construction site involves both intermittent and project processing.

2. There are three fundamental types of plant layout, respectively corresponding to the three different types of production operations situations. A product layout implies that a single product or else a single type of product, for example, automobiles, is manufactured on an assembly line, with the production tasks assigned to workstations along the line. A process layout involves the movement of batches of goods between departments via forklift truck, moving belt, or some other type of conveyance. A fixed-position layout is appropriate for a large end item such as a house or airplane, where all material is assembled to a major structure or product at a specified site.

3. Each type of layout has its own advantages and disadvantages. Production workers must learn to perform their jobs efficiently. However, if the tasks are overly repetitive and there is no opportunity for variety or for participation in the decision-making process, lethargy or antipathy can set in that would reduce the effectiveness of the best layout planning. That is why automation is advantageous; the machine takes over the highly repetitive jobs, while the employees concentrate on troubleshooting, machine maintenance and other operations requiring a combination of human logic and intuition.

4. Product layout such as that associated with Detroit automobile factories is a good idea when it is justified by the volume. The advantages of product layout are that it involves continuous flow of the work in process, minimum work-in-process inventory, maximum specialization, low material handling costs, efficient utilization of labor and equipment, and systematized routing, purchasing, accounting and inventory control. The disadvantages are dull repetitive jobs, inflexibility and susceptibility to frequent shutdowns.

5. A process layout allocates floor space to work centers so as to sustain a logical flow of semifinished goods, and minimize transportation and inventory costs. it is more flexible than product layout in the sense that a variety of products can be made without incurring extensive changeover costs. It also makes better use of the specialized skills of employees, so that incentive pay systems can be effective in enhancing productivity. Process layout is appropriate when each type of product or semifinished goods has low volume, but there are potentially high costs for unused equipment, excess inventory, slow or irregular movement, and a need for extensive production control paperwork.

6. A fixed-position layout is appropriate for large construction projects or for assembly of very large products such as airplanes, which are difficult to move. An example of a fixed position service system is a subway, which is an economical way to move large masses of people.

7. An assembly line is balanced to smooth the flow of semifinished goods, and to achieve the best possible utilization of both the labor force and the plant. The work is subdivided into groups of tasks, and each group is performed at some specific location along the line called a workstation. A workstation might be a single employee, or possibly a small cluster of employees, if the services of more than one person are required for the tasks.

8.   The cycle time is the span of time a unit of product is at a workstation. In balancing the line, we determine both the cycle time and the number of workstations, based on the number of units of product to be produced in a working day, the total of the times of the tasks needed to make one unit of product, and the amount of effective clock time available in a day, after allowing for rest periods, breaks and planned shutdowns of the line.

9.   There are several different meanings of the term "cycle." The minimum cycle time is the time required for the longest task. The maximum cycle is the sum of the task times for a single unit of product. The actual cycle time is somewhere between these two extremes; it is the amount of time at the workstation with the largest sum of task times.

10. The minimum number of workstations in the product layout is the sum of the task times for a single unit of product divided by the cycle time, to the next highest integer. Assigning tasks to workstations is done with heuristics (rules of thumb):

   a. Consider precedence; make sure that all jobs are done in a logical sequence.

   b. Try to keep all stations busy all of the time by filling up the cycle time with tasks. Do not assign a station more tasks than it has time to perform.

   c. The greatest positional weight rule, one of several heuristics for assigning tasks to stations, assigns tasks according to the greatest sum of remaining task times to a free station. Other heuristics are: most following tasks, most preceding tasks, and greatest sum of task times for tasks that precede.

11. Measures of effectiveness guide decision makers to satisfactory, but not necessarily optimum, decisions on process layouts. The simplest approach involves ranking of departments or work centers according to work flow (Distance x Number of loads carried), and assigning work center locations so as to minimize the total intraplant transportation costs.

12. The Muther grid is an alternative approach to process layout planning that allows for subjective opinions that consider multiple criteria on the closeness of work centers to one another. Work centers are rated in pairs on a six-point closeness scale from A (absolutely necessary) to X (undesirable). First the As are paired, and then the Xs are separated; then the Es (very important) are paired, etc., until all centers are accounted for.

GLOSSARY

assembly line: a product layout where a sequence of operations and tasks is performed on the end item at workstations strategically located at points along the length of the line.

balance delay: the percentage of idle time of a line.

cell: a group of machines assembled to perform the operations needed for a set of similar items (part families).

cellular manufacturing: see cell.

combination layout: a layout form that combines some of the features of both an assembly line for a product layout and the specialization of a process layout.

computer-aided manufacturing (CAM): manufacturing with some of the work performed by robots or cutting tools that are controlled by computer programs.

processing: refers to an assembly procedure such as a product layout that is dedicated to a single product or type of product.

cycle time: the span of time a unit of material Is at a workstation on an assembly line.

desired output rate: the effective demand for units of a product, translated into a daily rate of output.

fixed-position layout: a production layout such as for the construction of a house or the building of an airplane, with all material brought to the site where construction is being performed.

flow systems: see continuous processing.

group technology: grouping items that have similar design or processing characteristics into part families.

heuristic: a rule of thumb for setting priorities among a group of alternatives.

idle time: for a workstation the idle time in a cycle is the difference between the cycle time and the sum of the task times for the tasks performed at that station; for a plant, the idle time in a day is the sum of the workstation idle times multiplied by the number of cycles in a day.

industrial robot: a labor-saving device that performs highly repetitive production tasks such as spot welding or transferring material about over short distances, at very high speeds, under program control.

intermittent processing: refers to layouts for production of end items of one type in batches, with the same plant, equipment and personnel used to produce batches of another type of end item, possibly in a different configuration and sequence of operations.

job shop: see process layout.

line balancing: assigning tasks to workstations so as to have approximately the same amount of work performed at every workstation.

maximum cycle time: the sum of the task times required for one unit of product.

measure of effectiveness: in the context of process layouts, a measure of effectiveness of a proposed layout is a measure of the cost of the proposal in distance or time.

minimum number of workstations: the sum of the task times for all of the units of product produced in a day, divided by the operating time.

minimum cycle time: the time required by the longest task.

Muther grid: a chart that displays an index of closeness ratings for every pair of departments or work centers. It is used to assign work centers to positions in a process layout.

numerically controlled (NC) machines: cutting machines that are directed by a tape produced by a digital computer.

operating time: clock time available in a day of production, after subtracting scheduled stops and breaks.

precedence diagram: a diagram that shows the sequence of tasks to be performed on a unit of product in an assembly line.

process layout: a layout such as a job shop, with specialized workstations that perform activities or services on batches of material.

product layout: a layout such as an assembly line dedicated to the production of a single product or service or type of product or service.

project: nonroutine production or developmental planning and construction with relatively long task times for a network of tasks requiring specialized skills and services.

task time: the time required to perform a given task on a unit of product.

tiebreaker: when a decision process assigns identical priorities to two or more alternatives, a tiebreaker is a heuristic for deciding which priority is to be given first.

workstation: a location on an assembly line where a series of tasks is performed on units of a product.

work center: a location in a process layout where a specified group of tasks is performed on a unit or batch of material.

TRUE/FALSE QUESTIONS

1. Product layouts usually require less-skilled workers than process layouts.

2. The term *group technology* relates to the term *part families*.

3. Units Produced per day divided by Cycles per day equals Operating Time per day.

4. Cycle time is the average amount of clock time required to produce a unit of output.

5. A cycle is the same as the total of the task times needed to produce a single unit of output.

6. Subjective rating scales are not useful in process layouts.

7. The "greatest positional weight rule" assigns tasks according to the largest sum of preceding task times.

8. The percentage of idle time for a line is sometimes referred to as its balance delay.

9. One drawback of process layouts is that equipment utilization rates are lower than in a product layout.

10. The minimum cycle time in an assembly line is equal to the time for the longest task.

MULTIPLE-CHOICE QUESTIONS

1. Heuristic rules are usually used when:
   a. an optimum is necessary.
   b. a computer program isn't available,
   c. a program has a small number of possibilities.
   d. no optimizing routine is available.
   e. all other approaches have failed.

2. A production line is to be designed for a job with three tasks. The task times are 0.3 minutes, 1.4 minutes, and 0.7 minutes, respectively. The maximum cycle time, in minutes, is:
   a. 0.3   b. 1.4   c. 2.4   d. 2.8   e. none of the above

3. Which one of the following would not generally be regarded as a reason for redesign of a layout?
   a. Change in the volume of output or product mix
   b. Morale problems
   c. Accidents or safety hazards
   d. Inefficient operations
   e. All are potential reasons

4. A precedence diagram:
   a. shows the sequences in which tasks are performed.
   b. is in the shape of a network.
   c. shows all of the paths from beginning to end of completion of the product.
   d. a and c only.
   e. all of the above.

5. There are 9 assembly tasks for a product. The task times, predecessor relationships and workstation assignments are given in the following table.

Workstation	Task	Time (min.)	Predecessors
1	a	2	-
	b	7	a
	c	5	-
	d	2	-
2	e	15	c, d
	f	7	a, e
3	g	6	-
	h	4	b, g
	i	9	a

The cycle time for this product is:

a. 16 minutes.

b. 19 minutes.

c. 22 minutes.

d. 57 minutes.

e. none of the above choices is correct.

6. Which one of the following is not generally regarded as an advantage of product layouts?

a. Material handling costs per unit are low.

b. Labor costs are low per unit.

c. The system is fairly flexible to changes in volume of output.

d. Accounting, purchasing, and inventory control are fairly routine.

e. There is high utilization of labor and equipment.

PROBLEMS

1. Producing widgets involves fourteen production tasks, lettered a through n, below. For each task, the time required to accomplish it is given, and the immediately preceding task.

Production Task	Time (min.)	Preceding Task
a	.2	-
b	.4	a
c	.5	b
d	.4	c
e	1.0	a
f	.5	e
g	1.1	d, f
h	.7	g
I	.8	g
j	.4	h
k	1.2	I
l	.9	k
m	.6	l
n	.4	j, m
	9.1	

The manager expects to produce 300 widgets per eight-hour shift. The workers are allowed two 10-minute coffee breaks per shift, and 40 minutes is allocated to cleanup and maintenance tasks.

    a. Is it possible to accomplish the objective of 300 widgets per shift with one workstation?

    b. What is the maximum possible output with 14 workstations?

    c. Draw the precedence diagram for this process.

    d. What is the minimum number of workstations which will be required to achieve an output of 300 pieces per shift?

2.   Refer to the data in Problem 1.

    a. Assign the tasks to workstations according to the heuristic rule of the largest number of following tasks.

    b. How many workstations are required under the rule of the largest number of following tasks?

    c. What is the percent of idle time (or the balance delay) for this layout?

3.   Refer to the data in Problem 1.

    a. Assign the tasks to workstations according to the heuristic rule of the positional weight.

    b. How many workstations are required under the rule of the greatest positional weight?

    c. What is the percent of idle time (or the balance delay) for this layout?

4. The XYZ Co. manufactures a variety of specialized products according to the orders of the customers. The plant consists of 5 departments, numbered 1 through 5 below. While some variation in the work flow is experienced, depending on the composition of the orders received, the following matrix is considered to be representative of the traffic between the departments per five-day workweek, measured in the number of forklift loads or the number of pull truck loads.

From	1	2	3	4	5
1	0	100	50	0	30
2	70	0	60	0	80
3	10	30	0	140	10
4	50	40	0	0	60
5	50	40	80	10	0

The floor plan of the factory is displayed in the diagram below. (See next page). The plant has an L shape, and the lettered areas represent spaces that are to be occupied by the five departments.

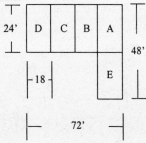

a. In how many ways can these five departments be arranged in the factory?

b. Obtain the distance matrix by measuring from the center of one space to the center of the other space. For example, the distance from area B to area E is 18 ft. + 24 ft. = 42 ft. The distances are the same, both ways.

c. Assign departments to the areas. Try to keep departments with heavy traffic close to each other.

d. Obtain the load-distance index for your layout. (The load-distance index is the sum of the products of the traffic between two departments and the distance between the two departments.)

e. Have you obtained the minimum value of the load-distance index?

5. (Advanced; based on matrix algebra) The textbook mentions some software packages which perform the lengthy computations involved in obtaining the load-distance index and which also test several layouts in search of a low value of the index. If you do not have access to any of these packages, you can obtain the load-distance index on your computer by multiplying the traffic matrix and the distance matrix. Let us symbolize the traffic matrix as $L(i,j)$ and the distance matrix as $D(i,j)$. Then the product matrix is: $P(i,j) = L(i,j)*D(i,j)$.

a. Show how to construct the traffic matrix and the distance matrix so as to perform this multiplication for the layout in 4-c. Hint: consider the traffic matrix to be fixed, and rearrange the distance matrix.

b. Show that the load-distance index is the trace of the product matrix.

6. Here is the Muther diagram for the departments in Problem 4.

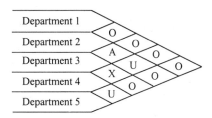

a. Assign the departments to the areas so as to satisfy, as far as possible, the conditions of the Muther diagram.

b. What is the value of the load-distance index of this layout?

CHAPTER 6   FACILITIES LAYOUT

True/False

Question	Answer	Glossary/ Key Idea	Textbook ref. page
1	T		264
2	T	G	269-70
3	F		273
4	T	G, 8	272-73
5	F	8, 9	272-73
6	F	12	283
7	F	G, 10	274
8	T	G, 10	275
9	T		266
10	T	9	273

Multiple-Choice

Question	Answer	Glossary/ Key Idea	Textbook ref. page
1	d	G	274
2	c		272-73
3	e		262
4	e	3	272
5	c		272-74
6	c		264

SOLUTIONS TO PROBLEMS

1.   a.   The operating time (OT) is (8)(60) - 20 - 40 = 420 minutes per shift. One work station would require 9.1 minutes to produce one widget. In one shift it could produce 420/9.1= 46 widgets, and the objective cannot be achieved.

     b.   With 14 workstations, the output is limited by the station with the longest time, which is station k with 1.2 minutes. In eight hours, fourteen stations could produce 420/1.2 = 350 widgets, which is more than adequate.

     c.

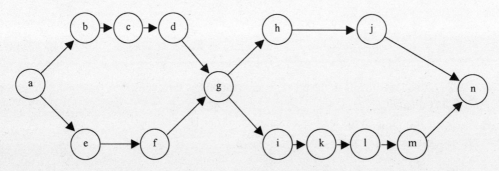

     d.   The minimum number of work stations = DΣt/OT = 300(9.1)/420 = 6.5 work stations.

2.   a.   Count the tasks which follow a particular task on a path through the precedence diagram which was obtained in #1c.

Task	Number Following
a	13
b	10
c	9
d	8
e	9
f	8
g	7
h	2
i	4
j	1
k	3
l	2
m	1
n	0

The cycle time (CT) = OT/D = 420/300 = 1.4 minutes. Each work station can spend a maximum of 1.4 minutes accomplishing a set of tasks.

Here is a set of feasible assignments. (It may not be the only one.) The idle time per station is the maximum total time (1.4 minutes) - the total station time.

Station	Tasks	Total time (minutes)	Idle time (minutes)
1	a,b,c	1.1	0.3
2	d,e	1.4	0
3	f	0.5	0.9
4	g	1.1	0.3
5	h,j	1.1	0.3
6	I	0.8	0.6
7	k	1.2	0.2
8	l	0.9	0.5
9	m,n	1.0	0.4
			3.5

b.   9 work stations are required.

c.   The percent of idle time = (Idle Time per Cycle)x100/(number of stations)×(maximum station time) = 3.5(100)[(9)(1.4)] = 27.78%.

3. a. The positional weight of a task is the sum of its own time and the times of all following tasks on the precedence diagram (#1 - c).

Task	Positional Weight
a	9.1 minutes
b	7.4
.	.
.	.
m	1.0
n	0.4

The assignment of tasks to work stations will be identical with Problem #2a. Because there must be a high correlation between the number of following tasks and the sum of the task times, these two rules must produce very similar layouts.

b. 9 work stations will be required.

c. The same as #3c.

4. a. 5! = 5(4)(3)(2)(1) = 120 possible layouts.

b. The distance matrix.

From

To	A	B	C	D	E
A	0	18	36	54	24
B	18	0	18	36	42
C	36	18	0	18	60
D	54	36	18	0	78
E	24	42	60	78	0

c. One layout is shown in the diagram below. This one starts with departments 3 and 4, since they have the heaviest traffic.

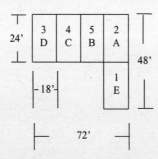

d. Find the products of the loads and distances for every pair of departments.

Departments	Loads	Areas	Distances	Products
3 to 4	140	D, C	18'	2,520
3 to 5	10	D, B	36'	360
.	.	.	.	.
.	.	.	.	.
1 to 5	30	E, B	42'	1,260
1 to 2	100	E, A	24'	2,400
Total (The Load-Distance Index)				30,600

    e. It is not known whether this is the minimum possible value among all of the 120 values of the load-distance index.

5. a. In the traffic matrix, the rows represented "from" and the columns represented "to." In the distance matrix, the rows will represent "to" and the columns will represent "from." Use the diagram in #4c to align the elements of the distance matrix with the elements of the traffic matrix. Thus, column 1 of the distance matrix must be "from E," since department 1 is in area E. Row 3 of the distance matrix must be "to D," since department 3 is in area D. Here is the rearranged distance matrix:

From

To	E	A	D	C	B
E	0	24	78	60	42
A	24	0	54	36	18
D	78	54	0	18	36
C	60	36	18	0	18
B	42	18	36	18	0

    b. Each element on the principal diagonal of the product matrix will be the sum of the products of

the traffic from each department and the distances from each department to all of the other departments.

6.   a. One assignment of departments to areas is shown in the diagram.

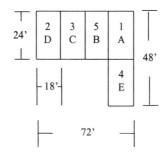

    b. The Load-Distance Index = 36,000. Compare this value with the value in #4d. The constraints on the locations of the departments have caused the value to increase.

CHAPTER 7
DESIGN OF WORK SYSTEMS

KEY IDEAS

1. This chapter covers both job design and work measurement; it brings together both qualitative and the quantitative aspects of designing a job and the working environment so as to achieve employee satisfaction and high productivity, and measuring the result.

2. Job design specifies the content of a job and the methods used, job design has significant effect upon the efficiency and productivity of the working force.

3. Job enlargement, which is sometimes called "horizontal loading," means diversifying tasks assigned to a worker. Job enrichment, which is also called "vertical loading," me increasing the skill level within the present job. Both job enlargement and job enrichment help sustain morale and improve efficiency and productivity, if the worker understand the reasons for the changes made in his assignments.

4. Automation is the substitution of mechanical or electronically controlled devices human energy in performing highly repetitive tasks. Although automation has been a important facet of production activity ever since the Industrial Revolution started over 250 years ago, it has become even more important in recent years because of t expanded usage of industrial robots.

5. Specialization is essential, because without it there would not be enough skill to sustain competitive position in the marketplace for goods or services, However, if specialization is too narrow, the employee does not learn very much about the production and operation system. For that reason, managers are frequently rotated in their assignments to provide depth as well as breadth.

6. Motion study provides guidelines for interfacing the worker, his tasks, and the environment. If there are substantial changes in the tasks or environment, new methods analysis may become necessary.

7. Flow process charts, work-machine charts and multiactivity charts are useful for methods analysis and balancing the work flow.

8. Properly scheduled work breaks help improve efficiency and morale.

9. The operations manager must ever be mindful of his or her responsibility to provide a safe working environment. The pressures that make this necessary are personal responsibility, public opinion, potential legal liabilities, possible interference with production due to lost-time accidents, industrial grievances, and OSHA (Occupational Safety and Health Administration) rules.

10. Time studies provide information on how much time a job can take. Since these studies involve repeated observations and measurements, the cost is justified if the task is repeated frequently and if there is substantial evidence that pre-existing time standards are not adequate. One of the problems of time study is worker resistance or non-cooperation, for example, by deliberately slowing down to give the analyst the impression that the job takes more time than it actually does.

11. In work sampling, a worker is observed at random times during working hours. Work sampling provides a measure of employee efficiency by showing what proportion of the time is spent working. It can be used to study nonrepetitive jobs. The sample size is a function of the proportion of idle time and how much confidence we want to have in the results.

GLOSSARY

allowance: the difference between normal time and standard time, which consists of planned nonworking time..

allowance factor: the proportion of time that the workers are taking breaks, or experiencing delays, etc..

automation: substituting mechanical and electronic devices for human energy in performing routine and highly repetitive jobs at very high speeds.

behavioral school: the school of thought that emphasizes the relationship between productivity and satisfying the wants and needs of the employee.

color coding: adopting a color scheme for the plant that enhances visibility and safety.

efficiency school: the school of thought, founded by F. W. Taylor, that emphasizes the relationship between productivity, pay incentives, and the configuration of the work space.

flow process chart: a symbolic chart that shows the sequence of operations and tasks performed by an employee in a particular job.

gang-process chart: a multiactivity chart showing a cross section of the tasks performed by a team of employees.

group incentive plans: incentive pay plans for all of the employees of a company based on savings in labor and material costs, or profit sharing; among the plans discussed in Chapter 7 are the Scanlon, Kaiser, Lincoln and Kodak plans.

job rotation: varying assignments among a group of employees by shifting tasks and responsibilities.

job design: assigning tasks and planning the working environment and system for an employee or a group of employees, taking into account the costs and benefits of the alternatives available.

job enlargement: giving an employee a greater number of tasks without a corresponding shift to another assignment or a higher level of responsibility.

job enrichment: increasing the level of responsibility of an employee as a motivation towards better performance.

knowledge-base d pay: paying workers for the level of knowledge and skill they master; workers are paid for their ability to perform multiple tasks or jobs.

methods analysis: studying the requirements of a job in order to propose new and possibly better ways to perform it.

motion study: a technique for studying the human motions needed to perform an operation or series of tasks, developed originally by Frank and Lillian Gilbreth.

normal time: the observed time adjusted by a rating factor for the worker's performance or speed in accomplishing the operation..

observed time: the average of the measured times for a task.

occupational Safety and Health Administration (OSHA): the federal agency that has the responsibility for administering laws relating to employee and environmental safety.

output-based systems: systems of incentive compensation to individuals based on output.

performance rating: a factor assigned by an analyst reflecting a judgment as to whether the worker was working rapidly or slowly..

quality of work: a term that characterizes the entire working environment, including facilities, work space and equipment, and the camaraderie among employees and between employees and supervisors.

random number table: a table of random numbers with many uses; in the context of Chapter 7, it is used to establish random times for making observations in work sampling.

specialization: division of labor so that each employee has the best opportunity to become proficient at the operations he will perform.

straight piecework: the worker is paid a set amount for each unit produced.

standard time: the normal time plus an allowance for breaks, maintenance, etc.

standard elemental times: standard times for jobs or tasks derived from historical data, rather than from current time-study data.

stopwatch time study: a widely used method of work measurement, developed by F. W. Taylor, for establishing the standard times for relatively small repetitive tasks.

therblig (Gilbreth spelled backward: an elementary unit of human motion in a motion study: common therbligs are: search *select, grasp,* hold, transport loaded, and release load.

time-based compensation systems: systems of compensation based on the amount of clock time an employee works.

work measurement: see stopwatch time study.

work sampling: a statistical technique developed by L. H. C. Tippett for determining what proportion of the time an employee is engaged in a task, by having the analyst walk through the area at random times; if the employee is engaged in a series of highly repetitive tasks, work sampling can be used to set standard task times.

worker-machine chart: a chart that displays the portions of a work cycle in which the worker and the machine are active or idle.

z-statistic: the unit normal deviate of the standard normal distribution that is used to look up probabilities in the normal probability table.

TRUE/FALSE QUESTIONS

1. Work sampling results in less disruption of work than time study does.

2. Time study results in less detail about the time taken for a given task than work sampling does.

3. The sample size needed for a work sampling study increases as the amount of error allowed increases.

4. Work sampling is performed by having the analyst spend a period of time with the employee and take measurements of the amount of time needed to complete tasks.

5. A flow process chart reveals the overall sequence of operations by focusing on the movement of materials on an assembly line.

6. A standard elemental time for a task is the standard time derived from historical data rather than current data.

7. Job enrichment is otherwise known as vertical loading.

8. It is usually difficult or impossible to perform time studies on creative or intellectual jobs such as those of a college professor.

9. The standard time for an activity is usually less than its normal time.

10. The allowance factor is designed to allow for defective products.

11. Job enrichment and job enlargement mean the same thing.

MULTIPLE-CHOICE QUESTIONS

1. The symbols of a flow process chart stand for:
    a. inspection, delay, transportation, storage, operation.
    b. transportation loaded, search, grasp, store, perform operation.
    c. release, transport. store, grasp, search.
    d. circle, arrow, pentagon, square, triangle.
    e. none of the above choices is correct.
2. Analysis of therbligs is most closely related to:
    a. methods analysis.
    b. simo chart.
    c. learning effect.
    d. motion study.
    e. all of the above choices are correct.
3. Which technique is useful for studying nonrepetitive jobs?
    a. methods analysis.
    b. time study.
    c. motion study.
    d. micromotion study.
    e. work sampling.
4. Task times derived from a firm's historical data are known as:
    a. predetermined times.
    b. standard elemental times.
    c. judgmental times.
    d. micromotion times.
    e. MTM.
5. Among the following, all are advantages of specialization except:
    a. simplifies training
    b. difficult to motivate quality
    c. high productivity
    d. relatively low wages
    e. all are advantages
6. Which of the following is not an advantage of specialization?
    a. low education/skill requirements
    b. little mental effort needed
    c. low wage costs
    d. work can be monotonous
    e. minimum responsibilities

7.   The following are true about stopwatch time except:

   a.   Several repetitions are usually timed.

   b.   A performance rating is usually necessary.

   c.   There is no record of the method used by the worker.

   d.   It is well-suited for repetitive jobs.

   e.   Jobs that have varying task requirements can pose some difficulty.

8.   Which one of the following statements concerning work sampling is not true?

   a.   Observations are made at random intervals.

   b.   A detailed description of activities is obtained.

   c.   Multiple observations are necessary.

   d.   It can be used to estimate the percentage of delay.

   e.   There is little or no disruption of work.

9.   The need for methods analysis might come from any of these sources except:

   a.   changes in seasonal demand.

   b.   changes in product design.

   c.   new products or services.

   d.   government regulations.

   e.   changes in tools and equipment.

10. Which of the following must be true in every case

   a.   the standard time > the normal time.

   b.   the normal time > the observed time.

   c.   the observed time < the mean time.

   d.   the mean time > the measured time of one performance of the operation.

   e.   the standard time < the normal time.

PROBLEMS

1.   A time study analyst is planning a work sampling study to estimate the percent of idle time in the packing department. The department consists of a foreman and three workers. The hourly wage of the foreman is $15 and the wage of the workers is $8. A time study technician has made 300 observations of these four employees at random times, producing the data below.

   Idle observations   60

   Working observations   <u>240</u>

   Total observations   300

   a.   What is the estimate of the percent of idle time?

   b.   What is the standard error of the percent?

   c.   Estimate the weekly loss due to idle time in the packaging department. The department works a 40-hour week.

   d.   Suppose that an estimate of idle time within 2 percentage points, either way, is required. How many more observations should be taken?

   e.   What will be the point estimate of the percent of idle time after the additional observations are taken?

2. In the course of manufacturing an amplifier, an off-on switch must be attached to the front panel. A time study analyst wishes to determine how long it takes an experienced employee to perform this operation; he therefore times a worker during several repetitions, producing the data below in minutes. The sample standard deviation, s = 0.7277 min.

Time (x)	Time (x)
9.5	8.5
8.2	10.0
9.0	8.5
8.8	10.0
9.3	8.7
9.8	8.0
8.0	8.9
7.9	<u>8.0</u>
Total	141.1

a. What is the true (population) mean time for attaching the off-on switch?

b. What is the observed time for attaching the off-on switch?

c. Suppose it was desired to estimate the mean time within 9 seconds either way. How may more observations would be required?

3. Use the data in Problem 2 to solve this problem.

a. The analyst has determined that the worker has a performance rating of 125 percent while being measured. What is the normal time?

b. Was this worker working rapidly or slowly?

c. The plant manager allows for these delays and interruptions during the working day.

Coffee breaks (2 per 8 hr. shift)	10 min. each
Personal time	20 min. per shift
Maintenance and adjustment of equipment	30 min. per shift
Delays and bottlenecks	20 min. per shift

What is the allowance as a percent of job time?

d. What is the standard time for attaching the off-on switch?

4. Use your work in Problem 3 to solve this problem. The workers who install the off-on switch are paid $10.00 per hour, with fringe benefits of 35 percent.

a. Estimate the number of off-on switches which one worker should be able to install in one 8-hour shift.

b. Determine the standard labor cost of installing the switch.

5. This problem uses the data of problems #2 and #3 to illustrate the use of working time allowances based on a full day's time (rather than on job time).

a. What is the allowance as a percent of working time?

b. What is the standard time for attaching the switch?

6. (One step beyond; based on your statistics course.) For the data in Problem #2 the standard deviation, s = 0.7277 min. Obtain the 95% confidence interval for the mean time for attaching the off-on switch.

    a. What is the standard error, $s_{\bar{x}}$?

    b. What is the 95% confidence interval?

    c. What is the interpretation of the confidence interval?

CHAPTER 7   DESIGN OF WORK SYSTEMS

True/False

Question	Answer	Glossary/ Key Idea	Textbook ref. page
1	T		337
2	F		337
3	F		335
4	F	G	333
5	F	G	317
6	T	G	332
7	T	G, 3	312
8	T		332
9	F		329
10	F		329-330
11	F		312

Multiple-Choice

Question	Answer	Glossary/ Key Idea	Textbook ref. page
1	a		318
2	d	G	320
3	f	11	333
4	b	G	332
5	b		312
6	d		312
7	c		327,333
8	b		337
9	c		316
10	a		329-330

SOLUTIONS TO PROBLEMS

1.   a. $\hat{p} = \dfrac{100(60)}{300} = 20\%$.

   b. $s_{\hat{p}} = \sqrt{\hat{p}(100 - \hat{p})/n} = \sqrt{20(100 - 20)/300} = 2.31\%$

   c.   The loss due to idle time will be the total of the loss due to the foreman's idle time and the loss due to the workers' idle time:

Foreman) .20(40 hrs.)($15.00)	$120.00
Workers) .20(40 hrs.)($8.00)(3 workers)	192.00
Total weekly loss	$312.00

   d. $n = z^2 \hat{p}(100 - \hat{p})/e^2 = (1.96)^2(20)(100 - 20)/2^2 \approx 1{,}537$. Therefore, 1,237 additional observations will be required.

   e.   The new value of $\hat{p}$ cannot be calculated until the additional observations are obtained.

2.   a.   The population mean is unknown.

   b. $OT = \dfrac{\sum x}{n} = \dfrac{141.1}{16} = 8.82$ min.

   c. $n = \dfrac{z^2 s^2}{e^2} = \dfrac{(1.96)^2(.7277)^2}{(.15)^2} \approx 91$. Therefore, 75 additional measurements of the task of installing the off-on switch will be needed.

3. a. Normal Time (NT) = OT x PR = 8.82(1.25) = 11.025 min.

    b. Because a performance rating of 125% is greater than 100%, the worker was working rapidly.

    c. The allowance percent (A) = 100(total allowance time)/(job time) = 100(20 + 20 + 30 + 20)/[(8(60) – 90] = 23.08% of job time.

    d. Standard Time (ST) = NT(1 + A) = 11.025(1 + .2308)= 13.57 minutes per installation.

4. a. Number of installations = $\dfrac{8(60)}{13.57} \approx 35$ switches.

    b. The standard labor cost = $\dfrac{13.57(\$10)(1.35)}{60} = \$3.05$.

5. a. The allowance percent (A) = 100(total allowance time)/(working time) = 100(90)/[8(60)] = 18.75%

    b. Standard time (ST) = NT/(1 – A) = 11.025/(1 – .1875) = 13.57 minutes per installation. (Compare to #3-d).

6. a. $s_{\bar{x}} = \dfrac{s}{\sqrt{n}} = \dfrac{.7277}{\sqrt{16}} = .1819$ min.

    b. The Lower Confidence Limit = $OT - z(s_{\bar{x}}) = 8.82 - 1.96(.1819) = 8.46$ min.

       The Upper Confidence Limit = $OT + z(s_{\bar{x}}) = 8.82 + 1.96(.1819) = 9.18$ min.

    c. There is a .95 probability that the true (population) mean time for installing the switch lies between 8.46 min. and 9.18 min.

CHAPTER 7S
LEARNING CURVES

KEY IDEAS

1. Repetitive operations performed by humans are subject to a learning effect that causes the time per repetition to decrease as the number of repetitions increases.

2. The improvements are due to the combined effect of actual learning by those performing the jobs and the contributions of indirect personnel (e.g., industrial engineers) who change work methods, job design, etc.

3. According to the learning curve theory, the time per repetition decreases at a constant percentage with every doubling of total number of repetitions. For instance, with an 80 percent curve, the time for the 10th unit will be 80 percent of the time needed for the 5th unit; and the time for the 16th unit will be 80 percent of the time needed for the 8th unit.

4. The textbook contains a table that can easily be used to obtain both individual times and cumulative times for selected learning rates.

5. Applications of the learning curve theory include negotiated purchasing, scheduling, pricing new products, budgeting, and inventory planning.

GLOSSARY

learning curve: a mathematical relationship used to describe the learning effect.

learning effect: the continued reduction in the amount of time required to complete a new task, sequence of tasks, or project, as a result of acquiring experience and skill in the job.

log-log scale: a type of graph paper that has logarithmic scales in both the horizontal and vertical directions.

natural logarithms: the logarithm of a number, x, to the base, e = 2.7183. That is, $e^{\ln x} = x$.

negotiated purchasing: used for special purchasing situations such as when a limited quantity of a customized product is involved.

unit time: the number of direct labor hours required for the nth unit in production.

TRUE/FALSE QUESTIONS

1. According to the learning curve, every time the cumulative output doubles, the learning rate increases.

2. A learning curve of 80 percent will result in more improvement than a 90 percent curve over a given number of units.

3. Learning curves only apply to humans, not to machinery.

4. Learning curve results are due strictly to worker learning.

5. Every time the cumulative output doubles, the time per unit will decrease by a constant percentage, assuming the learning curve is pertinent.

MULTIPLE-CHOICE QUESTIONS

1. If a learning situation has a learning curve of .80 and a time of 20 hours to build the initial unit, the estimated time for the 4th unit in hours is:

    a. 20   b. 16   c. 12.8   d. 10.24

2. In which of these activities would learning curves be least useful?

    a. budgeting

    b. pricing new products

    c. manpower planning

    d. assembly-line scheduling

    e. negotiated purchasing

3. A manager is trying to estimate the learning rate for a new job. The first unit required 16 hours and the fourth unit required just under 13 hours. The learning rate is:

    a. 70%

    b. 75%

    c. 80%

    d. 85%

    e. 90%

4. A job will have a learning rate of 75 percent. If the 3rd unit requires 10 hours, the 12th unit should require about this many hours:

    a. 5.6   b. 6.5   c. 7.4%   d. 8.3%   e. 9.2

PROBLEMS

1. Solve the following exercises by referring to Table 7S- I in your textbook.

    a. In the production of cargo planes, an 80 percent learning curve is experienced. It takes 2,000 direct labor hours to produce the first plane. Estimate the direct labor hours required to produce the 10th plane.

    b. In the above case, estimate the total direct labor hours required to produce the first 10 planes.

    c. In the construction of tract houses, a 90 percent learning curve is experienced. It takes 3,000 direct labor hours to construct the first house. Estimate the direct labor hours required to construct the 15th house.

    d. In the above case, estimate the total direct labor hours required to construct the first 6 houses.

2. The Emperor Shipyards Co. has a contract to build 20 identical oil tankers. The production manager believes that an 85 percent learning curve is appropriate for direct labor time. The wages of the workers average $12.00 per hour, with fringe benefits of 30 percent. The following accounting data have been accumulated on the first tanker.

    Direct labor   25,000 hr.

    Direct materials $200,000

    a. What is the interpretation of the 85 percent?

    b. Estimate the direct labor time required to build the 5th tanker.

    c. Estimate the total direct cost of the 5th tanker.

    d. Estimate the total direct labor time required to build all 20 tankers.

    e. Estimate the total direct cost of all 20 tankers.

    f. Find the price per tanker which is 150 percent higher than the total direct cost per tanker.

3   The formula for the learning curve is: $T_n = T_1 * n^b$, where:

    T_n = time f or the nth unit

    T_1 = time for the first unit

    b = ln(learning percent)/ln 2

    Use the e^x key or the lnx key on your calculator to solve these problems:

    a. ln 2 = ?

    b. Learning percent = 85%, Ln(learning percent) = ?

    c. b = ?

    d. $T_1 = 5,000$ hrs. $T_4 = ?$

4. Use the formulas in problem #3 to solve these problems:

    a. Learning percent = 82%, Ln(learning percent) = ?

    b. b = ?

    c. $T_1 = 7,000$ hrs. $T_5 = ?$

CHAPTER 7S   LEARNING CURVES

SOLUTIONS TO PROBLEMS

1. a. .477(2000) = 954 direct labor hours.

    b. 6.315(2000) = 12,630 direct labor hours.

    c. .663(3000) = 1,989 direct labor hours.

    d. 5.101(3000) = 15,303 direct labor hours.

2. a. Every time the output doubles, the time required to produce one unit is 85% as large as it was before the doubling occurred.

    b. .686(25000) = 17,150 direct labor hours.

    c. Direct Labor) 17,150 hrs.($12.00)   = $205,800.00

    Fringe Benefits) 205,800.00(.30)   =   61,740.00

    Direct Materials)   200,000.00

        Total $467,540.00

    d. 12.402(25000) = 310,050 direct labor hours.

    e. Direct Labor) 310,050 hrs.($12.00)   = $3,720,600.00

    Fringe Benefits) 3,720,600(.30)   =   1,116,180.00

    Direct Materials) 20($200,000)   =   4,000,000.00

        Total Cost $8,836,780.00

    f. The mean direct cost per tanker is estimated at 8,836,780/20 » $441,839.00. The price per tanker would be 441,839 x (2.50) = $1,104,598.00.

3. a. Ln 2 = 0.6931.

    b. Ln .85 = -0.1625.

    c. b = Ln .85/Ln 2 = -0.1625/0.6931 = -0.2345.

    d. $T_4 = T_1 * n^b = 5000(4^{-.2345}) = 5000(.7225) = 3,612$ hrs.

4. a. Ln .82 = -0.1985.

    b. b = Ln .82/Ln 2 = -0.1985/0.6931 = -0.2863.

    c. $T_5 = T_1 * n^b = 7000(5^{-.2863}) = 7000(.6308) = 4,415$ hrs.

CHAPTER 8
LOCATION PLANNING AND ANALYSIS

KEY IDEAS

1. A plant location decision is either a choice to expand existing productive facilities, add new locations, or substitute a new facility for an existing one. Subcontracting may also be used as a substitute for substantial plant expansion.

2 . A plant location decision can be made either before the capacity decision is made, concurrently with the capacity decision, or after it.

3. The criteria for choosing sites are not based solely on economics or cost. Many environmental and quality-of-life factors are relevant to the decision.

4. Service operations and public utility systems have different guidelines for choosing locations than do more conventional production operations. Service operations must concentrate upon accessibility to markets. A production facility decision is usually based on least cost, providing there are not some overriding considerations such as accessibility to raw materials or skilled labor, quality of life, etc.

5. There is a location problem at more than one level of decision making. Not only must a decision be made as to where to put the production facility, but also where to put the warehouses and distribution centers, and how to build support networks that take care of the relevant logistical problems.

6. In recent years multinational companies have been putting production facilities in foreign countries to take advantage of lower labor costs. In many cases, these plants produce semifinished goods and components to be integrated into larger products, via the production process. International operations management introduces new problems such as taxes, import duties, additional transportation costs, different sets of laws, foreign social and political structures, and trade practices and restrictions.

7. Localities frequently offer special incentives for industrial development by buying land for industrial districts, constructing special buildings, and offering favorable leases, tax incentives or loans.

8. Location preferences may reflect organizational policy on decentralization versus centralization.

9. Regional factors include location near the sources of raw materials, both for service and to minimize transportation costs.

10. Community location factors are primarily quality of life and quality of the work force available, as well as taxes, availability of public utilities, support for plant development, and whether or not there are costly local regulations. Special incentives offered by communities to attract industry are also relevant.

11. Site location factors include costs, access to all transportation media, zoning restrictions and land.

12. The factor rating scale method evaluates alternative locations by computing weighted averages of the factor rating scores of the various alternatives. The recommended location is the one with the highest weighted average.

13. The center of gravity method is useful in establishing an approximate (geographic) location for a distribution center. The method minimizes total shipping cost between the distribution center and multiple shipping points (destinations). if shipping quantities for all destinations are equal, the distribution center will be located at the arithmetic averages of the x and y coordinates of the destinations; if shipping quantities are unequal, the location of the distribution center is found by using a weighted average approach, where the weights are the quantities to be shipped.

GLOSSARY

center of gravity method: used to determine location for centralized distribution.

environmental regulations: regulations imposed by agencies such as the federal Occupational Safety and Health Administration (OSHA) or by local regulatory bodies that restrict the way a plant can be built or operated, based upon the potential effect on the environment.

factor rating: assigning numerical weights to factors in order to facilitate the plant location decision.

location: the site for a plant, raw materials, markets or a labor supply.

locational cost-volume analysis: break-even analysis adapted to the cost analysis of alternative plant

multinational company: a firm with plants in more than one country.

semi(finished goods: component parts or modules of an end item in the production system, that will require further processing.

tax abatement: reducing the tax base of a potential plant as a special incentive for the plant to locate in a particular region or community.

threshold: a minimum required value for an average factor rating score, if an alternative does not meet the threshold value, it is eliminated from further consideration,

TRUE/FALSE QUESTIONS

1. Factor rating scales is a proven method of choosing the best of a set of decision alternatives.

2. A location decision may be either to expand an existing facility, add a new one, or else replace an existing facility with another one.

3. The sum of factor weights in a rating scale can be greater than 100%.

4. A break-even point in location analysis is a case where two different locations have the same total cost.

5. It is more important for a service facility to be near the potential market than for a production facility.

6. Companies that use multiple plant strategies may have plants devoted to specific products, specific markets, or specific processes.

7. In choosing one of a set of location alternatives based on a factor rating scale, the scale usually does not accurately reflect dollar differences in costs between the various alternatives.

8. The center of gravity method is used to minimize production costs.

MULTIPLE-CHOICE QUESTIONS

1. Pick the statement about location decisions that is not true.

    a. They are often long term.

    b. Mistakes can be difficult to overcome.

    c. Both fixed costs and variable costs are usually affected.

    d. It is important to identify the optimal location.

2. Which of the following would not generally be classified as a regional factor in location decisions?

    a. Location of raw materials

    b. Location of markets

    c. Labor supply

    d. Taxes

    e. All are regional factors.

3. Which one of the following is more a community factor than a site factor?

    a. Rail access

    b. Zoning

    c. Environmental regulations

    d. Room for expansion

    e. Utility hookups

4. Here is a list of steps used in making location decisions. Which step should occur first?

    a. Identify a general region

    b. Identify factors that are important. such as location of markets

    c. Identify some community-site alternatives

    d. Identify criteria that will be used to evaluate alternatives

    e. Evaluate the alternatives

5. Which of the following would not usually be cited as a reason for U.S. companies locating in foreign countries?

    a. Increased quality of output

    b. Cheaper labor

    c. Availability of raw materials

    d. Access to markets

    e. All are reasons

6. Faced with the choice of location for a plant, a firm is considering four different possible alternatives. The decision will be made by using a scoring model. Give the order of preference for the four different locations based on the following data.

Criterion	Weight	Alternative			
		1	2	3	4
raw material availability	0.2	g	p	ok	vg
community support	0.1	ok	ok	ok	ok
transportation costs	0.5	vg	ok	p	ok
labor relations	0.1	g	vg	p	ok
quality of life	0.1	g	vg	p	ok

vg (very good) = 5 points;   ok (acceptable) = 3 points

g (good) = 4 points;   p (poor) = 1 point

The order of preference for the four alternatives is:

a. 1. 2, 3, 4.

b. 4, 3, 2, 1.

c. 1, 4, 2, 3.

d. 41 1, 3, 2.

e. 2, 1, 4, 3.

f. none of the above choices is correct.

PROBLEMS

1. Two plant locations are under consideration for a new battery factory. Here are estimates of the fixed and variable costs at each location.

Location	Fixed Cost per Year	Variable Cost per Unit
A	$1,500,000	$1.25
B	1,250,000	1.75

a. What is the total cost function for each location?

b. Plot the total cost functions on the same graph.

c. On the graph, identify the range of output for which each location has the least cost.

d. Which location should be selected for an output of 400,000 batteries per year.? 800,000 batteries per year?

e. Find the cutoff point algebraically.

2. Four plant locations arc under consideration for a new microchip plant. Here are estimates of the fixed and variable costs at each location.

Location	Fixed cost per year	Variable cost per unit
A	$3,500,000	$600
B	3,000,000	800
C	4,000,000	500
D	4,500,000	400

a. What is the total cost function for each location?

b. Plot the total cost functions for these locations on the same graph.

c. On the graph, identify the range of output for which each location has the least cost.

d. Which location should be selected for an output of 4,000 chips per year? 12,000 chips per year?

e. Find the cutoff points algebraically.

3. Two locations are under consideration for building a condominium. (A condominium is a building in which each apartment is owned by the resident, rather than rented.) One location is in suburb A of a large Eastern city, and the other is in suburb B. The marketing manager has identified the following factors which bear upon the location decision and their relative weights.

Factor	Desirable Status	Weight
1. Proximity to public transportation	Should be close	.20
2. Space for a parking lot	Should be large	.40
3. Property taxes	Should be low	.25
4. Electricity rates	Should be low	.15

Each factor will be rated on a scale of I = unsatisfactory to 10 = outstanding. Research has revealed the following information about each location, and the marketing manager has rated each factor at each location.

	Location		Rating	
Factor	A	B	A	B
1. Public transportation	1 block	6 blocks	9	2
2. Parking lot	1 acre	3 acres	3	7
3. Property taxes	$600/year	$800/year	6	4
4. Electric rates	$.09/kwh.	$.06/kwh.	5	8

a. Construct a rating analysis worksheet in the style of Example 2 in your textbook and determine the composite score for each location.

b. Where should the condominium be built? Why?

4. Business has been good for the Black & White News Company, which receives magazines from the publishers and distributes them to the news racks of drugstores and supermarkets. At present, it has five customers, each of which is serviced once a week; expired magazines are collected and new editions are displayed on the racks. (This problem is obviously artificially small.) Here are the x and y coordinates of the locations of the customers and the number of truck loads of magazines which go to each destination. The company operates out of a single warehouse, whose coordinates are also included. The company has outgrown the warehouse, and the partners are discussing whether to expand the present facilities or to construct a larger warehouse at a new site.

Customer	x	y	Weekly Loads
A	2	3	1
B	5	2	3
C	3	6	2
D	10	4	6
E	6	5	2
Warehouse	3	4	

a. Plot the locations of the customers on graph paper.

b. What is the mean of x?

c. What is the mean of y?

d. Plot the optimal location of the warehouse on your graph.

e. Based solely on this analysis, should the partners enlarge the present warehouse or construct a new one?

CHAPTER 8   LOCATION PLANNING AND ANALYSIS

SOLUTIONS TO PROBLEMS

1. a.   A) $C_A = 1,500,000 + 1.25x$

        B) $C_B = 1,250,000 + 1.75x$

    b, c.

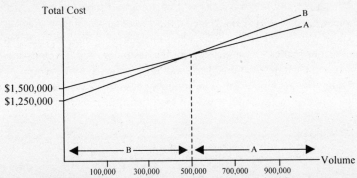

    d. For 400,000 batteries, location B is less expensive. For 800,000 batteries, location A is less expensive.

    e. At the cutoff point (Q), the total costs will be equal at both locations.

    $C_A = C_B$

    $1,500,000 + 1.25Q = 1,250,000 + 1.75Q$

    $Q = 500,000$ batteries.

2. a. A) $C_A = 3,500,000 + 800x$

B) $C_B = 3,000,000 + 500x$

C) $C_C = 4,000,000 + 500x$

D) $C_D = 4,500,00 + 400x$

b, c.

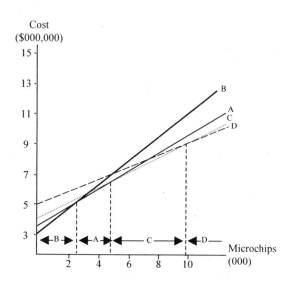

Cost ($000,000)

Microchips (000)

d. For 4,000 chips, location A is the least expensive. For 12,000 chips, location D is the least expensive.

e. $C_B = C_A$

$3,000,000 + 800Q = 3,500,000 + 600Q$

$Q = 2,500$ microchips.

At a lower volume, B is superior; at a higher volume, A is superior. The cutoff point between A and C is 5,000 microchips. The cutoff point between C and D is 10,000 microchips.

3. a.

Factor	Weight	Score A	Score B	Weighted score A	Weighted score B
1. Public Transportation	.20	9	2	1.80	0.40
2. Parking lot	.40	3	7	1.20	2.80
3. Property taxes	.25	6	4	1.50	1.00
4. Electricity rates	.15	5	8	0.75	1.20
				5.25	5.40

b. The condominium should be built in suburb B, since it has the higher composite score.

4. a.

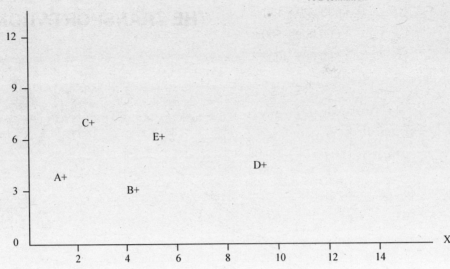

Problem No. 4-a
+ = A Destination

b. $\bar{x} = \dfrac{\sum Qx}{\sum Q} = \dfrac{1(2) + 3(5) + 2(3) + 6(10) + 2(6)}{1 + 3 + 2 + 6 + 2} = 6.78$.

c. $\bar{y} = \dfrac{\sum Qy}{\sum Q} = \dfrac{1(3) + 3(2) + 2(6) + 6(4) + 2(5)}{1 + 3 + 2 + 6 + 2} = 3.93$

d.

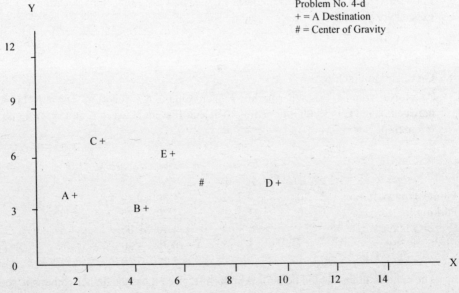

Problem No. 4-d
+ = A Destination
# = Center of Gravity

e. The partners should build a new warehouse at $\bar{x} = 6.78$ and $\bar{y} = 3.93$, since shipping expenses should be lower from the new warehouse.

CHAPTER 8S
THE TRANSPORTATION MODEL

KEY IDEAS

1.   A transportation problem involves distributing stocks or supplies from multiple sending points (origins) to multiple receiving points (destinations) in such a way that the total transportation cost is minimized.

2.   The transportation model is a special-purpose linear programming model that permits manual solution of fairly large problems with relative ease. Problems must be set up in tabular fashion, such as shown in the textbook.

3.   The first step in a transportation problem is to make sure that supply and demand are equal. If they are not, add a dummy row or column with a supply (row) or demand (column) equal to the difference between supply and demand. Assign a zero transportation cost to each cell in the dummy row or column.

4.   Next, obtain an initial feasible solution. Use the intuitive method.

5.   Evaluate the solution to determine if it is optimal. Use either the stepping-stone method or the MODI method.

6.   If all cell evaluations are positive or zero, the solution is optimal. A zero cell evaluation signifies the existence of an alternate solution that will result in the same total cost as the current solution. One or more negative cell evaluations indicate a non-optimal solution. Use the stepping-stone method to obtain an improved solution.

7.   Repeat steps 5 and 6 until the optimal solution has been obtained.

8.   One application of the transportation model is for location decisions. In such cases, two (or more) competing location alternatives are each used in a different version of the transportation table to see which one will provide the lowest total cost solution.

GLOSSARY

See also GLOSSARY for Chapter 5S on "linear programming."

cell: a location at the i-th row and the j-th column of a transportation matrix that identifies a shipment from the i-th source of supply to the j-th destination.

completed cell: an assigned shipment from source, i, to destination, j. under the solution of the transportation model for the current iteration.

degenerate solution: for the transportation model, a solution that is feasible, but does not have the required number of shipments to make possible a test for optimality; in that case, an E (nearly zero) shipment is assigned to one of the empty cells to make possible further progress in verifying the solution.

dummy: see unequal supply and demand.

empty cell: a cell that does not contain a shipment.

epsilon (ε): when the solution is degenerate, an ε (nearly zero) shipment is assigned to one of the empty cells; the ε is placed so as to facilitate the tests for feasibility and optimality.

feasible solution: a solution that exhausts the available supply capacities and at the same time satisfies all of the demand requirements.

intuitive approach: assigning units to cells, lowest cost first, to obtain an initial feasible solution of a transportation model.

iteration: improved feasible solutions of the transportation model are obtained in a series of stages called iterations; the term iteration comes from the fact that the same procedure is followed for each successive stage of improvement.

modified distribution (MODI) method: an efficient method for evaluating a feasible solution of a transportation problem based on index numbers.

optimal solution: the feasible solution with the smallest total transportation cost.

solution: a set of shipments which satisfies the constraints.

stepping-stone: a method for improving a feasible solution by shifting shipment amounts at right angles around a closed path so as to reduce the overall transportation cost.

suboptimal solution: a feasible solution that is not optimal.

transportation matrix: a table consisting of m rows, each row representing a source of supply, and n columns, each column denoting a destination, and each (i, j) cell (i = 1, 2,..., m, j = 1,2,..., n) contains cost data about a shipment from the i-th source of supply to the j-th destination.

transportation model: a linear programming technique for minimizing the overall transportation cost of shipments of a commodity from m sources, such as warehouses, with limited capacities, to n destinations, such as stores, with specified minimum demand requirements.

unequal supply and demand: a situation where the total of the capacities of the m sources of supply and the total of the demand requirements for the n destinations are not equal; in that case it is necessary to assign a dummy row or else a dummy column in order to balance the transportation model; if there is a surplus, the sum of the capacities or availabilities exceeds the sum of the requirements-in that case a dummy column absorbs the unused demand; if there is a shortage, a dummy row absorbs the backorders for unsatisfied demand.

TRUE/FALSE QUESTIONS

1. The transportation model of linear programming assumes homogeneous commodities, deterministic supply, deterministic demand, that every source is capable of shipping to every destination, and that there is a known per-unit shipping cost from every source to every destination.

2. The transportation model is used to identify the optimum shippng plan for a given transportation problem.

3. The steppingstone method of cell evaluation involves making a series of alternating additions and subtractions of equal amounts to occupied cells, and to the cell being evaluated.

4. When an empty cell is filled artificially in order to complete a degenerate solution of the transportation model, the filled cell is called a dummy.

5. When developing an improved solution, quantities can be shifted horizontally, vertically, or diagonally.

6. The total transportation cost of a set of shipments for the transportation model is the sum of the products of the per-unit shipping costs multiplied by the shipment amounts.

7. A dummy origin or destination is used when the supply and demand are not equal.

MULTIPLE-CHOICE QUESTIONS

1. In a transportation cell-evaluation path, plus and minus signs alternate in order to:
    a. preserve equality of supply and demand.
    b. assure equality of + and - signs.
    c. increase the probability of optimality.
    d. none of the above.

2. A transportation model has 6 rows and 5 columns. What is the required number of occupied cells?
    a. 9.
    b. 10.
    c. 11.
    d. 12.
    e. 30.

3. A transportation model has S = 600 and D = 500. What does the transportation matrix require:
    a. adding a dummy origin for 100 units
    b. adding a dummy destination for 100 units.
    c. deleting 100 units of the supply.
    d. deleting 100 units of the demand.
    e. It depends on how many origins and destinations there are.

4. In a transportation minimization problem, the optimal solution is reached when:
    a. The number of rows equals the number of columns.
    b. The total supply equals the total demand.
    c. All empty cells have been evaluated.
    d. No cells with a value of zero occur.
    e. None of the above.

5. In a transportation model, an alternate optimal solution exists if:
    a. The values of all of the unoccupied cells are positive.
    b. The values of some cells are positive and the rest are negative.
    c. The value of at least one unoccupied cell is zero.
    d. The values of all of the unoccupied cells are negative.
    e. An alternative optimal solution never exists.

6. In the linear programming version of the transportation model:
    a. all constraints are $\geq$.
    b. all constraints are $\leq$.
    c. some constraints are $\geq$ and some are $\leq$.
    d. all constraints are $=$.
    e. some constraints are $\geq$ and some are $=$.

PROBLEMS

1. A firm has four factories, # 1, 2, 3, 4, which ship their output to two warehouses, A and B. The capacities of the factories for one month, the requirements of the warehouses for one month, and the costs of shipping one unit from each factory to each warehouse are given below.

Factory (Rows)	Capacity (units)	Warehouse (Columns)	Requirements (units)
1	250	A	600
2	400	B	700
3	450	Total	300
4	350		
Total	1,450		

To:	A	B
1	12	10
From 2	14	11
3	9	12
4	8	7

Determine the least-cost shipping schedule for the month by the stepping-stone algorithm.

a. Set up the transportation matrix.

b. Find the initial solution by the intuitive (lowest-cost) method.

c. What is the cost of the initial solution?

d. What is the optimum shipping schedule?

e. What is the cost of the optimum schedule?

f. What is the interpretation of the 150 items in the dummy column?

2. Solve Problem 1 by the MODI method.

a. Find the row and column indexes for the occupied cells.

b. Find the row and column indexes for the unoccupied cells.

c. What is the optimum shipping schedule?

d. What is the cost of the optimum schedule?

3. A firm has two factories, # 1 and 2, which ship their output to four warehouses, A, B, C, D. The capacities of the factories for one month, and the requirements of the warehouses for one month, and the costs of shipping one unit from each factory to each warehouse are given below.

Factory (Rows)	Capacity (units)	Warehouse (Columns)	Requirements (units)
1	500	A	300
2	900	B	200
Total	1,400	C	400
		D	200
		Total	1,100

Shipping From	to	Cost	Shipping From	to	Cost
1	A	$15	2	A	$9
1	B	13	2	B	11
1	C	13	2	C	12
1	D	10	2	D	16

Determine the least-cost shipping schedule for the month by the stepping-stone method. This problem is degenerate.

   a. Set up the transportation matrix.

   b. Find the initial solution by the intuitive (lowest-cost) method.

   c. What is the cost of the initial solution?

   d. What is the optimum shipping schedule?

   e. What is the cost of the optimum schedule?

   f. What is the interpretation of the 300 units in the dummy column?

4.   Solve problem #3 by using an EXCEL spreadsheet.

   a. What is the objective function of the linear programming version of the problem?

   b. What are the constraints in the linear programming version of the problem?

   c. How do you enter the problem on the EXCEL spreadsheet?

   d. How do you enter the objective function?

   e. How do you enter the constraints?

   f. What is the solution?

   g. What is the total cost?

   h. Did you get the same answer as in #3?

CHAPTER 8S   THE TRANSPORTATION MODEL

True/False

Question	Answer	Glossary/ Key Idea	Textbook ref. page
1	T		390
2	T	1	390
3	T		393-394
4	F	G, 3	403-404
5	F		395
6	T		400
7	T	3	402

Multiple-Choice

Question	Answer	Glossary/ Key Idea	Textbook ref. page
1	a		394
2	b		394-395
3	b		402
4	e		399
5	c		394
6	d		406

SOLUTIONS TO PROBLEMS

4.   a,b.

To: From:	A		B		Dummy		Supply
1		12		10		0	
1	250						250
2		14		11		0	
2	350		50				400
3		9		12		0	
3			450				450
4		8		7		0	
4			200		150		350
Demand	600		700		150		1450

Here are the values of the unoccupied cells, along with one plus-minus path.

To: From:	A	B	Dummy	Supply
1	12 / 250	10 / (+1)	0 / (-2)	250
2	14 / 350	11 / 50 (−)	0 / (-4) (+)	400
3	9 / (-6)	12 / 450	0 / (-5)	450
4	8 / (-2)	7 / 200 (+)	0 / 150 (−)	350
Demand	600	700	150	1450

c.

From	To	Quantity	Cost	Product
1	A	250	$12	$ 3,000
2	A	350	14	4,900
2	B	50	11	550
3	B	450	12	5,400
4	B	200	7	1,400
4	DUMMY	150	0	0
	Total Cost		$15,250	

d.

To: From:	A	B	Dummy	Supply
1	12 / (+1)	10 / 250	0 / (+1)	250
2	14 / (+2)	11 / 250	0 / 150	400
3	9 / 450	12 / (+41)	0 / (+3)	450
4	8 / 150	7 / 200	0 / (+41)	350
Demand	600	700	150	1450

e. Here is the total cost of the optimum shipping schedule.

From	To	Quantity	Cost	Product
1	B	250	$10	$2,500
2	B	250	11	2,750
2	DUMMY	150	0	0
3	A	450	9	4,050
4	A	150	8	1,200
4	B	200	7	1,400
		Total Cost		$11,900

f. Because 150 units are to be sent to the dummy destination, they will not be produced. Factory #2 will have idle time.

2. a. For occupied cells, use the formulas:

column index =cell cost - row index; or row index = cell cost - column index.

Begin with the cost for the first row, and let the first row index, R_1, be 0.

Cell	Cell Cost	Row/column Index	Cell/column Index
1-A	12	$R_1 = 0$	$C_1 = 12$
2-A	14	$C_1 = 12$	$R_2 = 2$
2-B	11	$R_2 = 2$	$C_2 = 9$
3-B	12	$C_2 = 9$	$R_3 = 3$
4-B	7	$C_2 = 9$	$R_4 = -2$
4-D	0	$R_4 = -2$	$C_3 = 2$

b. For unoccupied cells, use the formula: cell index = cell cost - row index - column index.

Cell	Cell Cost	Row Index	Column Index	Cell Index
1-B	10	$R_1 = 0$	$C_2 = 9$	
1-Dummy	0	$R_1 = 0$	$C_3 = 2$	
2-Dummy	0	2	2	
3-A	9	3	12	
3-Dummy	0	3	2	
4-A	8	-2	12	

Compare the cell indexes with the circled numbers in the matrix for #1b. Because some of the cell indexes are negative, a cheaper shipping schedule exists.

c. Solve this problem by finding the plus-minus path for the cell with the most negative index and reallocating the quantities to be shipped. At each iteration, find the indexes for the occupied cells by using the technique of #2a; find the indexes for the unoccupied cells by using the technique of #2b. The answer will be the same as #1d.

d. Same as #1e.

3. a, b.

To: From:	A		B		C		D		Dummy		Supply
		15		13		13		10		0	
1	300		200		(-1)		(-8)		(-2)		500
		9		11		12		16		0	
2	(-4)		ε		400		200		300		900
Demand	300		200		400		200		300		1600

c.

From - To	Quantity	Cost	Product
1 - A	300	$15	$ 4,500
1 - B	200	13	2,600
2 - C	400	12	4,800
2 - D	200	16	3,200
2 DUMMY	300	0	0
		Total Cost	$15,100

d.

To: From:	A		B		C		D		Dummy		Supply
		15		13		13		10		0	
1	(+6)		ε		(+1)		200		300		500
		9		11		12		16		0	
2	300		200 + ε		400		(+6) 15 0		(+2)		900
Demand	300		200		400		200		300		1600

e.

From - To		Quantity	Cost	Product
1	D	200	$10	$ 2,000
1 - DUMMY		300	0	0
2	A	300	9	2,700
2	B	200	11	2,200
2	C	400	12	4,800
		Total Cost		$11,700

f. Factory #1 will have idle time.

4. a. Min $Z = 15x_{1A} + 13x_{1B} + 13x_{1C} + 10x_{1D} + 0x_{1E} + 9x_{2A} + 11x_{2B} + 12x_{2C} + 16x_{2D} + 0x_{2E}$

    b. ST: 1) $x_{1A} + x_{1B} + x_{1C} + x_{1D} + x_{1E} = 500$

               2) $x_{2A} + x_{2B} + x_{2C} + x_{2D} + x_{2E} = 900$

               A) $x_{1A} + x_{2A} = 300$

               B) $x_{1B} + x_{2B} = 200$

               C) $x_{1C} + x_{2C} = 400$

               D) $x_{1D} + x_{2D} = 200$

               E) $x_{1E} + x_{2E} = 300$

    c.

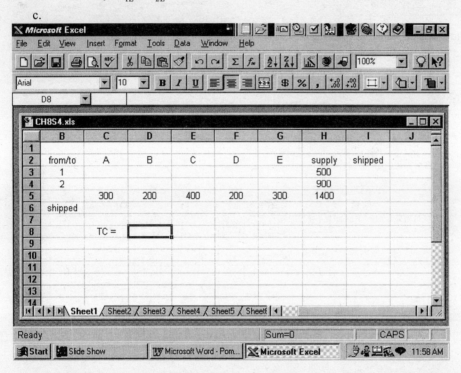

    d. In cell D-8: =15*C3+13D3+13E3+10F3+0G3+9C4+11D4+12E4+16F4+0G4.

    e. In cell I-3: =C3+D3+E3+F3+G3

        In cell I-4: =C4+D4+E4+F4+G4

        In cell C-6: = C3+C4

        In cell D-6: = D3+D4

        In cell E-6: = E3+E4

        In cell F-6: = F3+F4

        In cell G-6: = G3+G4

        Click on Tools; Click on Solver. Set target cell: D8; Min; by changing cells C3:G4.

        Click on Add; Cell Reference C3:G4, >=; 0

        Click on Add; Cell Reference I3; =; 500

Click on Add; Cell Reference I4: =; 900

Click on Add; Cell Reference C6; =; 300

etc.

Click on Solve; Highlight Answer Report

EXCEL cell F3 = matrix cell D1 = 200 units

etc.

g. $11,700.

CHAPTER 9
INTRODUCTION TO QUALITY MANAGEMENT

KEY IDEAS

1. An organization's reputation for superior quality can give it a competitive advantage in the marketplace. Superior quality can also reduce the risk of liability claims, reduce costs, and increase productivity.

2. Quality is defined as the ability of a product or service to consistently meet or exceed the expectations of the customer. Operational definitions of quality generally refer to one or more dimensions of quality. These include performance, special features, conformance to expectations, reliability, durability, and service after delivery.

3. The determinants of quality are design, conformance to design, ease of use, and service after delivery.

4. The consequences of poor quality relate to image/reputation, liability, productivity, and costs. Costs can be categorized as failure costs, appraisal costs, and prevention costs.

5. Quality can be improved by R & D efforts (explained in Chapter 5 of the textbook), by efforts of improvement teams, and by suggestions from employees and customers. Management plays a key role in improving and maintaining good quality.

6. Modern quality management stresses prevention of mistakes rather than finding and correcting mistakes after they occur. This has placed increased emphasis on both product design and process design. Quality gurus such as Deming, Juran, Crosby, and Ishikawa have greatly influenced current thinking and practice of quality management.

7. Quality awards, such as the Malcolm Baldrige Award and the Deming Prize have generated interest in quality improvement, and helped to focus attention on the importance of quality. They have also helped to educate business people on quality management.

GLOSSARY

appraisal costs: costs related to appraising quality, such as inspection, testing, and so on.

Baldrige Award: created by Congress to stimulate efforts to improve quality, and to recognize quality achievements. Limited to U.S. companies.

Deming Prize: named in honor of American W. Edwards Deming. A Japanese prize that recognizes successful quality efforts.

dimensions of quality: used for operational definitions of quality. included are performance, special features, reliability, durability, perceived (or reputed) quality, and service after the sale..

external failure costs: costs incurred because of defective products or faulty services which are discovered after the sale.

internal failure costs: costs incurred because of defective products or faulty services which are discovered before the sale.

ISO 9000: a series of standards that outline the requirements for quality management systems. Developed by the International Organization for Standardization, which is comprised of 91 countries, including the U.S. Essential for companies that want to deal with the European Economic Community (EC).

ISO-14000: a set of standards which was introduced by the International Organization for Standardization. It is intended to assess a company's performance in terms of environmental responsibility.

liability: the legal responsibility of a producer for defects of a product or service that cause injury, harm, or property damage

prevention costs: costs associated with attempts to prevent mistakes from occurring. These include planning and administrative costs, training costs, monitoring operations, working with vendors, and so on.

quality at the source: making each employee responsible for the quality of his or her own work.

quality of conformance: achieving the intent of design in producing a product or delivering a service.

quality of design: the extent to which a product or service possesses features that can meet or exceed customer expectations.

zero defects: any level of defects is too high; management must install programs that help the organization move towards the elimination of defects.

TRUE/FALSE QUESTIONS

1. In the phrase *quality of conformance*, conformance refers to meeting customer specifications.

2. The Deming prize is limited to U.S. companies.

3. One definition of quality is fitness for use.

4. Service after the sale is one dimension of quality.

5. Liability claims can result from poor quality.

6. One criticism of the Baldrige Award is that applicants sometimes spend tremendous amounts of time and money vying for it.

7. Quality at the source refers to each worker being responsible for the quality of his/her work.

8. Reworking items that fail to pass inspection is an example of an appraisal cost.

9. ISO1400 is a set of environmental standards.

MULTIPLE-CHOICE QUESTIONS

1. Which one of these reflects an internal failure cost?
   a. inspection
   b. rework
   c. liability claim
   d. customer complaint
   e. replacement of defective products

2. Although closely associated with quality, this name is not on the list of quality gurus:
   a. W. Edwards Deming
   b. Philip Crosby
   c. Malcolm Baldrige
   d. J. M. Juran
   e. Kaoru Ishikawa

3. Which name is associated with the phrase "fitness for use"?
    a. Deming
    b. Crosby
    c. Baldrige
    d. Juran
    e. Ishikawa

4. Which name is associated with a list of 14 points?
    a. Deming
    b. Crosby
    c. Baldrige
    d. Juran
    e. Ishikawa

5. Which name is associated with a cause-and-effect diagram?
    a. Deming
    b. Crosby
    c. Baldrige
    d. Juran
    e. Ishikawa

6. Which name is associated with a Japanese Prize?
    a. Deming
    b. Crosby
    c. Baldrige
    d. Juran
    e. Ishikawa

7. Which name is associated with the phrase, "quality is free"?
    a. Deming
    b. Crosby.
    c. Baldridge.
    d. Juran.
    e. Ishikawa.

8. Which one of these would not be considered a determinant of quality?
    a. Ease of use
    b. Service after delivery
    c. Design
    d. Conformance to design
    e. Focus groups

9.   Which of the following would not normally be included in a list of the major ways quality affects an organization?

a.   Liability
b.   Reputation
c.   Costs
d.   Productivity
e.   All are factors

CHAPTER 9 INTRODUCTION TO QUALITY MANAGEMENT

True/False

Question	Answer	Glossary/ Key Idea	Textbook ref. page
1	T	G, 3	423
2	F		432
3	T		427
4	T	2	422
5	T	1	424
6	T		431
7	T	G	
8	F		424-425
9	F		436

Multiple-Choice

Question	Answer	Glossary/ Key Idea	Textbook ref. page
1	b		425
2	c	6	425
3	d		430
4	a		430
5	e		430
6	a		432
7	b		432
8	e		422-423
9	e		424

CHAPTER 10
QUALITY CONTROL

KEY IDEAS

1. There are two principal types of ways of measuring quality: attributes (counting the number of occurrences in one or two categories) and variables (measuring a characteristic or the deviation from a standard).

2. There are two principal types of Quality Assurance: sampling inspection of incoming outgoing materials (acceptance sampling) and control charts for ongoing processes (process control). Each type may be applied to attributes or variables.

3. Control charts differentiate between the process being in control (within an accept range of random variation) and out of control (outside the acceptable range). Process control involves making frequent small sample inspections to detect whether the process in control or out of control. Out of control means either above the upper control limit below the lower control limit.

    The limits for control charts are established first by obtaining 20 to 25 small samples of same size at different times from the process. This forms the basis for judging future samples.

4. The four types of control charts described in this chapter are: x-bar chart for means, R charts for ranges, *p-charts* for attributes with proportion defectives, and c-charts for the number of defects.

    a. The x-bar charts are based on the mean and a known standard deviation. The UCL and LCL are frequently based on ±2-sigma or 95.5% limits or ±3-sigma or 99% limits of the normal distribution.

    b. Use range to simplify calculations by using the range instead of the standard deviation. Tables of control chart factors A_2, D_3, D_4 are used in conjunction with range data to obtain control limits for x-bar charts.

    c. A c-chart for attributes gives the number of defects in a standard small sample for very large lots. It is based on the theory that the number of defects, c, has a Poisson distribution, so that $\bar{c}$ is the mean number of defectives in the sample, and the standard deviation the number of defects is $\sqrt{c}$.

5. To be effective, controls may need to be revised from time to time to reflect such factors a changes in the process due to changing standards, technological changes, etc.

6, Run tests such as the number of runs with respect to the median, and the number of runs up and down, can be useful in checking for nonrandomness. Run tests should be used in conjunction with control charts. Both approaches test for randomness. A process that is in control will exhibit randomness in a sequence of observations; the appearance of nonrandomness suggests that the process is not random (i.e., not in control).

7. A process capability ratio provides an indication of the ability of the process to meet specifications. It is computed as the ratio of a specified dimension to the process width on that dimension. A value of 1.00 means the two are equal; the greater the value of the ratio, the more likely it is that the process output will fall within the allowable variation (specification).

TIPS FOR PROBLEM SOLVING

A frequent issue in problems in this chapter involves determining the value of z that will be used to calculate upper and lower control limits for mean, p, and $\bar{c}$ charts. Here are some typical ways the information is given, and how to obtain the value of z:

1. "Use 2-sigma limits." The "2" refers to z; hence use $z = 2$.

2. "Determine control limits such that 95% of the sample values will fall within the limits when the process is in control." To obtain z, divide the percentage by 2 (e.g., .95/2 = .4750) and then locate this value in Appendix Table A. That enables you to determine the value of z (for .4750, the value is 1.96).

3. Some problems refer to an alpha risk, or the risk of making a Type I error (e.g., 5%). Note that these two terms both essentially refer to the area in the tails of a normal distribution. In these cases, subtract the percentage from 100%, divide by 2, and find the value of z in Appendix Table A (e.g., 1.00 - .05 = .95; .95/2 = .4750; $z = 1.96$).

4. If a problem does not contain a probability or a z-value for control limits, simply use a reasonable value such as $z = 2$ or 3.

Note that for control chart problems, Appendix Table A is the preferred table rather than Table B.

GLOSSARY

attribute: a characteristic that has just two choices, e.g., defective or acceptable.

c-chart: for a continuous process, a type of control chart based on the number of defects per unit.

conformance: the characteristics of the product satisfy the established standard for the characteristics.

control chart: a technique devised by Walter Shewhart to monitor the quality level of work in process.

control limit: see upper control limit and lower control limit.

inspection: examining material in process or finished products to determine conformance to standard.

liability: the legal responsibility of a producer for defects of a product or service that causes injury, harm, or property damage.

lower control limit (LCL): in a Shewhart-type control chart, the lower limit of the random scatter of a sample statistic, to define whether a process is in control or out of control.

p-chart: for attribute process control, a type of control chart based on the proportion of defective items in a sample.

process capability: the variation allowed by the design specification relative to the inherent variability of process output.

process capability ratio: a measure of the capability of the manufacturing process to meet the specifications of the product. It is the ratio of the specification width to the process width.

process control: automated computer-controlled operations in a production process; for example, a chemical plant refinery.

quality: a measure of the conformance of a product to an established standard; quality may be defined either qualitatively or quantitatively.

range (R): the range of values of the observations in a sample.

range chart: a control chart for variation in the ranges of output samples.

tolerances: specifications pertaining to a dimension or characteristic of a product.

Type I error: incorrectly concluding a process is out of control.

Type II error: incorrectly concluding a process is in control.

upper control limit (UCL): in a Shewhart-type control chart, the upper limit of the random scatter of a sample statistic, to define whether a process is in control or out of control.

variable: any measurable characteristic; for quality assurance, it usually means a measurable characteristic on a continuous scale, such as height. weight, pressure, speed, etc.

x-bar chart: a type of control chart for variables, based on the mean and standard deviation of a sample.

TRUE/FALSE QUESTIONS

1. Two key issues is inspection are how much to inspect and how often.

2. The cost of inspection may outweigh the benefits of 100 percent inspection.

3. Range and p-charts both deal with sampling for attributes.

4. An attribute is counted rather than measured.

5. An attribute control chart can have a computed negative LCL.

6. As the sample size gets larger, the standard deviation of the sampling distribution of means gets smaller.

7. x-bar charts are based on the normal distribution.

8. x-bar and range charts are used with measurement data.

9. The theoretical basis for a control chart is a sampling distribution.

10. Acceptance sampling is performed primarily on products during production.

11. If the process capability ratio has a value less than 1, the process is capable of turning out the product.

MULTIPLE-CHOICE QUESTIONS

1. Which one of the following is not usually an advantage of centralized inspection?

   a. Special testing equipment

   b. Quick decisions

   c. More favorable testing environment

   d. All are advantages

   e. None are advantages

2. Which term is most closely associated with the term , "sampling distribution"?

   a. 100% inspection.

   b. On-site inspection.

    c.   Quality at the source.

    d.   Control chart.

3.   What type of control chart would be used to monitor the number of defects in the output of a process for making rope?

    a.   x-bar chart.

    b.   p chart.

    c.   c chart.

    d.   R chart.

4.   What type of control chart would be used to monitor the number of defectives in the output of a process for making iron castings?

    a.   x-bar chart.

    b.   p chart.

    c.   c chart.

    d.   R chart.

5.   Tolerances are:

    a.   statistical limits.

    b.   limits on inherent process variability.

    c.   limits of natural variability.

    d.   limits established by customers.

    e.   b and c.

6.   The number of runs up and down in the data set 8 9 12 10 11 12 is:

    a.   2

    b.   3

    c.   4

    d.   5

    e.   none of these.

7.   The number of runs with respect to the median in the data set 8 9 12 10 11 12 is:

    a. 2   b. 3   c. 4   d. 5   e. none of these.

8.   An x-bar chart is best suited for this type of data:

    a.   Count.

    b.   Attribute.

    c.   Measurement.

    d.   None of these.

9.   Tolerances refer to:

   a. Control limits.

   b. Specifications.

   c. Process capability.

   d. Process variability.

10.   Process capability calculations take into account the process width and:

   a. Process standard deviation.

   b. Process dispersion.

   c. Specifications.

   d. Control limits.

PROBLEMS

Note: Control chart factors can be found in Table 10-2 of your textbook and in Table D of this study guide.

1.   The Perfect Circle Company manufactures bushings. Once each hour a sample of 125 finished bushings is drawn from the output; each bushing is examined by a technician. Those which fail are classified as defective; the rest are satisfactory. Here are data on ten consecutive samples taken in one week:

Sample no.	1	2	3	4	5	6	7	8	9	10
Defective	15	13	16	11	13	14	20	25	30	45

   a. What type of control chart should be used here?

   b. What is the center line of the chart?

   c. What is the lower control limit (LCL)? The upper control I

   d. What statistic should be plotted on the control chart for

   e. Draw the control chart on a piece of graph paper.

   f. Is this system under control?

   g. What should the quality control engineer do?

2.   Use the data in Problem #1 in this problem. Assume that an assignable cause has been found for Sample #10 and has been corrected.

   a. What is the value of the center line of the revised control chart?

   b. What is the lower control limit of the revised chart?

   c. What is the upper control limit of the revised chart?

   d. Compare the revised control chart to the original control chart.

3. The Take-Charge Company produces batteries. From time to time a random sample of six batteries is selected from the output and the voltage of each battery is measured, to be sure that the system is under control. Here are statistics on 16 such samples.

Sample	Mean	Range	Sample	Mean	Range
1	4.99	0.41	9	5.01	0.49
2	4.87	0.57	10	5.19	0.56
3	4.85	0.59	11	5.40	0.44
4	5.26	0.74	12	5.15	0.63
5	5.09	0.74	13	5.00	0.35
6	5.02	0.21	14	4.89	0.45
7	5.13	0.56	15	4.99	0.54
8	5.09	0.92	16	5.05	0.33

   a. What type of control chart should be used here? Why?

   b. What is the center line of the chart?

   c. What is the lower control limit? The upper control limit?

   d. What statistic should be plotted on the control chart for each sample?

   e. Draw the control chart on a piece of graph paper.

   f. Is this system under control?

   g. What should the quality control engineer do?

4. Use the data in Problem 3 to draw an R chart.

   a. What is the lower control limit? The upper control limit?

   b. What statistic should be plotted on the control chart for each sample?

   c. Draw the control chart on a piece of graph paper.

   d. Is this system under control?

   e. What should the quality control engineer do?

5. Assume that an assignable cause has been found and corrected for sample # 11 in Problem 3.

   a. What is the value of the center line of the revised control chart?

   b. What is the lower control limit of the revised chart? The upper control Limit?

   c. Compare the revised control chart to the original control chart.

6. Tinker Belle Peanut Butter is sold in .50 kilograms jars. The plant produces thousands of jars of peanut butter per working day; the process is rather simple and quite standardized, and is thought to be highly stable, with a standard deviation of .016 kg. Management has specified that the jars should fall within .054 kg of the label value.

   a. What is the process capability index?

   b. Is this process capable?

7. Occasionally, a random sample of five jars of Tinker Belle Peanut Butter (see problem #6) is selected from the output and weighed, to be sure that the system is under control. Here are data on ten such samples. Measurements are in kilograms.

Sample	1	2	3	4	5	6	7	8	9	10
	.50	.50	.50	.51	.51	.51	.50	.50	.51	.50
	.47	.48	.49	.51	.50	.50	.51	.52	.48	.51
	.50	.48	.51	.52	.49	.52	.49	.47	.50	.49
	.49	.48	.47	.51	.52	.51	.50	.49	.49	.50
	.51	.47	.49	.51	.50	.51	.48	.49	.50	.47
	2.47	2.41	2.46	2.56	2.52	2.55	2.48	2.47	2.48	2.47

a. What type of control chart should be used here? Why?

b. What is the center line of the chart?

c. What is the lower control limit? The upper control limit?

d. What statistic should be plotted on the control chart for each sample?

e. Draw the control chart on a piece of graph paper.

f. Is this system under control?

g. What should the quality control engineer do?

8. (One step beyond. Use Table D in this study guide.) Use the data in Problem 6 to construct an R chart.

a. What is the lower control limit? The upper control limit?

b. What statistic should be plotted on the control chart for each sample?

c. Draw the control chart on a sheet of graph paper.

d. Is this system under control?

e. What should the quality control engineer do?

9. The Poseidon Fabric Co. produces large beach towels (among other things): they are supposed to be brightly colored and have a fringe on each end. From time to time, a towel is selected from the finished goods and subjected to an intense inspection in search of any and all defects. A defect is a stain, a badly dyed spot, a hole, a missing fringe, etc., each occurrence counts as a distinct defect. Here are data on 12 sample towels.

Towel	1	2	3	4	5	6	7	8	9	10	11	12
Number of defects	2	1	3	0	1	4	0	1	3	2	3	1

a. What type of control chart should be used here? Why?

b. What is the center line of the chart?

c. What is the lower control limit? The upper control limit?

d. What statistic should be plotted on the control chart for each sample?

e. Draw the control chart on a piece of graph paper.

f. Is this system under control?

g. What should the quality control engineer do?

10.   Here is an x-bar chart with 20 sample means plotted on it. Use this chart to perform a test for runs above and below the center line. See next page.

a.   What is the expected number of runs?

b.   What is the standard deviation of the number of runs?

c.   What is the actual number of runs?

d.   What is the z-statistic?

e.   What are the critical values of z for 95 percent?

f.   Is this process under control? Explain.

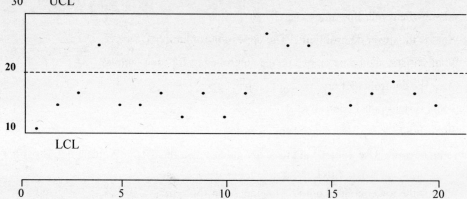

CHAPTER 10   QUALITY CONTROL

<table>
<tr><td colspan="4">True/False</td><td colspan="4">Multiple-Choice</td></tr>
<tr><td>Question</td><td>Answer</td><td>Glossary/
Key Idea</td><td>Textbook
ref. page</td><td>Question</td><td>Answer</td><td>Glossary/
Key Idea</td><td>Textbook
ref. page</td></tr>
<tr><td>1</td><td>T</td><td></td><td>441</td><td>1</td><td>b</td><td></td><td>443</td></tr>
<tr><td>2</td><td>T</td><td>4</td><td>440-441</td><td>2</td><td>d</td><td></td><td>445</td></tr>
<tr><td>3</td><td>F</td><td>4</td><td>448</td><td>3</td><td>c</td><td>4</td><td>454</td></tr>
<tr><td>4</td><td>T</td><td>G, 1</td><td>447</td><td>4</td><td>b</td><td>4</td><td>452</td></tr>
<tr><td>5</td><td>T</td><td></td><td>452</td><td>5</td><td>d</td><td>G</td><td>460</td></tr>
<tr><td>6</td><td>T</td><td></td><td>448</td><td>6</td><td>b</td><td></td><td>456-457</td></tr>
<tr><td>7</td><td>T</td><td></td><td>448</td><td>7</td><td>c</td><td></td><td>456-457</td></tr>
<tr><td>8</td><td>T</td><td></td><td>448-449</td><td>8</td><td>c</td><td>4</td><td>448</td></tr>
<tr><td>9</td><td>T</td><td></td><td>445</td><td>9</td><td>b</td><td>G</td><td>460</td></tr>
<tr><td>10</td><td>F</td><td>2</td><td>440</td><td>10</td><td>c</td><td>7</td><td>461</td></tr>
<tr><td>11</td><td>F</td><td>7</td><td>462</td><td></td><td></td><td></td><td></td></tr>
</table>

SOLUTIONS TO PROBLEMS

1. a. Use the p chart. This is attribute data with the categories of satisfactory and defective bushings.

   b. $CL = \bar{p} = \dfrac{100(15 + 13 + \cdots + 45)}{125 + 125 + \cdots 125} = \dfrac{100(202)}{1250} = 16.16\%$.

   c. $\hat{\sigma}_p = \sqrt{\dfrac{\bar{p}(100 - \bar{p})}{n}} = \sqrt{\dfrac{16.16(100 - 16.16)}{125}} = 3.29\%$.

   $LCL = \bar{p} - 3\hat{\sigma}_p = 16.16 - 3(3.29) = 6.29\%$

   $UCL = \bar{p} + 3\hat{\sigma}_p = 16.16 + 3(3.29) = 26.03\%$

   d.

Sample No.	Statistic (p)	Sample No.	Statistic (p)
1	16/125 = 12%	6	11.2%
2	10.4	7	16.0
3	12.8	8	20.0
4	8.8	9	24.0
5	10.4	10	36.0

e.

	UCL
26.03	

(control chart with UCL at 26.03, center line at 16.16, LCL at 6.29, x-axis from 0 to 10)

f. No. Sample #10 falls above the UCL.

g. He should look for an assignable cause for sample #10.

2. a. The revised center line will be obtained by deleting sample #10 and recalculating the value of $\overline{p}$ on the basis of the remaining nine samples.

$$\text{revised } \overline{p} = \frac{100(202-45)}{(1250-125)} = 13.96\%$$

b. Revised $\hat{\sigma}_p = \sqrt{\dfrac{\overline{p}(100-\overline{p})}{n}} = \sqrt{\dfrac{13.96(100-13.96)}{125}} = 3.10\%$

Revised $LCL = \overline{p} - 3\hat{\sigma}_p = 13.96 - 3(3.10) = 4.66\%$

Revised $UCL = \overline{p} + 3\hat{\sigma}_p = 13.96 + 3(3.10) = 23.26\%$

c. The revised control limits have lower values than the original control limits, and they are slightly closer to the center line.

3. a. Use the x-bar chart; this is measurement data.

b. $CL = \overline{\overline{x}} = \dfrac{\sum \overline{x}}{k} = \dfrac{4.99 = 4.87 + \cdots + 5.05}{16} = 5.06$ v.

(k = the number of samples)

c. Because the value of the population standard deviation is unknown, use $\overline{R}$ and the A_2 control chart factor.

$$\overline{R} = \frac{\sum R}{k} = \frac{0.41 + 0.57 + \cdots + 0.33}{16} = 0.53 \text{ v.}$$

$$LCL = CL - A_2\overline{R} = 5.06 - .48(.53) = 4.81 \text{ v.}$$

$$UCL = CL + A_2\overline{R} = 5.06 + .48(.53) = 5.31 \text{ v.}$$

d.   The sample mean.

e.

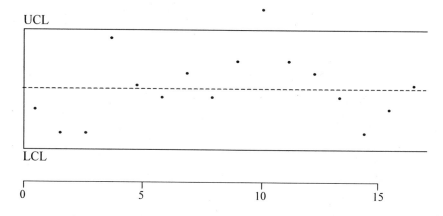

f.   No, sample #11 is out of control.

g.   He should look for an assignable cause for sample #11.

4.   a.   Because s is unknown, use $\overline{R}$ and the factors, D_3 and D_4 from the Table of Control Chart Factors.

$$LCL = D_3\overline{R} = 0(.53) = 0 \text{ v.}$$

$$UCL = D_4\overline{R} = 2.00(.53) = 1.06 \text{ v.}$$

b.   The sample ranges.

c.

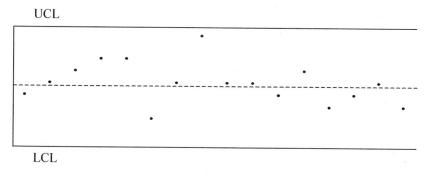

d.   Yes.

e. No action is needed.

5.   a.   v.

      b. LCL = 5.03 − .48(.53) = 4.78 v.

          UCL = 5.03 + .48(.53) = 5.28 v.

      c. The new control limits are lower but are still the same distance from the center line.

6.   a.   (specification width)/(process width) = .054/(3(.016)) =1.125.

      b. Yes, but not by much.

7.   a. Use the x-bar chart; this is measurement data.

      b.   kg.

      c. Because the value of the population standard deviation is known, find the standard error of
          the sample means and use z = ±3s.

                                    kg.

                                                        kg.

                                                        kg.

      d. The sample mean. Here are the first few.

              Sample No.   Mean

                    1   kg.

                    2   kg.

      e.

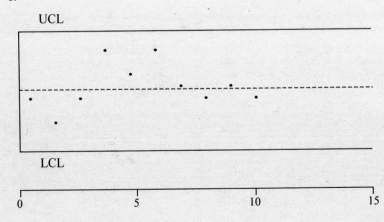

      f. Yes.

g. No action is necessary.

8. a. Because σ is known, use the factors, D_1 and D_2, from the Table of Control Chart Factors in this Study Guide.

$LCL = D_1\sigma = 0(.016) = 0$ kg.

$UCL = D_2\sigma = 4.916(.016) = .0787$ kg.

b. Plot the ranges. Here are the first few of them.

Sample No. Range (R)

1      $R = x_{l\,arg\,est} - x_{smallest} = .51 - .47 = .04$ kg.

2      $R = x_{l\,arg\,est} - x_{smallest} = .50 - .47 = .03$ kg.

c.

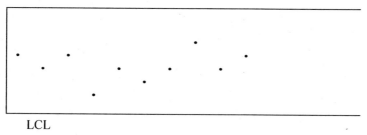

UCL

LCL

0   5   10   15

d. Yes.

e. No action is necessary.

9. a. Use a c-chart, because the data consists of the number of defects per unit; a unit is a towel.

b. $CL = \bar{c} = \dfrac{\sum c}{k} = \dfrac{21}{12} = 1.75$ defects per towel

c. $LCL = \bar{c} - 3\sqrt{\bar{c}} = 1.75 - 3\sqrt{1.75} = -2.2186 \rightarrow 0$

$UCL = \bar{c} + 3\sqrt{\bar{c}} = 1.75 + 3\sqrt{1.75} = 5.7186$.

d. The number of defects per towel.

e.

     UCL

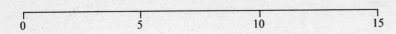

LCL

0	5	10	15

f. Yes.

g. No action is necessary.

10.   a. $E(r)_{med} = (k/2) + 1 = (20/2) + 1 = 11$ runs

(N = the number of samples)

      b. $\sigma_{med} = \sqrt{(N-1)/4} = 2.18$ runs

      c.   r = 5 runs.

      d. $z_{med} = (r - E(r))/\sigma_{med} = (5-11)/2.18 = -2.75$

      e. $z = \pm 1.96$.

      f.   No; $-2.75 < -1.96$.

CHAPTER 10S
ACCEPTANCE SAMPLING

KEY IDEAS

1.   The optimal level of inspection balances the cost of inspection and the cost of allowing undetected defectives to pass through the system.

2.   Each situation calls for a different type of inspection process; the stages of production where inspection may take place include: raw materials and purchased parts, finished product end items, before costly operation, before taking an irreversible step, or before painting or plating or some other covering that hides potential defects. Also some inspections take place at the production site and others at the customer's designated location, or in a laboratory.

3.   Acceptance sampling pertains to incoming batches of raw materials (or purchased parts) and to outgoing batches of finished goods. Current emphasis in quality assurance is away from acceptance sampling and towards 1) improving the process so that there is less need for inspection, and 2) improving supplier quality so that there is less need for inspection of incoming goods.

4.   Acceptance sampling can be applied to either attributes or variables. Attributes are those characteristics of a product or service that are counted (e.g., pass-fail, defective-nondefective), and variables are characteristics that are measured (e.g., width, thickness, weight).

5.   The technical starting point for an acceptance sampling plan is the operating characteristic (OC) curve, which gives probability of acceptance, P_{ac} vs. quality level (i.e., the proportion of defects p). The higher p is or the greater the deviation from standard, the lower P. is. A widely used type of OC curve has two clearly identifiable points, the AQL, acceptable quality level, a designated "good" quality, and the LTPD, lot tolerance percent defective, a designated "bad" quality.

For the AQL, $P_{ac} = 1 - \alpha$, where α is the probability of rejecting a lot with quality AQL. For the LTPD, $P_{ac} = \beta$, where β is the probability of accepting a lot with quality LTPD.

6.   The AOQ is the average outgoing quality, frequently shown as a curve with AOQ as a function of p. When rejected lots are inspected 100 percent to remove all defective items and the defectives are replaced with good items, the AOQ is better than with intermediate quality lots because of the extra inspection.

For lots where the number sampled, n, is small relative to the lot size, N, the $AOQ \approx P_{ac} * p$, p is the fraction defective in the lot. The highest AOQ (poorest outgoing quality) for a sampling plan is known as the average outgoing quality limit or the AOQL.

GLOSSARY

acceptable quality level (AQL): for a given sampling plan, a specified quality level for which there is a low probability of rejecting a good lot.

acceptance number: in attributes sampling, for a given sample size, the maximum number of allowable defectives for acceptance.

acceptance sampling: sampling of lots of incoming material to determine conformance to standard.

attribute: a characteristic that has just two choices, e.g., defective or acceptable.

average outgoing quality (AOQ): given the sampling plan, for a specified incoming lot quality level, a function showing the average quality level of the outgoing lot, as a result of it, replacing defective units of material by good ones.

conformance: the characteristics of the product satisfy the established standard for the characteristics.

consumer's risk: the probability that a lot that has a quality worse than the lot tolerance percent defective will be accepted, or passed.

inspection: examining material in process or finished products to determine conformance to standard.

lot tolerance percent defective (LTPD): for a given sampling plan, a specified quality level for which there is a low probability of accepting a bad lot.

operating characteristic (OC): a mathematical function that yields, for a given sampling plan, the probability of accepting the lot, as a function of the percent defective.

producers risk: the probability that a lot that has an acceptable quality level will be rejected.

quality: a measure of the conformance of a product to an established standard; quality may be defined either quantitatively or quantitatively.

sampling plan: a procedure that identifies a lot . as being of either acceptable or rejectable quality; for example, with attributes, a typical acceptance sampling plan would specify for a given lot size, the sample size and the maximum number of allowable defects for acceptance.

Type I error: rejecting a good lot.

Type II error: accepting a bad lot as good.

variable: common usage is any measurable characteristic; for quality assurance, it usually means a measurable characteristic on a continuous scale, such as height, weight, pressure, speed, etc.

TRUE/FALSE QUESTIONS

1. Acceptance sampling can be applied to attributes or to variables.

2. The ability of a sampling plan to discriminate between good and bad lots is described by its operating characteristic curve.

3. Acceptance sampling is performed primarily on products during production.

4. An "accept" decision for a lot of material implies that the lot does not contain any defectives.

5. The AQL is the probability of rejecting a lot of material that is of acceptable quality.

6. The acceptance number in a sampling inspection plan is the lot tolerance percent defective.

7. The AOQL is the worst case of outgoing quality.

MULTIPLE-CHOICE QUESTIONS

1. Acceptance sampling is used for all but which one of these?
    a. Incoming raw material.
    b. Intermediate production.
    c. Final goods.
    d. Incoming purchased parts.

2. In which instance would acceptance sampling not be appropriate?
    a. Destructive testing is required.
    b. The cost consequences of passing defectives is low.
    c. A large number of items must be processed in a short period.
    d. Fatigue and boredom lead to inspection errors.
    e. All are appropriate applications.

3. The letters AQL stand for:
    a. average quality limit.
    b. average quality level.
    c. acceptable quality limit.
    d. acceptable quality level.
    e. average quality of lots.

4. Which is a list of the elements of an acceptance sampling plan?
    a. The lot size, the sample size, and the lot tolerance percent defective.
    b. The lot size, the sample size, and the acceptance number.
    c. The sample size, the acceptance number, and the lot tolerance percent defective.
    d. The sample size, the acceptance number, and the average outgoing quality limit.
    e. The acceptance number, the lot tolerance percent defective, and the AOQL.

PROBLEMS

1. A 10 ampere fuse is a weak link in an electrical circuit; if the fuse is defective. it could fail to blow, even though the current exceeded 10 amps, thereby risking damage to equipment and personal injury. An electrical manufacturer uses enormous quantities of 10 ampere fuses in its products, which are purchased in lots of 100,000 from an outside supplier. The contract provides that each lot will be examined by the buyer according to this acceptance sampling plan: a random sample of 20 fuses will be drawn from the lot and tested by being subjected to a current of 10 amperes; if 0 or 1 of them fail to blow, the lot will be accepted; if 2 or more of them fail to blow, the lot will be returned.

   a. Which probability distribution should be used here? Why?

   b. Calculate some points on the operating characteristic curve for this sampling plan.

   c. Draw the OC curve on a piece of graph paper. Use Table D in your textbook.

   d. The acceptable quality level (AQL) is 5 percent defective fuses. What type of sampling error might be made at the AQL?

   e. What is the probability of suffering a sampling error at the AQL? What is the name of this probability?

   f. The lot tolerance percent defective (LTPD) is 15 percent defective fuses. What type of sampling error might be made at the LTPD?

   g. What is the probability of suffering a sampling error at the LTPD? What is the name of this probability?

2. The Major Convenience Appliance Company produces small appliances, such as drip coffee makers, for home and office use. It purchases the indicator lights, which indicate whether the appliance is off or on, from an outside supplier. Indicator lights are bought in lots of 10,000, the contract specifies that each lot will be examined by the buyer according to this acceptance sampling plan: a random sample of 150 indicator lights will be drawn from the lot and tested, if five (or fewer) defective lights are found, the batch will be accepted; if more than five defective lights are found, the batch will be returned.

   a. Which probability distribution should be used here? Why?

   b. Calculate some points on the operating characteristic curve for this sampling plan.

   c. Draw the OC curve on a piece of graph paper.

   d. The acceptable quality level (AQL) is 2 percent defective lights. What type of sampling error might be made at AQL?

   c. What is the probability of suffering a sampling error at the AQL? What is the name of this probability?

   f. The lot tolerance percent defective (LTPD) Is 6 percent defective lights. What type of sampling error might be made at the LTPD?

   g. What is the probability of suffering a sampling error at the LTPD? What is the name of this probability?

3.   Calculate some points on the AOQ curve for the acceptance sampling plan in Problem 2.

a.   Draw the AOQ curve on a piece of graph paper.

b.   What is the approximate value of the average outgoing quality limit (AOQL)

c.   What is the significance of the AOQL?

CHAPTER 10S   ACCEPTANCE SAMPLING

True/False			
Question	Answer	Glossary/ Key Idea	Textbook ref. page
1	T	4	479
2	T	G, 1	480
3	F	3	479
4	F		481
5	F	G, 5	481
6	F	5	482
7	T	G, 6	485

Multiple-Choice			
Question	Answer	Glossary/ Key Idea	Textbook ref. page
1	b	3	479
2	e		479
3	d	G	484
4	b		479

SOLUTIONS TO PROBLEMS

1. a. Use the binomial distribution. This is attribute data with the categories of satisfactory and defective fuses, and the sample size is small.

    b. Use Table D in your textbook.

    Assumed Percentage
    of Defective Fuses $P(x < 1)$

0%	1.0000
5%	0.7358
10%	0.3917
15%	0.1756
20%	0.0692
100%	0.0

    c. Operating Characteristic Curve.

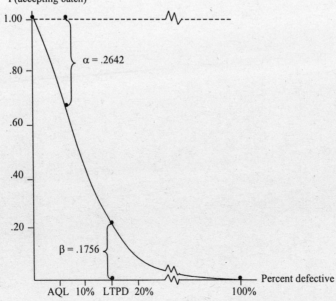

d.   A Type I sampling error, consisting of rejecting a satisfactory batch.

e.   p(Type I sampling error) = α = 1 - .7358 = .2642.

f.   A Type II sampling error, consisting of accepting an unsatisfactory batch of fuses.

g.   p(Type II sampling error) = ß = .1756.

2.   a.   Use the Poisson distribution. This is attribute data with the categories of satisfactory and defective indicator lights, and the sample size is large.

b.   Use Table C in your textbook, with a mean, μ = np.

Assumed Percentage of Defective Items	Mean = np	P(x < 5)
0%	0	1.000
1%	1.5	0.996
2%	3.0	0.916
4%	6.0	0.446
6%	9.0	0.116
100%	150.0	0

c.   Operating Characteristic Curve.

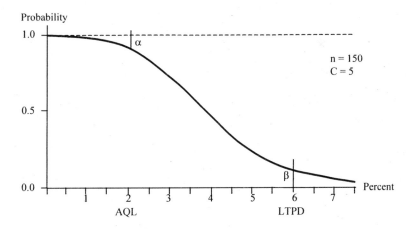

d.   A Type I sampling error, consisting of rejecting a satisfactory batch of fuses.

e.   A Type I sampling error, consisting of rejecting a satisfactory batch of indicator lights.

f.   p(Type I sampling error) = α = 1 - .916 = .084.

g.   A Type II sampling error, consisting of accepting an unsatisfactory batch of indicator lights.

h.   p(Type II sampling error) = ß = .116.

Use the formula, $AOQ \approx P_{ac} * p$, since the batch size is large compared to the sample size.

Assumed Percent of Defective Items	p(accepting the lot)	AOQ
0%	1.000	0
1%	0.996	0.996%
2%	0.916	1.832%
3%	0.703*	2.109%
4%	0.446	1.784%
5%	0.242	1.210%
100%	0	0

*Interpolate in Table C: (.720 + .686)/2 = .703.

a.

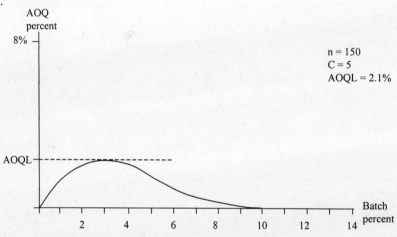

b.   AOQL = 2.109% defective lights.

c.   Because this acceptance sampling plan is applied to incoming indicator lights, those batches which are used in production will not include over 2.109% defective lights, on the average.

CHAPTER 11
TOTAL QUALITY MANAGEMENT

KEY IDEAS

1. Total Quality Management (TQM) is a philosophy that says that quality is the responsibility of everybody in the organization. The focal point is customer satisfaction. Important features include continuous improvement (described in supplement of this chapter), benchmarking, employee empowerment, the use of teams for problem solving, and knowledge of tools (described in chapters 3S and 9 in the textbook).

2. Continuous improvement is a philosophy towards the improvement of quality that many organizations have adopted: The quest for higher and higher levels of quality should never end. Continuous improvement provides a structured approach to quality improvement. It is directed primarily at improving the *process.*

3. The conceptual basis for continuous improvement is the plan-do-check-act (PDCA) cycle: *Plan* by studying and documenting the current process. Collect data on the process. Develop a plan. *Do* refers to implementing the plan, and collecting data. *Check* involves evaluating the data collected during the do phase. *Act* means to standardize the new method if it is judged to be successful. Also, consider repeating it in other similar situations, communicate it to others, and implement training for the new method. The PDCA cycle is also known as the Shewhart cycle or the Deming wheel.

4. Among the key tools and techniques that are used for continuous improvement are flow charts, check sheets, Pareto analysis, brainstorming, control charts, interviewing, quality circles, benchmarking, cause-and-effect diagrams, and run charts.

5. A basic concept in both decision making and problem solving is that some elements or factors are more important than others. Typically, a relatively few of these are very important, and many are relatively unimportant. This is known as the Pareto phenomenon. The implication for decision makers and problem solvers is that it is important to identify the few key elements of factors and then give them special attention or emphasis.

6. Organizations need to avoid the trap of over-emphasizing TQM, personnel and paperwork costs can quickly mount. A balanced approach is generally the best approach, giving measured emphasis to quality while continuing to give appropriate attention to other aspects of the organization.

GLOSSARY

benchmarking: using another organization's processes as a standard to improve your own process. The benchmark need not be in the same type of business, and need not be a competitor.

brainstorming: an idea generating method where a group of people cooperate in a freethinking session, building on each other's ideas.

Cause-and-effect diagram: also called a fishbone diagram; a problem solving tool resembling the skeleton of a fish.

conformance: the characteristics of the product satisfy the established standard for the characteristics.

continuous improvement: the attitude adopted by many organizations that strives to continually improve quality. The primary emphasis is on process improvement.

fishbone diagram: see cause-and-effect diagram.

5W2H approach: A set of basic questions, five that begin with a W (Who? What? Where? When? Why?) and two that begin with an H (How? and How much?). Used as a basis for process improvement.

inspection: examining material in process or finished products to determine conformance to standard.

liability: the legal responsibility of a producer for defects of a product or service that causes injury, harm, or property damage.

Pareto analysis: analysis that organizes categories of items according to degree of importance or frequency of occurrence. The purpose is to direct efforts to those items which have the greatest potential for improvement.

Plan-do-study-act (PDSA) cycle: is the conceptual basis for continuous improvement. It provides a structure for improvement efforts.

total quality management (TQM): a philosophy that involves everyone in an organization in a quest for quality.

TRUE/FALSE QUESTIONS

1. The Total Quality Management philosophy applies only to production workers.

2. Satisfying the customer includes meeting the requirements of the next person in the production process.

3. The plan-do-study-act cycle is also known as the Shewhart wheel or the Deming wheel.

4. The 5W2H approach is a method used for asking questions about a process.

5. The 5W2H approach provides a graphical representation of the key steps in a process.

6. A check sheet is a simple tool used for problem identification.

7. Another name for a cause and effect diagram is a fishbone diagram.

8. The Pareto chart is based on the idea that a few factors usually account for a large percentage of the total number of cases.

MULTIPLE-CHOICE QUESTIONS

1. Which one of these terms is associated with studying another organization's products or operations?
   a. Brainstorming
   b. Benchmarking
   c. Pareto analysis
   d. Continuous improvement

2. Which one of these is the conceptual basis for continuous improvement?
   a. Benchmarking
   b. Cause-and-effect diagram
   c. Pareto analysis
   d. The plan-do-study-act cycle

3. Which one of these is a tool for problem solving?
   a. Benchmarking.
   b. Cause-and-effect diagram.
   c. Pareto analysis.
   d. The plan-do-study-act cycle.

4. The term "80-20 rule" is most closely associated with:
   a. Control charts
   b. Pareto analysis
   c. Check sheets
   d. Brainstorming

PROBLEMS

1. The Modern Styles Furniture Company produces a line of disassembled furniture which comes in a carton. The buyer is required to assemble the pieces into a usable object. One of the products is a two-shelf bookcase. Here is the parts list for the product:

   1 back panel   2 middle shelves   1 package of screws
   1 top shelf   2 side panels   1 cardboard carton

This problem is concerned only with the cardboard carton and its contents, The pieces of the bookcase are assumed to be satisfactory, but some may be missing in some cartons. This constitutes a simplification, of course, since it ignores the problem of defective or damaged parts. The company provides an 800 number on the carton to assist customers who experience difficulties. Recently, there has been a rash of calls concerning missing parts. The Company promptly ships the missing part(s) to the aggrieved customer.

Management is concerned about the poor reputation which the Company's products are developing and about the extra expense of the shipments, which should be unnecessary. In an attempt to pinpoint the problem, some employees have been detailed to check every carton before it is sealed up and to keep a record of their findings on a check sheet. Any parts discovered to be missing are replaced before the carton is shipped. Here is a table of their findings for one week.

Piece	Mon.	Tues.	Wed.	Thurs.	Fri.	Total
Back panel	3	1	2	1	1	
Top shelf	2	2	3	1	2	
1 Middle shelf	6	4	7	4	10	
2 Middle shelves	2	-	3	1	-	
1 side panel	7	10	4	8	6	
2 side panels	-	2	1	3	1	
Screws	3	4	5	5	4	
Carton	-	-	-	-	-	
Total						

    a.   Fill in the totals in the Table.

    b.   Which piece is most often omitted?

    c.   Suggest a corrective action for the piece in b.

    d.   Which piece is the next most often omitted?

    e.   Suggest a corrective action for the piece in d.

    f.   Which day is most prone to errors in packing?

    g.   Suggest a corrective action for the worst day.

2.   Using the data in Problem #1, construct a Pareto diagram for the missing pieces.

3.   Assume that action has been taken to resolve the problem of the missing pieces in Problem #1, according to the suggestions in the answers to Problem #1. In order to find out whether the corrections were effective, all cartons produced in one week have been checked, producing the data in the table, below.

Piece	Mon.	Tues.	Wed.	Thurs.	Fri.	Total
Back panel	1	2	1	2	1	
Top shelf	3	2	3	1	3	
1 Middle shelf	-	-	-	-	-	
2 Middle shelves	1	2	1	-	1	
1 side panel	-	-	-	-	-	
2 side panels	2	1	1	3	1	
Screws	5	6	3	3	5	
Carton	-	-	-	-	-	
Total						

    a.   How much progress has been made in solving the missing pieces problem?

    b.   Which piece is now the most often omitted?

    c.   Suggest a corrective action for the piece in b.

CHAPTER 11 TOTAL QUALITY MANAGEMENT

True/False

Question	Answer	Glossary/ Key Idea	Textbook ref. page
1	F	1,G	492
2	T		492
3	T	G, 3	497
4	T	G	510
5	F	G	510
6	T	G	498
7	T	G	503
8	T	G	502

Multiple-Choice

Question	Answer	Glossary/ Key Idea	Textbook ref. page
1	b	G	509
2	d	G, 3	497
3	b	G	503
4	b	G	502

SOLUTIONS TO PROBLEMS

1.   a.

Piece	Total
Back- panel	8
Top shelf	10
1 Middle shelf	31
2 Middle shelves	6
1 Side panel	35
2 Side panels	7
Screws	21
Carton	0
Total	118

Weekday	Total
Monday	23
Tuesday	23
Wednesday	25
Thursday	23
Friday	24
Total	118

    b. 1 side panel.

    c. Perhaps a worker could be delegated to tape the panels together in sets of two, so that the packer must pick up both of them. You may be able to think of something better.

    d. 1 middle shelf.

    e. Perhaps a worker could be delegated to tape the panels together in sets of two.

    f. The day totals are all about the same, and no day appears to be particularly error prone.

    g. No action is needed.

2.

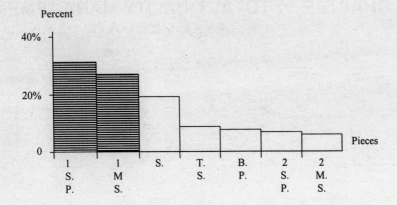

3. a. The rate of missing pieces has been reduced from 118 per week to 54, which is an improvement of 64 pieces, or 54%.

    b. The package of screws.

    c. Perhaps a brightly colored tag could be attached to the package, to make it noticeable. You may be able to think of something better.

CHAPTER 12
AGGREGATE PLANNING

KEY IDEAS

1. Aggregate planning is intermediate range planning of general levels of employment and output to balance supply and demand.

2. The term "aggregate" implies that planning is done for groups of products, or product types (i.e., product "families") rather than for specific or individual products.

3. Planners take into account projected demand, capacity, and costs of various options in devising an aggregate plan.

4. Among the variables available to planners are adjustments in output rate, employment level, overtime/undertime, and subcontracting.

5. The goal of aggregate planning is to achieve output objectives at the lowest possible cost.

6. Due to the nature of aggregate planning, it is seldom possible to structure a plan that is guaranteed optimal. Instead, planners usually resort to trial-and-error methods to achieve an acceptable plan.

7. Among the strategies aggregate planners might try are to:

    a. maintain a level work force and meet demand variations in some other manner.

    b. maintain a steady rate of output, and use some combination of inventories and subcontracting to meet demand variations.

    c. match demand period by period with some combination of work force variations, subcontracting, and inventories.

    d. use a combination of decision variables.

    Note: It is unlikely that planners would attempt to match demand period by period by vary employment levels alone because that would tend to be costly, disruptive, and result in low employee morale.

8. Choosing a strategy usually depends on the cost entailed and company policy.

9. In order to effectively plan, in addition to knowledge of company policy, estimates of the following items must be available to planners:

    a. Demand for each period

    b. Capacity for each period

    c. Costs (regular time, overtime, subcontracting, backorders, etc.)

10. In order to translate an aggregate plan into meaningful terms for production, it must be disaggregated (i.e., broken down into specific product requirements) to determine labor, material, and inventory requirements.

11. A master schedule indicates the desired quantity and timing of deliveries. A master production schedule takes into account planned production, as well as on-hand inventory.

12. There are three basic inputs to the master schedule: Beginning inventory, forecasts for each period in the schedule, and customer orders. Outputs of the scheduling process include projected inventory, production requirements, and the amount of uncommitted inventory, which is referred to as available-to-promise (ATP) inventory.

GLOSSARY

aggregation: forming groups of similar commodities, represented by a single common unit of measurement, without identifying specific product names.

available-to-promise (ATP) inventory: uncommitted inventory.

chase strategy: adjusting capacity to match demand period by period.

cumulative graph: a graph that displays accumulated output and sales over a period of time such as a year, showing where the periods of shortage and surplus occur.

disaggregation: breaking down an aggregate plan into specific products.

intermediate planning: production planning covering a period of from two to twelve months.

long-range planning: planning for production, covering a period of time of more than twelve months.

master schedule: shows the desired quantity and timing of end items over the schedule horizon.

master production schedule: shows the quantity and timing of planned production, taking into account desired delivery quantities as well as inventory on-hand.

overtime: working time for an employee beyond the normal 40-hour week.

pure strategy: a strategy with a single focal point (e.g., maintain a level work force).

regular time: working time during the normal 40-hour workweek.

short-range planning: planning for production, covering a period of time less than two months.

spreadsheet: a budgeting and scheduling matrix, with the rows representing categories of production or activity and the columns representing time periods.

subcontracting: permitting a portion of the production activity to be carried on by an outside vendor, under a contractual agreement as to price and production levels.

time fences: stages or phases of a master production schedule.

TRUE/FALSE QUESTIONS

1. Aggregate planning is long-range planning (2 years or more) for large products.

2. Aggregate planning is concerned with both the quantity and timing of anticipated demand.

3. Overtime is not considered as a variable in aggregate planning.

4. Keeping a constant level of production in every time division of a planning period (month, week, etc.) is one possible strategy for aggregate planning.

5. The cost of either a backlog, or a large inventory, or of subcontracting production, is usually very nearly proportional to the number of units involved.

6. The transportation method of linear programming is used differently in developing an aggregate plan as described in Chapter 12, than in solving the conventional transportation model, as described in Chapter 8S.

7. Disaggregating an aggregate plan involves creating a master schedule for production of the end items included in the aggregate plan.

8. A "chase" strategy involves matching demand and capacity in each period.

9. Available-to-promise inventory is uncommitted inventory.

MULTIPLE-CHOICE QUESTIONS

1. All of the following are reasonable strategies aggregate planners might try except:
    a. maintain a level work force and meet demand variations in some other manner.
    b. maintain a steady rate of output, and use some combination of inventories and subcontracting to meet demand variations.
    c. match demand period by period with some combination of work force variations, subcontracting, and inventories.
    d. vary the workforce period by period to match demand.

2. In order to effectively plan, estimates of each of the following items must be available to planners except:
    a. Inventory lot sizes.
    b. Demand for each period
    c. Capacity for each period
    d. Costs (regular time, overtime, subcontracting, backorders, etc.)

3. Which of the following is not a technique used for aggregate planning?
    a. Linear programming
    b. Simulation
    c. Trial-and-error charting
    d. Double smoothing

4. Which term is most closely associated with disaggregation?
    a. Backorders
    b. Overtime
    c. Subcontracting
    d. Master schedule
    e. Trial and error

5. Which one of the following is not a basic option for altering capacity?
    a. Hire and fire workers
    b. Use overtime
    c. Use subcontracting
    d. Use backorders
    e. All are options for altering capacity

6. All of the following are basic options for altering demand except:
    a. pricing.
    b. promotion.
    c. backorders.
    d. inventories.
    e. all are "demand" options.

7.   Which statement is false?

    a.   Aggregate planners are concerned with the quantity and timing of expected demand.

    b.   The basic problem of aggregate planning is balancing supply and demand.

    c.   Aggregate planners rely heavily on the master schedule to guide their efforts.

    d.   All of these statements are true.

8.   Which one of these is not a master scheduling input?

    a.   Forecasts

    b.   Planned inventory

    c.   Customer orders

    d.   Beginning inventory

9.   Which one of these is not an output of a master production schedule?

    a.   Production requirements

    b.   Projected inventory

    c.   Customer orders

    d.   Available-to-promise inventory

PROBLEMS

1.   The Snow Mountain Ski Company produces pairs of skis. Its business is highly seasonal, and for the next fiscal year it has the following forecasts of the demand for pairs of its skis for each month. The fiscal year runs from July 1 to June 30.

Month	Forecast	Month	Forecast
July	125	January	500
August	150	February	450
September	300	March	200
October	350	April	150
November	400	May	50
December	600	June	25
		Total Demand	3,300

The company has a beginning inventory on July 1 of 50 pairs of skis. The company has a capacity of 16 pairs of skis per eight-hour shift, and it works one shift per day, for 48 five-day weeks per year. Here are financial data on producing, storing, and selling skis.

    Variable cost during the day shift (8 AM to 5 PM): $60.00 per pair

    Variable cost during the night shift (5 PM to 2 AM): $70.00 per pair

    Cost of storing skis for one month: $2.00 per pair in the average inventory

    Cost of acquiring skis from a supplier: $64.00 per pair

    The selling price of skis: $150.00 per pair

Skis may not be backordered, since they must be available during the skiing season. In case of shortages, the company does have options, however. It may schedule half of a night shift (four hours, with a capacity of 8 pairs of skis); or it may schedule a full night shift (8 hours with a capacity of 16 pairs of skis); or it may purchase from an outside supplier. In the event of surplus production, the company may reduce the day shift to half-time (4 hours per day, with a capacity of 8 pairs of skis). It will not close the plant entirely.

a. Construct an aggregate planning schedule for the fiscal year in the style of Example 1 of Chapter 12 of your textbook. Assume that the company schedules one 8-hour shift per working day with no outside purchases. Unsold pairs of skis will be kept in inventory.

b. How many sales will be lost under the plan in a above?

c. How much gross margin will be made per month under the plan in a? For the entire year? (Gross margin = Revenue - Cost of goods sold - Storage costs.)

d. It is proposed to schedule half of the night shift beginning in the month in which a shortage appears in the schedule in a (for four weeks) and continuing until the month in which the shortage disappears (for two weeks). Prepare the aggregate planning schedule in the style of Example 1 in your textbook.

e. How many sales will be lost under the plan in part d?

f. How much gross margin will be made under the plan in d per month? For the entire year? Compare this amount to the gross margin in part c.

g. What is one obvious improvement that could be made in the plan in part d.

h. What other options might be explored?

2. Use the data in Problem 1 to .draw a cumulative graph of demand and the inventory, by months, in the style of Figure 12-3 in your textbook, for the plan in la.

3. Use the data in Problem 1 to answer this question. Formulate the production problem in the style of the transportation model, as shown in Table 12-4 of your textbook. Construct the table for the months of October, November, December, and January. In each period the alternatives are to produce skis during the day shift, or during the night shift, or both. Backorders are not allowed. You may ignore the beginning and ending inventory. Do not solve.

4. As large as the matrix is in Problem #3, EXCEL can solve it.

a. How do you enter the problem in an EXCEL spreadsheet?

b. How do you enter the objective function?

c. How do you enter the constraints?

d. What is the solution?

e. What is the cost of the solution?

5. Here is information on the Caribou Beer Company regarding sales of its six-packs for the period of May and June. It is now April 30, and the inventory contains 60 six-packs. The forecasts for each week of the period are given below, along with the firm orders.

Week	ending	Forecast	Orders
May	6	500	400
	13	500	450
	20	500	450
	27	500	1,000
June	3	550	500
	10	550	500
	17	600	600
	24	600	650

Six-packs are produced in lots of 1,200, once a week, if needed.

a. Construct the Master Production Schedule for May and June.

b. When should the Production Manager plan on producing more six-packs?

CHAPTER 12   AGGREGATE PLANNING

True/False				Multiple-Choice			
Question	Answer	Glossary/ Key Idea	Textbook ref. page	Question	Answer	Glossary/ Key Idea	Textbook ref. page
1	F	1	524	1	d	7	
2	T		527	2	a	9	593-94
3	F	8	529	3	d		598-608
4	T	7	530	4	d	G	608-609
5	T		534	5	d	4	594-96
6	T		534	6	d		593-94
7	T		543	7	c	1	608-609
8	T	G	530	8	b		610
9	T	G	544	9	c		610

SOLUTIONS TO PROBLEMS

1. a,b.

Month	J	A	S	O	N	D	6 Month Total
Forecast	125	150	300	350	400	600	1925
Production	320	320	320	320	320	320	1920
Inventory							
Beginning Balance	50	245	415	435	405	325	
Ending Balance	245	415	435	405	325	45	
Average Balance	147.5	330	425	420	365	185	
Lost Sales							
(Pairs of Skis)							

Month	J	F	M	A	M	J	12 Month Total
Forecast	500	450	200	150	50	25	3300
Production	320	320	320	320	320	320	3840
Inventory							
Beginning Balance	45	0	0	120	290	560	
Ending Balance	0	0	120	290	560	855	
Average Balance	22.5	0	60	205	425	707.	
Lost Sales	135	130					265
(Pairs of Skis)							

c.

Month	J	A	S	O	N	D	6 Month Total
Sales Volume	125	150	300	350	400	600	1925
Sales Dollars	$18750	22500	45000	52500	60000	90000	$288750
Cost of Goods Sold	7500	9000	18000	21000	24000	36000	115500
Cost of Storage	295	660	850	840	730	370	3745
Total Costs	7795	9660	18850	21840	34730	36370	119245
Gross Margin	$10955	12840	26150	30660	35270	53630	169505

Month	J	F	M	A	M	J	12 Month Total
Sales Volume	365	320	200	150	50	25	3035
Sales Dollars	$54750	48000	30000	22500	7500	3750	$455250
Cost of Goods Sold	21900	19200	12000	9000	3000	1500	182100
Cost of Storage	45	0	120	410	850	1415	6585
Total Costs	21945	19200	12120	9410	3850	2915	188685
Gross Margin	$32805	28800	17880	13090	3650	835	$266565

d,e.

Month	J	A	S	O	N	D	6 Month Total
Forecast	125	150	300	350	400	600	1925
Production (Day)	320	320	320	320	320	320	1920
Production (Night)							
Total Production							
Inventory							
Beginning Balance	50	245	415	435	405	325	
Ending Balance	245	415	435	405	325	45	
Average Balance	147.5	330	425	420	365	185	
Lost Sales							
(Pairs of Skis)							

Month	J	F	M	A	M	J	12 Month Total
Forecast	500	450	200	150	50	25	3300
Production (Day)	320	320	320	320	320	320	3840
Production (Night)	160	160	80				400
Total Production	480	480	400	320	320	320	4240
Inventory							
Beginning Balance	45	25	55	255	425	695	
Ending Balance	25	55	255	425	695	990	
Average Balance	35	40	155	340	560	842.	
Lost Sales							
(Pairs of Skis)							

f.

Month	J	A	S	O	N	D	6 Month Total
Sales Volume	125	150	300	350	400	600	1925
Sales Dollars	$18750	22500	45000	52500	60000	90000	$288750
Cost of Goods Sold							
(Day)	7500	9000	18000	21000	24000	36000	115500
Cost of Goods Sold							
(Night)							
Cost of Storage	295	660	850	840	730	370	3745
Total Costs	7795	9660	18850	21840	34730	36370	119245
Gross Margin	$10955	12840	26150	30660	35270	53630	169505

Month	J	F	M	A	M	J	12 Month Total
Sales Volume	500	450	200	150	50	25	3300
Sales Dollars	$75000	67500	30000	22500	7500	3750	$495000
Cost of Goods Sold							
(Day)	20400	17400	7200	9000	3000	1500	174000
Cost of Goods Sold							
(Night)	11200	11200	5600				28000
Cost of Storage	70	80	310	680	1120	1685	7690
Total Costs	31670	28680	13110	9680	4120	3185	209690
Gross Margin	$43330	38820	16890	12820	3380	565	$285310

g. The day shift might be reduced to half-time during the spring months, to reduce the inventory build-up.

h. Peak demand might be met by obtaining skis from a supplier. Or the night shift might be scheduled to begin earlier, say in December, to anticipate the winter demand for skis.

2.   X = Calendar Time; Y = The cumulative demand or production from July 1 up to date.

The month's initial refers to the last day of the month. Graph the following points:

Month	Production	Demand	Month	Production	Demand
O	0	0	J	2240	2425
J	320	125	F	2560	2875
A	640	275	M	2880	3075
S	960	575	A	3200	3225
O	1280	925	M	3520	3275
N	1600	1325	J	3840	3300
D	1920	1925			

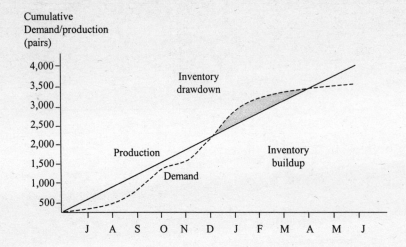

3. Place the months in the columns; the column totals will be the monthly demand. A dummy column will be needed. Place the day shifts and the night shifts in the rows; the row totals will be the monthly capacities of each shift. A different row will be needed for each shift for each month. The costs will be the variable cost per pair of skis plus the cost of storage. Thus, skis produced by the day shift in July and stored until September will cost $60 + $2 + $2= $64. Because it is not possible to produce skis in November for sale in October, enter a large cost ($100) in the October column and November row, in order to exclude those cells from the solution.

	Oct.	Nov.	Months Dec.	Jan.	Dummy	Capacity
Day shift October	60	62	64	66	0	320
Night shift October	70	72	74	76	0	320
Day shift November	100	60	62	64	0	320
Night shift November	100	70	72	74	0	320
Day shift December	100	100	60	62	0	320
Night shift December	100	100	70	72	0	320
Day shift January	100	100	100	60	0	320
Night shift January	100	100	100	70	0	320
Demand	350	400	600	500	710	2560

4. a.

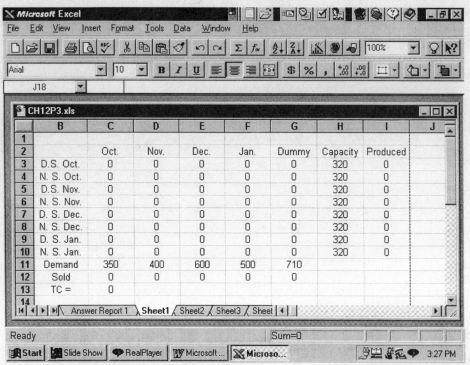

In the spreadsheet (CH12P3.xls), the table reads:

	B	C	D	E	F	G	H	I	J
1									
2		Oct.	Nov.	Dec.	Jan.	Dummy	Capacity	Produced	
3	D.S. Oct.	0	0	0	0	0	320	0	
4	N. S. Oct.	0	0	0	0	0	320	0	
5	D.S. Nov.	0	0	0	0	0	320	0	
6	N. S. Nov.	0	0	0	0	0	320	0	
7	D. S. Dec.	0	0	0	0	0	320	0	
8	N. S. Dec.	0	0	0	0	0	320	0	
9	D. S. Jan.	0	0	0	0	0	320	0	
10	N. S. Jan.	0	0	0	0	0	320	0	
11	Demand	350	400	600	500	710			
12	Sold	0	0	0	0	0			
13	TC =	0							

b. In cell C13:

$=60*C3+62*D3+64*E3+66*F3+0*G3+70*C4+72*D4+74*E4+76*F4+0*G4+100*C5+60*D5+62*E5+64*F5*0*G5+100*C6+70*D6+72*E6+74*F6+0*G6+100*C7+100*D7+60*E7$
$+$
$62*F7+0*G7+100*C8+100*D8+70*E8+72*F8+0*G8+100*C9+100*D9+100*E9+60*F9+0*G9+100*C10+100*D10+100*E10+70*F10+0*G10.$

c. In cell I3: =SUM(C3:G3)

etc. Hint: use the copy and paste facilities of EXCEL.

In cell C12: =SUM(C3:C10)

etc. Hint: use the copy and paste facilities.

d.

Month	Shift	Pairs of Skis
Oct.	Day	320
Oct.	Night	30
Nov.	Day	320
Nov.	Night	80
Dec.	Day	320
Dec.	Night	280
Jan.	Day	320
Jan.	Night	180

e. $116,700.

5.   a.

60	May			
	6	13	20	27
Forecast	500	500	500	500
Customer Orders	400	450	450	1,000
Projected Inventory	760	260	960	1,160
MPS	1,200		1,200	1,200

	June			
	3	10	17	24
Forecast	550	550	600	600
Customer Orders	500	500	600	650
Projected Inventory	610	60	660	10
MPS			1,200	

b.   Six-packs will produced in the weeks of May 6, May 20, May 27, and June 17

CHAPTER 13
INVENTORY MANAGEMENT

KEY IDEAS

1.   The chapter describes several different ways of classifying inventory:

   a.   raw materials, finished goods, parts, etc.

   b.   independent and dependent demand

   c.   dollar volumes and sizes: A, B, C. etc.

2.   Inventories are held for a variety of reasons, such as customer demand for end items, smoothing production, decoupling internal operations, a hedge against stockouts and price increases, and economical purchasing.

3.   The requirements for effective inventory management are:

   a.   an accounting system to keep track of on-hand and on-order merchandise

   b.   reliable forecasting of demand

   c.   estimates of lead times between placing an order and receiving goods, and lead-time variability

   d.   estimates of inventory holding costs, ordering costs and shortage (backorder) costs

   e.   a classification system

4.   There are numerous examples of electronic automation in retail inventory management, such as UPC scanners, J. C. Penney scanners, and airline reservation systems.

5.   The question of how much to order is often answered using some form of an EOQ model. The fundamental variants of the deterministic economic order quantity model include:

   a.   EOQ for purchased end items or semifinished goods acquired from outside vendors

   b.   economic run length for internal production orders in batch processing and noninstantaneous replacement

   c.   quantity discounts

   In variants *a* and *b* the order quantity is set at a level such that *total holding costs = total ordering costs;* unit acquisition (purchase) cost is considered indirectly, but only insofar as it is used to

   calculate holding cost. In variant *c* order a quantity that minimizes the sum of three costs: acquisition, holding, and ordering costs. In order to implement a quantity discount model, it is only necessary to calculate total cost at an EOQ if it falls between two price breaks, or at a price break. A price break is a quantity at which there is a change in price.

6.   An EOQ model tells you how much to order, but it does not say when to place an order. With uncertainties in delivery schedules and usage rates, there is no guarantee that there will always be material in stock to service production operations. This is where reorder point (ROP) models come into the picture. There are four variants of ROP:

   (1) constant demand rate and lead time

   (2) variable demand, constant lead time

   (3) constant demand, variable lead time

   (4) variable demand and variable lead time

The approach to (1) is simple, place the order when the stock gets to a level such that what is in stock now will all be used up when the new shipment arrives. Variants (2), (3), and (4), however, add realism by allowing the decision maker to set a safety stock as a buffer against uncertainty. The size of this safety stock depends upon whether the uncertainty is in the demand rate, the lead time, or both, and how much risk of a stockout the decision maker finds acceptable. In (2), (3), and (4) the fundamental relationship is:

ROP = Expected demand during lead time + Safety stock.

The size of the safety stock is determined by the "service level," the probability of no stockout, that is:

Service level = 1.00 - Stockout risk.

There are two fundamental assumptions:

(1) daily demands in lead time are independent

(2) the daily demand rates are normally distributed

In (3), "constant demand, variable lead time," the uncertainty is with the length of the period rather

than the demand rate. The lead time (number of days) is assumed to be normally distributed.

7. Chapter 13 includes a discussion of relationships between shortages and service levels for reorder models with fixed lead time (LT) and variable demand. This approach introduces the order quantity (Q) as an element that influences safety stock decisions, and shows the interrelationship between Q, service level (SL), safety stock (SS), annual demand (D), and the standard deviation of demand in LT (σ_{dLT}). The greater Q is, all other things being the same, the smaller the safety stock necessary to achieve a specified level of service over the long run.

Table 13-3 gives the unit normal loss function, E(z,), associated with both the corresponding z-value and the lead-time service level (LTSL). For a normally distributed lead-time demand, E(z) is a scale factor that is multiplied by σ_{dLT} to calculate the expected shortage in lead time, E(n). The expected annual shortage, E(N), is the product of E(n) and the number of cycles in a year, D/Q.

Since
$$E(N) = (1 - SL_{annual})D$$
$$SL_{annual} = 1 - E(N)/D$$
$$SL_{annual} = 1 - E(n)/Q$$
$$SL_{annual} = 1 - (E(z) * \sigma_{dLT}/Q)$$

8. When ordering is constrained to fixed times, the fixed-order-interval model applies. With the fixed-order-interval model, the safety stock is greater than with the other models, because the ordering is done at fixed time intervals regardless of the stock level.

9. The single-period model is appropriate for cases in which one order is to be placed that is intended to satisfy demand for an entire period. The period can be a day, week, or other interval. Often, the items involved are perishable (e.g., fresh seafood), or otherwise have a limited shelf life (e.g., daily newspapers). Other examples include spare parts for equipment and inventories of rental equipment.

10.   Regardless of the application, the single-period model involves computation of a theoretical service level, which is the ratio of unit shortage cost to the sum of unit shortage and excess costs:

$$SL = \frac{C_S}{C_S + C_E}$$

TIPS FOR SOLVING PROBLEMS

This chapter has numerous models, and it can be very difficult in some instances to know which model to use. Part of the difficulty relates to the fact that each model contains several elements, and any one of the elements might be the unknown that solves the problem.

There are two things you can do to enhance your ability to solve these problems. One is to familiarize yourself with the circumstances under which each model is appropriate, and the other is to learn the components of each model and to be able to recognize them in a problem setting. Together, these two skills will greatly contribute to your being able to correctly select the appropriate model.

One way to develop these skills is to refer to Table 13-4 in your textbook. Most of the models are listed, along with the basic formulas and definitions of symbols. Note that the symbols are the components of the models. Thus, you have a list of most of the components. When trying to solve a problem, you might want to begin by listing the symbols and values of as many components as you can from the information given in the problem. By comparing your list to the formulas in Table 13-4, you should be able to determine which value or values are missing or unknown, and hence, what you need to solve for. Also, make it a point to know which part of an ROP formula relates to risk, to service level, to safety stock, and so on.

Example 1

A company produces small motors which it uses in assembling pumps. It can produce the motors at the rate of 200 per day. Motors are used in assembling pumps at the rate of 50 a day. Because the production rate of motors exceeds the usage rate, excess motors are stored in inventory until they are needed for pump assembly. Answer these questions.

1. What is the production rate?
2. What is the usage rate?
3. At what rate does the inventory build up?
4. If a production run size for motors is 2,000, how many days does it take to produce a run?
5. If production of motors temporarily ceases after each production run, how many motors will be in inventory when production ceases, if beginning inventory was zero motors?
6. How many days after the production ceases will a new run be needed (i.e., how long will the supply of motors last)?

Solution to Example 1

1. $p = 200$ motors per day.
2. $u = 50$ motors per day.
3. Buildup $= p - u = 100 - 50 = 150$ per day.
4. At 200 motors per day, it will 10 days to produce 2,000 motors.
5. At a buildup rate of 150 motors per day, there will be 1,500 motors in inventory in 10 days.

6.   Motors are used at the rate of 50 per day. A supply of 1,500 motors will last 1,500/50 = 30 days.

Example 2

A pharmacy dispenses an average of 50 milligrams of a generic drug per day, with a standard deviation of 5 milligrams per day. The prescription manager is willing to accept to more than a 1% risk of a stockout during lead time, which is 4 days. Assume that the distribution of prescriptions is normal. The mean usage during lead time is:

$$D_{LT} = D_d * LT = 50 * 4 = 200 \text{ mg.}$$

The standard deviation of lead time demand is:

$$\sigma_{dLT} = \sqrt{LT} * \sigma_W = \sqrt{4}*5 = 10 \text{ mg.}$$

and the lead-time service level (LTSL) is 99%. Therefore, z = 2.33, the safety stock (SS) = 23.3 mg. and the reorder point is ROP = 223.3 mg.

1.   Suppose Q = 500 mg; what is the annual service level?

2.   What value of Q would yield $SL_{annual} = 99\%$? What are the corresponding values of the safety stock (SS), the reorder point (ROP) and the order interval?

3.   Assuming that Q = 500 mg, what LTSL would correspond to $SL_{annual} = 99\%$? What are the corresponding values of SS and ROP?

Solution to Example 2

1.   In Table 13-3, for LTSL = 0.99, $E(z)$ = 0.003; therefore:

$$SL_{annual} = 1 - (E(z) * \sigma_{dLT}/Q) = 1 - (.003 * 10/500) = .99994$$

2.   In this case the unknown is Q, a formula is derived by algebra:

$$Q = \frac{E(z)* \sigma_{dLT}}{1 - SL_{annual}} = \frac{.003 * 10}{.01} = 3 \text{ mg.}$$

Since z = 2.33, both SS and ROP are identical to the original solution: 23.3 mg and 223.3 mg, respectively. Q, however, is very small, just three milligrams, or 3/50 of a day's demand. This means that the order interval is 3/50 of a day and that it would be necessary to place orders 17 times a day.

3.   With Q = 500 and an annual service level of 99%, in order to solve the LTSL, it is first necessary to find $E(z)$.

$$E(z) = Q(1 - SL_{annual})/\sigma_{dLT} = 500(1-.99)/10 = .5 .$$

The corresponding z value (from Table 13-3) is approximately -0.20. and the LTSL is 42%.

$$SS = z\sigma_{dLT} = -0.2(10) = -2 \text{ mg.}$$

$$ROP = D_{LT} + SS = 200 - 2 = 198 \text{ mg.}$$

An order will be placed approximately every 10 days.

In Example 1. the standard deviation of daily demand and lead-time demand are small, the LT is small and the LTSL is 99 percent. This results in both a large safety stock and frequent orders; therefore, the holding costs are relatively high. Part 3 of Example 1 shows that in the long run needs can be satisfied with only a 1 percent probability of running out of stock, with an LTSL less than 50 percent.

Example 3

In an electronics assembly plant a robotic cart used in production operations moves on a fixed track from one workstation to another, in a preprogrammed way, transferring certain supplies and tools. The circular outer rims of the wheels of the cart have gear teeth that mesh with the gear teeth of the track. Because there are very frequent stops and starts, the gear teeth wear out rapidly and it is necessary to have a stock of them on hand in order to facilitate replacement. The supplier of the gear teeth operates a Japanese-style 'Just-in-time*' inventory system, and keeps a very low stock of teeth, servicing orders largely out of new production rather than stock.

Management's policy is to operate a reorder system with an annual service level of 95 percent. The lead time between placing an order for new gear teeth and receiving the order is 2 days; the daily average wearout is 100 gear teeth with a standard deviation of 50 gear teeth, and the gear teeth are ordered in standard lot sizes of 500 units.

What are the safety stock, reorder point and the corresponding lead-time service level?

Solution to Example 3

The standard deviation of lead-time demand is $\sigma_{dLT} = \sqrt{LT} * \sigma_d = \sqrt{2} * 50 = 70.71$

$E(z) = (1 - SL_{annual})Q/\sigma_{dLT} = (.05 * 500)/70.71 = 0.3535$

Referring to Table 13-3, $z \approx 0.12$ and $LTSL \approx 55\%$.

SS = 0.12 x 70.71 = 8.49 gear teeth;

ROP = 200 + 8 = 208.

GLOSSARY

carrying cost: see holding cost.

classification system: the A-B-C system classifies inventory items as follows:

    A: small percentage of items, but account for greatest proportion of annual dollar usage or other measure of importance.

    B: middle-size percentage of items, accounting for middle percentage of value or importance.

    C: large percentage of items, accounting for small proportion of annual dollar usage or importance.

continuous system: keeping the count of available stock in an electronic or mechanical device that records additions or removals as they occur.

cycle counting: physically counting items in inventory.

decoupling (internal operations): strategic placement of inventories so that one section of the plant is not adversely affected by bottlenecks in other sections.

demand: the rate at which stock is used.

demand rate variability: is commonly expressed as a standard deviation.

dependent demand: demand estimates for components and raw materials are determined by demand estimates for finished items.

economic lot size: the lot size that balances holding costs against ordering or setup costs, so as to minimize the net cost of stocking inventory.

economic run size: an economic order quantity, when stock replenishment occurs through production rather than by purchase.

electronic scanner: a device that reads and interprets barcodes.

excess cost: the unrecovered cost per unit of items that are left in inventory at the end of the period.

fixed-order-interval model: a model for inventory control that assumes orders will be place at fixed intervals of time.

hedge: holding inventory as a protection against future possible shortages or price increase.

holding cost: the monetary cost, per unit, of holding a unit of stock for a stated period of time.

independent demand: demand estimates for an item of inventory that are not governed controlled by demand estimates for any other item.

inventory accounting system: a file that records all transactions relevant to inventory management, and from which reports are periodically processed and prepared.

lead time: the length of time between the placing of an order and receiving it.

lead-time variability: in those cases where the lead time is not known with certainty, lead time variability is measured by the standard deviation of the number of days in lead time.

lot sizing: deciding how many units to order.

optimal stocking level: the quantity for which the service level achieved equals or exceeds the ratio of shortage cost to the sum of shortage and excess cost (see formula in Key Ideas).

periodic inventory system: counting available stock at stated periods of t

pricebreak: where quantity discounting is practiced, a price break is a quantity at which a lower price is offered.

purchased parts: assembled or partially assembled components of a product, that have had extensive prior processing and are purchased from subcontractors or suppliers.

quantity discount: a reduction in price per unit, as an incentive for making purchases in larger quantities.

raw materials: components of a product that are used in the production process in bulk.

reorder point: a level of stock at which a replenishment is ordered.

safety stock: a stock level over and above average usage in lead time, maintained as a hedge against unusually high demand.

salvage value: the recoverable cost of an item that remains in inventory at the end of the period. This may be negative; there may be an additional cost to dispose of an item.

service level: defined as the probability of being able to satisfy any order during the normal order cycle from stock on hand.

setup cost: the monetary cost of each production or purchase order placed, not including the purchase price or the costs of direct charges for production.

shortage cost: the loss per unit incurred when demand exceeds supply of an item during a period.

single-period model: inventory model used when items in inventory cannot be carried over from one period to the next. Examples include items with limited shelf lives, and spare parts for machines.

smoothing production: relatively steady usage of production resources.

standard normal distribution: the distribution of the standard normal statistic z, with a mean of zero and a variance of one.

stockout: running out of stock, before the next replenishment is received.

supplies: expendable purchased or manufactured elements that are not explicitly incorporated into end items, but are a necessary part of the operation of the plant.

two-bin system: a form of inventory management that is especially useful for C-type items: the first bin is used until it is depleted, then the second bin; when the second bin is opened, an order is placed for replenishment.

UPC system: using electronic scanners to read the Universal Product Code of every item purchased, in order to facilitate pricing, order preparation and continuous inventory management.

work-in-process inventory: partially completed, assembled or processed material that is not classified as an end item, purchased part, or raw material.

z-statistic: the random variable of the standard normal distribution.

TRUE/FALSE QUESTIONS

1. A pricebreak is an order quantity at which the purchaser is offered a lower price per unit by purchasing that quantity or more.

2. If the supplier does not offer quantity discounts, the unit cost will not directly affect the decision of how many units to order, but may do so indirectly if the holding cost is measured as a percentage of the acquisition cost.

3. All reorder-point models assume constant lead time.

4. The two-bin system is a form of a reorder-point model

5. The basic EOQ model assumes that each order is delivered at a single point in time.

6. With the quantity-discount model, an order level might not be at an EOQ.

7. In a reorder-point model, the order amount is the EOQ.

8. The ROP is equal to expected demand during lead time plus safety stock.

9. In the single-period model, the service level is equal to the ratio of "excess cost" divided by " excess cost plus shortage cost."

10. In the single-period model, the greater the shortage cost relative to the excess cost, the higher the service level.

11. In a discrete model, the actual number of units short must be an integer, while the expected number of units short does not have to be an integer.

MULTIPLE-CHOICE QUESTIONS

1. In a reorder model the daily demand rate is normally distributed with a mean of 50 units and a standard deviation of 5 units. The lead time is 9 days, Q = 500 units, and the leadtime service level (LTSL) is 90%. What are approximate values for SS and ROP?

    a. 19, 69
    b. 4, 69
    c. 6, 469
    d. 19, 469

2.   If both the lead time and daily demand are constant, the ROP is equal to:
   a.   Safety stock
   b.   Expected demand minus safety stock.
   c.   Expected demand plus safety stock.
   d.   Daily demand times lead time.
   e.   None of these.

3.   The quantity discount model is most similar to which one of these models?
   a.   ROP.
   b.   EOQ.
   c.   Fixed interval.
   d.   Single period.
   e.   Noninstantaneous replenishment.

4.   Which inventory model does not provide an order quantity??
   a.   EOQ.
   b.   ROP
   c.   Single-period.
   d.   Fixed-interval
   e.   Quantity discount

5.   Which one of the following is not a reason for holding inventories?
   a.   To decouple stages of production
   b.   As a hedge against inflation
   c.   To be able to buy in economical lot sizes
   d.   To meet projected demand
   e.   All are reasons

6.   Which one of the following is not a requirement for effective inventory management?
   a.   A system to keep track of inventory on hand
   b.   A classification system for inventory items
   c.   Reasonable estimates of holding and shortage costs
   d.   Using an EOQ model for determining order quantity
   e.   All are requirements

7.   Which one of the following would not appear on a list of relevant costs of inventory?
   a.   Shortage   b.   Carrying   c.   Order   d.   Holding   e.   Overtime

8.   Which one of the following would not be included in a list of assumptions of the basic EOQ model?
   a.   Lead time does not vary.
   b.   There are no quantity discounts.
   c.   Demand is spread uniformly throughout the year.
   d.   Annual demand is a known quantity.
   e.   All are assumptions.

9.	Which one of the following is a true statement concerning the relationship between holding and ordering costs in the basic EOQ model?

    a.	The two arc always equal at the EOQ.

    b.	Holding cost is sometimes equal to ordering cost, and sometimes greater at the EOQ.

    c.	Holding cost is sometimes equal to ordering cost, and sometimes less at the EOQ.

    d.	Holding cost is always greater than ordering cost at the EOQ.

    e.	There is no relationship between the two.

10.	In the quantity-discount model, if the total cost curves all reach their minimum levels at the same order quantity, this implies that:

    a.	holding costs are constant per unit.

    b.	holding costs are a percentage of unit price.

    c.	ordering costs are constant.

    d.	ordering and setup costs are equal.

    e.	none of these.

The following three questions refer to this information: A bakery makes a limited number of croissants each day for sale in its coffee shop. The croissants cost $.35 each to produce and sell for $1.50 each. Leftover croissants are sold in the bakery the following day for $1.00 each, and all of those are sold.

11.	The excess cost is:

    a.	$.35

    b.	$1.50

    c.	$1.00

    d.	$1.15

    e.	$0

12.	The salvage value is:

    a.	$.35

    b.	$1.50

    c.	$1.00

    d.	$1.15

    e.	$0

13.	The shortage cost is:

    a.	$.35	b.	$1.50	c.	$1.00	d.	$1.15	e.	$0

14.	Demand for a perishable item can be described by a uniform distribution that ranges from 18 units per period to 30 units per period. If shortage and excess costs are equal, the optimal stocking level would be:

    a.	18	b.	30	c.	24	d.	impossible to say.

PROBLEMS

1. An automobile manufacturer uses about 60,000 pairs of bumpers (front bumper and rear bumper) per year, which it orders from a supplier. The bumpers are used at a reasonably steady rate during the 240 working days per year. It costs $3.00 to keep one pair of bumpers in inventory for one month, and it costs $25.00 to place an order. A pair of bumpers costs $150.00.

   a. Which inventory model should be used here: the instantaneous model, the noninstantaneous model, or the single-period model? How do you know?

   b. Write the annual carrying cost function.

   c. Write the annual ordering cost function.

   d. Write the annual total cost function.

   e. What is the EOQ?

   f. What is the significance of the EOQ?

   g. What is the total annual expense of ordering the EOQ every time?

   h. How many orders will be placed per year?

   i. What is the total annual expense of ordering 600 pairs of bumpers every time? How much is saved per year by ordering the EOQ?

2. The Acme Bumper Co. manufactures bumpers for automobiles for one of the big three auto companies. About 60,000 pairs of bumpers (front bumper and rear bumper) are ordered by the auto company per year, at a price of $150.00 per pair. Pairs of bumpers are produced at a rate of about 400 per working day, and the company operates 240 days per year. The company manufactures other products, and it must set up the manufacturing system for a production order for pairs of bumpers, which costs $250.00. It costs $2.50 to store one pair of bumpers for one month.

   a. Which inventory model is appropriate here: the instantaneous model, the noninstantaneous model, or the single-period model? How do you know?

   b. Write the annual carrying cost function.

   c. Write the annual setup cost function.

   d. Write the annual total cost function.

   e. What is the EOQ?

   f. What is the significance of the EOQ?

   g. What is the total annual expense of producing the EOQ every time?

   h. How many production runs will be required per year?

   i. What is the total annual expense of manufacturing 3,000 pairs of bumpers per production run? How much is saved per year by producing the EOQ every time?

3. Use the data from Problem 1 to solve this problem, in addition to the data below. The supplier offers a system of quantity discounts, as follows:

Order Quantity	Cost per Pair	Discount
1 to 299 pairs	$150.00	0%
300 to 499 pairs	$150.00	4%
500 or more pairs	$150.00	10%

a. Which inventory model is appropriate here: the instantaneous model, the quantity discount model, or the single-period model? How do you know9

b. Write the annual total cost function for orders for less than 300 pairs.

c. Write the annual total cost function for orders for 300 to 499 pairs.

d. Write the total cost function for orders for at least 500 pairs.

e. Draw the graph of the three total cost functions on a piece of rectangular coordinate paper.

f. What is the EOQ?

g. What is the total annual expense, including the purchasing cost of ordering the EOQ every time?

4. The purchasing agent has ascertained that the usage of floppy disks in the company is approximately normally distributed, with a mean of 30 per working day and a variance of 16. The company operates 240 days per year. Floppy disks are obtained from a supplier who is very reliable, when an order is placed (on day 0), it is always received on the fifth working day. The company cannot afford to run out of floppy disks, and the purchasing agent has established a 99.5 percent service level.

a. Which reorder-point model is appropriate here, fixed lead time and variable demand, variable lead time and fixed demand, or variable demand and variable lead time?

b. What is the mean usage during lead time?

c. What is the standard deviation of the usage during lead time?

d. What is the reorder point? Draw a diagram like the one in Figure 13-11 in your textbook.

e. What is the significance of the reorder point?

f. What is the safety stock?

5. The purchasing agent has ascertained that the employees use about 50 pencils per day, with very little variation. Pencils are ordered from a supplier whose shipments are irregular. They are normally distributed with a mean of 10 working days and a variance of 4. He has established a 95 percent service level for pencils.

a. Which reorder-point model is appropriate here: variable demand and fixed lead time, fixed demand and variable lead time, or variable demand and variable lead time?

b. What is the mean usage during lead time?

c. What is the standard deviation of usage during lead time?

d. What is the reorder point? Draw a diagram in the style of Figure 13-13 in your textbook.

e. What is the significance of the reorder point?

f. What is the safety stock?

6. The purchasing agent has ascertained that the usage of letterhead paper has an approximately normal distribution with a mean of 200 sheets per working day and a standard deviation of 13 sheets. Letterhead paper is ordered from a printer whose deliveries are variable, with a mean of 25 working days and a variance of 4 working days. The purchasing agent has established a 99 percent service level for letterhead paper.

a. Which reorder-point model is appropriate here: variable demand and fixed lead time, fixed demand and variable lead time, or variable demand and variable lead time?

b. What is the mean usage during lead time?

c. What is the standard deviation of usage during lead time?

d. What is the reorder point? Draw a diagram in the style of Figure 13-13 in your textbook.

e. What is the significance of the reorder point?

f. What is the safety stock?

7. (One step beyond; based on statistics) The Whirlwind Appliance Store sells freezers for home use. These are large, upright units which resemble a refrigerator. They differ in operation in that the entire interior is kept at a freezing temperature. The store orders the freezers from the factory, which is very reliable and will deliver the order within one week (7 calendar days) almost invariably. Here are the volumes of sales for the past 50 weeks: 2, 1, 4, 5, 2, 0, 3, 6, 7, 3, 4, 2, 2, 4, 3, 5, 5, 1, 3, 6, 4, 5, 1, 0, 1, 4, 3, 5, 7, 6, 3, 5, 4, 1, 5, 5, 4, 5, 6, 4, 3, 2, 5, 4, 1, 5, 2, 5, 4. Future sales are expected to be similar. The store manager wishes to establish a 95 percent service level.

a. What is the frequency distribution for this data? Does it appear to be approximately normal?

b. What are the mean sales of freezers per week?

c. What is the empirical probability distribution?

d. What is the cumulative probability distribution?

e. What is the reorder point? (Hint: use the cumulative probability distribution.)

f. What is the safety stock?

8. An appliance store knows that the distribution of monthly sales of 50" TV sets is approximately normal with a mean of 6 sets and a standard deviation of 1.5 sets. The sets cost $2,750 each, and are priced at $4,000. The sets are ordered from the manufacturer on the 10th of the month (or the preceding business day), and there is a lead time of seven business days. There are 20 business days in a typical month. The manager wishes to maintain a 90 percent service level. The store is open six days a week and Sunday afternoons. On March 31, the store had five 50" TV sets on hand. Here is data regarding sales for the next three months:

Month	Sales
April	4 sets
May	8 sets
June	7 sets

a. Which inventory model is appropriate here: the fixed quantity and variable order interval model, the variable quantity and fixed order interval model, or the single period model?

b. How many sets should be ordered on April 10?

c. What will be the ending inventory on April 30?

d. How many sets should be ordered on May 10?

e. What will be the ending inventory on May 31?

f. How many sets should be ordered on June 10?

9. Use Table 13-3 in your textbook to answer these questions.

    a. What is the expected number of units short per cycle in Problem 4?

    b. What is the implication of the expected number of units short in Problem 4?

    c. What is the expected number of units short in Problem 5?

    d. What is the significance of the expected number of units short in Problem 5?

10. Here is a list of 15 items, containing the annual volume of sales and the unit price, An A-B-C inventory system is to be established on the basis of the annual dollar value of each item. Classification A will contain about 60% of the dollar value; B will contain about 30%; and C will contain about 10%. Determine the items which belong in each category.

Item	Annual Volume	Unit Price	Annual Dollar Value
a	800	26	
b	300	20	
c	9,000	7	
d	7,000	5	
e	200	65	
f	100	83	
g	1,000	42	
h	1,800	6	
i	450	18	
j	7,500	10	
k	350	9	
l	700	28	
m	500	95	
n	750	30	
o	900	72	

    a. Determine the annual dollar value for each item and the total annual dollar value.

    b. Which items should be assigned to the A category? To the B category? To the C category?

11. A delicatessen sells potato salad from trays in the cooler cabinet; the salesperson packs the salad into cardboard containers according to the customers' orders. The supervisor prepares one batch of salad in the morning and disposes of any leftover salad at closing time. Potato salad sells for $1.49 per pound, and costs $0.80 to prepare. Sales of potato salad are believed to be normally distributed with a mean of 60 pounds per day and a variance of 256.

    a. Which inventory model is appropriate here: the single-period model, the instantaneous model, or the quantity discount model? How do you know?

    b. What is the shortage cost, C_s?

    c. What is the excess cost, C_e?

    d. How large a batch should the supervisor mix up in the morning?

12. Kerey White operates a booth which sells specialty merchandise at the State Fair. This year she is planning to sell t-shirts which are inscribed:

FAMILY FUN

THE STATE FAIR

FOR ALL AGES

The price of the t-shirts will be $25.00.each. Ms. White buys plain white t-shirts from a factory at a cost of $864 per gross (144 shirts), with a 3% discount for payment within 10 days, which she always takes. Ms. White inscribes the design on the t-shirts, herself, and estimates that her labor is worth $4.00 per shirt. Unsold T-shirts are useless, but can be sold to a scrap dealer for $0.16 per pound; there are eight t-shirts in a pound. The number of t-shirts which will be sold at the State Fair is, of course, unknown. But, based on previous experience, Ms. White estimates that the mean sales are 3 gross, and that the probability of selling more than 3 gross decreases as the quantity increases.

a. Which inventory model should be used here-the instantaneous model, the quantity discount model, the single period model?

b. Which probability distribution should be used here?

c. What is the shortage cost, C_s?

d. What is the excess cost, C_e?

e. What is the service level?

f. How many t-shirts should Ms. White prepare (in gross)?

g. Estimate Ms. White's profits for your answer in f.

CHAPTER 13   INVENTORY MANAGEMENT

True/False

Question	Answer	Glossary/ Key Idea	Textbook ref. page
1	T	G	574
2	T	5	571
3	F	6	582
4	T	G, 6	562.579
5	T		572
6	T		579
7	T	6	579
8	T	6	580
9	F		590
10	T		590
11	T		591

Multiple-Choice

Question	Answer	Glossary/ Key Idea	Textbook ref. page
1	d	9	581-582
2	e		581
3	b	6	576
4	b		579
5	e	2	559
6	d	3	561
7	e	5	563-564
8	e		567
9	a	5	570
10	a		575
11	c		589
12	e		589
13	d		5589
14	c		590-591

SOLUTIONS TO PROBLEMS

1. a. Use the instantaneous model.

   b. The annual carrying cost = HQ/2 = 3(12)Q/2 = 18Q.

   c. The annual ordering cost = DS/Q = 60000(25)/Q = 1500000/Q.

   d. The annual total cost = 18Q + 1500000/Q.

   e. $Q = \sqrt{\dfrac{2DS}{H}} = \sqrt{\dfrac{2(60,000)25}{36}} \approx 289$ pairs of bumpers.

   f. Every time the company places an order, it should order 289 pairs of bumpers.

   g. The annual total expense = (Q/2)H + (D/Q)S = (289/2)36 + (60,000/289)25 = $10,392.00 per year.

   h. The number of orders = D/Q = 60000/289 $\approx$ 208 per year.

   i. The annual total expense = 18(600) + 1500000/600 = $13,300. The annual savings are $13,300 – $10,392 = $2,908.00.

2. a. Use the noninstantaneous model.

   b. The annual carrying cost = (HQ/2)[(P-U)/P] = (2.50(12)Q/2)[(400 - 60000/240)]/400 = 5.625Q.

   c. The annual setup cost = DS/Q = 60000(250)/Q = 15000000/Q.

   d. The annual total cost = 5.625Q + 15000000/Q.

   e. $EOQ = \sqrt{\dfrac{2DS}{H}} \sqrt{\dfrac{p}{p-u}} = \sqrt{\dfrac{2(6000)250}{30}}$ x $\sqrt{\dfrac{400}{400-250}}$ = 1,633 pairs of bumpers.

f. The company should place a production order for 1,633 pairs of bumpers every time.

g. The annual total cost = 5.625EOQ + 15000000/EOQ = 5.625(1633) + 15000000/1633 ≈ $18,371.00 per year.

h. The number of production runs = D/EOQ = 60000/1633 = 36.74 runs per year.

i. The annual total cost = 5.625(3000) + 15000000/3000 = $21,875.00. The annual savings are $21,875.00 - $18,371.00 = $3,504.00.

3. a. Use the quantity discount model.

b. The annual total cost = 18Q + 1500000/Q + 150D.

c. The net price = 150(1 - d) = 150(1 - .04) = $144.00. The annual total cost = 18Q + 1500000/Q + 144D.

d. The net price = 150(1 - d) = 150(1 - .10) = $135.00. The annual total cost = 18Q + 1500000/Q + 135D.

e.

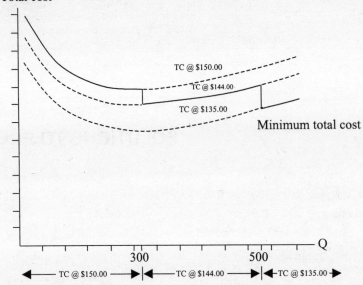

f. The EOQ is the minimum feasible point, which is 500 pairs of bumpers.

g. The annual total cost = 18(500) + 1500000/500 + 135(500) = $79,500.00

4. a. Use the fixed lead time and variable demand model.

b. The mean usage during lead time = $\bar{d}$ (LT) = 30(5) = 150 floppy disks.

c. The standard deviation = $\sigma_d \sqrt{LT}$ = $4\sqrt{5}$ = 8.94 floppy disks.

d. ROP = $\bar{d}$ (LT) + z(standard deviations) = 150 + 2.58(8.94) = 173.08 floppy disks.

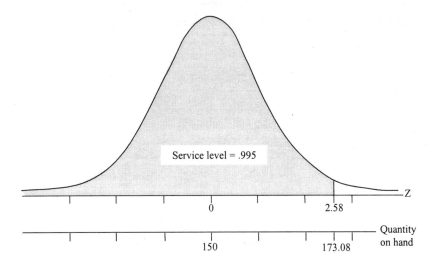

Service level = .995

2.58

Z

0

Quantity
on hand

150   173.08

e. When the quantity of floppy disks on hand falls to 173.08 disks (or fewer) place an order for the economic order quantity.

f. The safety stock = ROP - mean usage = 173.08 - 150 = 23.08 floppy disks.

5. a. Use the fixed demand and variable lead time model.

b. The mean usage during lead time = $d\,\overline{LT}$ = 50(10) = 500 pencils.

c. The standard deviation = $d\sigma_{LT}$ = 50(2) = 100 pencils.

d. ROP = $\bar{d}$ (LT) + z(standard deviations) = 500 + 1.65(100) = 665 pencils.

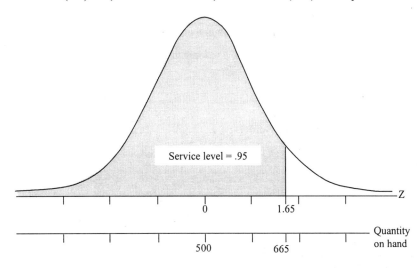

Service level = .95

1.65

Z

0

Quantity
on hand

500   665

e. When the quantity of pencils on hand falls to 665 (or fewer), place an order for the economic order quantity.

f. The safety stock = ROP – the mean usage = 665 – 500 = 165 pencils.

6. a. Use the variable demand and variable lead time model.

b. The mean usage during lead time = $\bar{d}$ (LT) = 200(25) = 5,000 sheets.

c. The standard deviation = $\sqrt{LT\sigma_d^2 + \bar{d}^2\sigma_{LT}^2}$ = $\sqrt{25(169) + 40000(4)}$

$$= \sqrt{4225 + 160000} = 405.25 \text{ Sheets.}$$

d. ROP = The mean usage + z(standard deviations) = 5000 + 2.33(405.25) = 5,944.23 sheets.

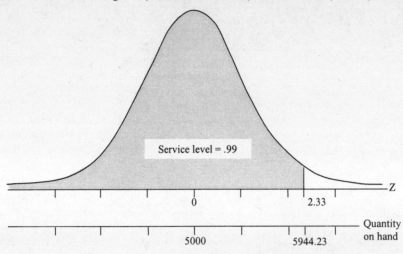

e. When the quantity of letterhead paper on hand falls to 5,944.23 sheets (or fewer) place an order for the Economic Order Quantity.

f. The safety stock = ROP - the mean usage = 5,944.23 - 5,000 = 944.23 sheets.

7. a,b,c

Freezer Sales (x)	f	fx	p	Cumulative p
0	2	0	.04	.04
1	6	6	.12	.16
2	6	12	.12	.28
3	8	24	.16	.44
4	10	40	.20	.64
5	12	60	.24	.88
6	4	24	.08	.96 ←
7	2	14	.04	1.00
	50	180	1.00	

The frequency distribution is highly skew negative and is not approximately normal.

d. $\bar{x} = \sum fx / \sum f$ = 180/50 = 3.60 freezers per week.

e. The first cumulative probability which exceeds .95 is .96, and the reorder point is 6 freezers.

f. The safety stock = 6 - 3.6 = 2.4 freezers.

8. a. Use the fixed order interval and variable quantity model.

    b. The expected demand = $\bar{d}\,(OI + LT)$ = 6 sets.

    The safety stock = $z\sigma_d\sqrt{OI + LT}$ = 1.28(1.50) = 1.92 sets.

    The order quantity = the expected demand + the safety stock - the quantity on hand
    $$= 6 + 1.92 - 5 \approx 3 \text{ sets.}$$

    c. The ending inventory on April 30 will be 5 + 3 - 4 = 4 sets.

    d. The order quantity = the expected demand + the safety stock - the quantity on hand
    $$= 6 + 1.92 - 4 \approx 4 \text{ sets.}$$

    e. The ending inventory on May 31 will be 4 + 4 - 8 = 0 sets.

    f. The order quantity = the expected demand + the safety stock - the quantity on hand
    $$= 6 + 1.92 - 0 \approx 8 \text{ sets.}$$

9. a. $E(z) = E(2.58) = .002$

    $E(n) = E(z)(\text{standard deviations}) = .002(8.94) = .02$ floppy disks.

    b. The mean number which will be short per order cycle is .02 floppy disks. In other words, no shortage should be experienced in most order cycles, but very rarely there may be a shortage of one disk.

    c. $E(z) = E(1.65) \approx .020.$

    $E(n) = E(z)(\text{standard deviations}) = .020(100) = 2$ pencils.

    d. The mean number which will be short per order cycle is 2 pencils. In other words, sometimes there will be a shortage of around 2 pencils (e.g., 1, 2, 3, or 4, but probably not more, pencils).

10. a.

Item	Annual Dollar Value
a	$20,800*
b	6,000
.	.
.	.
n	22,500
o	64,800
Total	$372,050

    * (800 x $26.00)

    b. Rearrange the items in the order of decreasing annual dollar value. Calculate the cumulative totals and the cumulative percents. Here are the first few items:

Item	Annual Dollar Value	Cumulative Dollar Value	Cumulative Percent
o	$64,800	$ 64,800	17.41%
c	63,000	127,800	34.35*
m	47,500	175,300	47.11
g	42,000	217,300	58.41
d	35,000	252,300	67.81

    *34.35% = 100(127,800)/372,050. Classification A will contain items o, c, m, and g. B will contain items d, n, a, l, e, and h. C will contain items f, i, j, b, and k.

11. a. Use the single period model.

b. C_s = Revenue per unit - cost per unit = $1.49 -$0.80 = $0.69 per pound.

c. C_e = Cost per unit = salvage value per unit = $0.80 - 0 = $0.80.

d. The service level = $C_s/(C_s + C_e)$ = .69/(.69 + .80) = .46.

e. The value of z for the service level = -0.04. The batch size = the mean demand + z(standard deviations) = 60 - 0.04(16) = 59.36 pounds of potato salad.

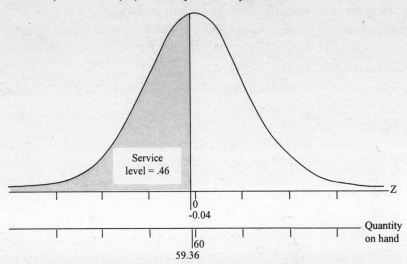

12. a. The single-period model, since the t-shirts are salable only at one event.

b. The Poisson distribution displays decreasing probabilities as the value of the random variable increases.

c. C_s = revenue per unit - cost per unit = 25(144) - 864(.97) = 3600 - 838.08 = $2761.92.

d. C_e = cost per unit - salvage value per unit = 864(.97) - .02(144) = 838.08 - 2.88 = $835.20.

e. The service level = $C_s/(C_s + C_e)$ = 2761.92/(2761.92 + 835.20) =.7678 .

f. Use the cumulative Poisson distribution with $\mu = 3$, in Table C to obtain these values:

x	P(x)
0	.050
1	.199
2	.423
3	.647
4	.815←
5	.916
6	.966
7	.988
8	.996
9	.999
10	1.000

Because P(x) = .815 is the lowest probability to exceed .7678, Ms. White should prepare 4 gross of t-shirts.

g. Profits = revenues – expenses = 4(3600) – 4(838.08) = 4(2761.92) = $11,047.68. It is improper to count Ms. White's labor as an expense.

CHAPTER 14
MATERIAL REQUIREMENTS PLANNING

KEY IDEAS

1. Manufacturing is performed to meet anticipated needs for future delivery of end items to customers, according to a master schedule that summarizes both the firm orders and the forecasted needs, and translates these into requirements at specified time "buckets" (frequently defined as calendar weeks), for a specified planning period.

2. An end item is a hierarchy of components, assemblies, subassemblies, finished goods and semifinished goods, some of them purchased from outside vendors and some assembled inside the plant. The relationships between elements at different levels are exhibited in a bill of materials (BOM) or its graphical equivalent, a product-structure tree.

3. Low-level coding of a product-structure tree puts a given type of assembly at the same level in the tree, no matter what levels the "parents" may be at, a parent is the next higher level of assembly.

4. MRP releases either internal production orders or external purchase orders for components, assemblies, subassemblies, etc., time phased so as to permit arrival of goods at the next higher level of assembly when they are needed.

5. The three principal computerized files in an MRP system are a master schedule, a bill of materials and an inventory record. The inventory record contains, for each element: (a) the lead time, safety stock and lot size, and for every time bucket in the planning period, (b) the gross requirements, available quantities, net requirements, scheduled receipts from past orders and planned releases of orders for future production.

6. For elements that go into multiple parents, MRP "pegs" (traces) requirements to specific parents. Low-level coding of the product-structure tree facilitates these assignments.

7. An MRP schedule must be periodically reviewed and updated. The two principal types of review are regeneration and net change. Regeneration periodically revises the plan, recording all changes, and net change makes the changes as they are needed.

8. MRP generates useful information and reports for a variety of management purposes, but there is some potentially useful information it cannot produce. For example, it cannot show which departments are to be assigned a specific production workload. In order to insure that the plan is consistent with departmental and plant workload capacities, it should be tested for realism by being simulated several times with different proposed master schedules, to see which schedule yields the best results.

9. Part-period balancing is a technique for setting order sizes for a component or an end item in a situation of dynamic dependent demands, such as is usually associated with MRP, based on some of the significant theoretical considerations that underlie independent inventory systems. Recall that in Chapter 13, it is shown that the minimum stocking cost for an item is attained when the EOQ or economic lot size is set at a level such that the total of the holding costs is equal to the total of order or setup costs. Part-period balancing attempts to satisfy this same objective by setting the order interval and the size of an order such that the total order cost is equal to the total holding costs.

10. Capacity Requirements Planning is used in conjunction with MRP. It helps to insure that the MRP production plans are realistic, and that they are consistent with management objectives of smooth flow of materials, continuity of the labor force and balanced workloads between departments. The resulting revisions of the MRP schedules may affect either the master schedule, the rough-cut capacity plan, or the overall production plan, or a combination of several of these plans.

11. MRP II systems actively integrate marketing and finance into rough-cut capacity planning, capacity requirements planning and setting up MRP master schedules.

GLOSSARY

assembly-time chart: displays for an end item, the time phasing of how components are integrated into levels of assembly, including both the lead time and the next level of assembly for every component.

available: inventory on hand, plus scheduled receipts that are available for use within the current time bucket.

bill of materials (BOM): the structural relationship between all the components of an assembly or end item, showing the quantities of components that are needed to assemble one unit of the end item.

capacity requirements planning: adjusting and modifying MRP plans to sustain a free flow of materials and effective utilization of the labor force and plant.

component: any ingredient of a product; this could include, for example, a raw material, subassembly, assembly or end item.

dependent demand: demand for an item derived from the demand for some item or items at a higher level of assembly.

exploding a BOM: printing a BOM, showing all components and their levels.

frozen master schedule: a firm master schedule not subject to modification.

gross material requirements: required minimum size of a lot to be dispatched to the next higher level of assembly.

independent demand: the demand for finished goods, or the demand for products or services which are not incorporated into other products or services.

inventory records file: a record maintained for every component, assembly, subassembly, raw material or end item, of planned and actual order releases and material receipts, and of the customary lead times.

level: in a product-structure tree, a code that assigns a stage number of an assembly, showing how many stages there are between the component and the end item: 0 for end item, 1 or first level, 2 for second level, etc.

level-by-level processing: a search for all the components of a given type at the same level of assembly.

load report: a bar chart that shows planned and actual production releases over a given span of time.

lot-for-lot ordering: MRP with planned-order releases and planned-order receipts matching net requirements exactly.

lot sizing: determining an order size.

low-level coding: a bill of materials or product-structure tree drawn so that all units of a given type of component are at the same level of assembly.

lumpy demand: sporadic, uneven demand resulting in nonuniform batch sizes and usage rates.

MRP (Material Requirements Planning): a computer-based information system designed to handle ordering and scheduling of dependent demand components.

MRPII (Manufacturing Resource Planning): not a replacement for MRP nor an improved version, it is an expansion of the scope of production planning to include other areas of the firm, especially marketing and finance.

master schedule: a schedule that specifies the quantity and timing of end items that are to be produced.

net-change system: MRP that is updated continuously, every transaction is posted by the computer, and the changes in available quantities and requirements are made in real time.

net material requirements: the difference between gross material requirements and amount onhand.

part-period balancing: a technique for lot sizing that incorporates economic lot sizes for all components into production planning, based on setting lot sizes such that total holding cost is approximately the same as total setup cost.

pegging: tracing a given set of gross requirements, identifying all of the parents that generated those requirements.

planned-order receipt: a lot of material to be received, based on a prior planned-order release.

planned-order release: a production order for a lot of material, placed a lead time ahead of the planned-order receipt of that lot.

primary reports: reports prepared based on standard MRP parameters, such as planned-order schedules, order releases, and changes to planned orders.

projected on hand: the expected amount of inventory that will be on hand at the *beginning* of each period.

product-structure tree: a graphical representation of a bill of materials showing at each level of assembly the number of components of each type that are the ingredients for the assembly at the next level.

regenerative system: MRP that is updated at regular intervals of time.

safety stock: stock maintained over and above that needed to satisfy net requirements. safety time: additional time allowance to compensate for variable lead time.

scheduled receipts: lots scheduled for arrival that are available for use within the current time period; scheduled receipts differ, for example, from planned-order receipts in that scheduled receipts represent executed (instead of "planned") order releases.

secondary reports: reports such as performance control, planning and exception reports, that can be prepared from MRP data.

simulation: computerized studies of the mathematical models of the plant operation, systematically varying the parameters so as to determine the effects of changes in these parameters upon costs, schedules or profits.

stacked lead time: the cumulative lead time required to complete the assembly of all components and subassemblies that go into an end item.

time bucket: a unit of time (e.g.. a week), for purposes of measuring the duration of an MRP operation, such as receiving or releasing an order, or the lead time.

time fences: A series of time intervals in which restrictions are placed on changes to the master schedule. The nearest time fence is the most restrictive.

time phasing: scheduling of the completion of a batch of material, to arrive at the next higher level of assembly, just ahead of the time this material is incorporated into the assembly.

TRUE/FALSE QUESTIONS

1. A departmental load report is one of the primary reports of an MRP system.

2. A bucket in MRP refers to a time period, such as a week, two-week period, etc.

3. Net requirements = Gross requirements - Scheduled receipts - Projected onhand.

4. Low-level coding puts the components and raw materials at the bottom of a product structure tree.

5. Level-by-level processing scans the inventory-status record file in order to determine in which time bucket the scheduled requirements are to be placed.

6. Because of the pyramid relationship for all components in an MRP system, it is appropriate to provide safety stocks at all levels, since this would help to reduce the setup costs.

7. Regeneration as a means of updating an MRP is a better way to update an unstable MRP than net change.

8. There is no relationship between MRP and plant capacity utilization.

9. Safety stock is generally avoided in MRP because it can result in unnecessary inventory buildup.

10. The three principal computerized files maintained for an MRP system include the bill of materials, the product-structure tree and an inventory record.

11. An inventory record file is maintained in MRP for every raw material, component, assembly, subassembly or end item.

12. MRP has been replaced by MRPII.

13. Lead time is the time between placing an order and receiving the material, it makes no difference whether the order is one to purchase the material or a production order.

14. An MRP worksheet is essentially a "worksheet" showing all the various requirements on hand, planned releases and planned receipts for every item and for every time bucket covered by the current master schedule.

15. In part-period balancing, the size of an order and the length of the order interval are set so that the total of the order costs is approximately equal to the total of the holding costs.

MULTIPLE-CHOICE QUESTIONS

1. The principal files that are incorporated into a computerized MRP system are:
    a. inventory record, master schedule, BOM, MRP computer program.
    b. inventory record, master file, part-period balancing program.
    c. end items, components, and load reports.
    d. capacity requirements planning file, master schedule, inventory record.
    e. MRP computer program, master schedule, capacity requirements planning file.

2. Which of the following statements concerning the level of assembly is correct?
   a. Gross requirements are derived from the planned-order releases at the next higher level.
   b. Gross requirements are derived from the planned-order releases at the next lower level.
   c. Gross requirements are derived from the planned-order receipts at the next higher level.
   d. Gross requirements are derived from the planned-order receipts at the next lower level.
   e. None of the above is correct.

3. Which one of these would not be a possible lot size?
   a. EOQ.
   b. Gross requirements.
   c. Net requirements.
   d. An amount less than net requirements.
   e. All are possible lot sizes.

4. Linking a part with a specific parent is referred to as:
   a. lot sizing.
   b. pegging.
   c. kanban.
   d. capacity planning.
   e. leveling.

5. A list of all parts and materials needed to assemble one unit of a product is called:
   a. a master schedule.
   b. a kanban.
   c. an inventory record file.
   d. MRP.
   e. a bill of materials.

6. Which phrase or term is most clearly associated with the acronym BOM?
   a. Master schedule
   b. Net requirements
   c. Scheduled receipts
   d. Product-structure tree
   e. Inventory record file

7. Which of the following correctly describes the computation of net requirements?
   a. Gross requirements - Scheduled receipts
   b. Gross requirements - On hand + Scheduled receipts
   c. Gross requirements - Scheduled receipts - On hand
   d. Gross requirements - Scheduled receipts + Planned order receipts

PROBLEMS

1. Here are the parts list and the lead time for product TT.

Component/Subassembly	Number Required	Lead time
Product TT		
Subassembly A	2	1 week
Component B	1	2 weeks
Subassembly A		
Component B	3	2 weeks
Component C	1	1 week
Component D	2	1 week

    The master schedule for product TT is:

Week Number	1	2	3	4	5	6
Quantity	0	0	0	25	50	75

    a. Construct the product-structure tree for product TT.
    b. Determine the quantity of each subassembly and component that will be required.
    c. Construct the time-phased plan for each subassembly and component in the style of Figure 14-10 in your textbook; four of them will be required.

2. Use the data in Problem 1 to solve this problem. During the fourth week, an equipment breakdown delayed the production of component D for one week. Thus, the 300 units which were to go into production in the fourth week and be received in the fifth week must be postponed to the fifth and sixth weeks.

    a. Construct a new master schedule for the fourth and subsequent weeks.
    b. Construct new time-phased plans for each subassembly and component for the fourth and subsequent weeks.

3. Here is the usage schedule for component K.

Period	1	2	3	4	5	6
Quantity	60	50	80	70	30	50

    It costs $500 to set up the equipment to produce K. and it costs $2 to store one unit of K for one period.

    a. What is the cumulative demand schedule?
    b. What is the economic part-period (EPP)?
    c. What is the lot size (based on the EPP)?

Master Schedule	Week	1	2	3	4	5	6	7	8
	Quantity								

	1	2	3	4	5	6	7	8
Gross requirements								
Scheduled receipts								
Projected on hand								
Net requirements								
Planned-order receipts								
Planned-order releases								

	1	2	3	4	5	6	7	8
Gross requirements								
Scheduled receipts								
Projected on hand								
Net requirements								
Planned-order receipts								
Planned-order releases								

	1	2	3	4	5	6	7	8
Gross requirements								
Scheduled receipts								
Projected on hand								
Net requirements								
Planned-order receipts								
Planned-order releases								

	1	2	3	4	5	6	7	8
Gross requirements								
Scheduled receipts								
Projected on hand								
Net requirements								
Planned-order receipts								
Planned-order releases								

CHAPTER 14   MATERIAL REQUIREMENTS PLANNING

True/False

Question	Answer	Glossary/ Key Idea	Textbook ref. page
1	F		633
2	T	G, 1	621
3	T		625
4	F	G, 3	623-624
5	F	G	623
6	F		633
7	F	G	631
8	F	10	636
9	T		633
10	F	5	620
11	T	5	621
12	F		641
13	T		621
14	T		628
15	T	9	635

Multiple-Choice

Question	Answer	Glossary/ Key Idea	Textbook ref. page
1	a	5	620
2	a	G, 6	626
3	d		626
4	b	G, 6	631
5	e	G	621
6	d	G, 2	621
7	c		625

SOLUTIONS TO PROBLEMS

1.   a.

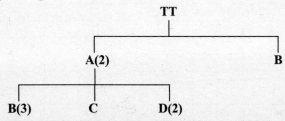

b.   The master schedule calls for 150 units of product TT.

Subassembly/component	Quantity	
Product TT		
Subassembly A	300	(150 x 2)
Component B	150	
Subassembly A		
Component B	900	(300 x 3)
Component C	300	
Component D	600	(300 x 2)

The list may be condensed by combining the quantities for Component B:

Subassembly/componen	Quantity
Product TT [t]	
Subassembly A	300
Component B	1050
Component C	300
Component D	600

c.

Subassemby A LT = 1 wk.	1	2	3	4	5	6
Gross requirements				50	100	150
Scheduled receipts						
Projected on hand						
Net requirements				50	100	150
Planned-order receipts				50	100	150
Planned-order releases			50	100	150	

Component B LT = 2 wk.	1	2	3	4	5	6
Gross requirements			150	325	500	75
Scheduled receipts						
Projected on hand	100	100	100			
Net requirements			50	325	500	75
Planned-order receipts			50	325	500	75
Planned-order releases	50	325	500	75		

Component C LT = 1 wk.	1	2	3	4	5	6
Gross requirements			50	100	150	
Scheduled receipts						
Projected on hand						
Net requirements			50	100	150	
Planned-order receipts			50	100	150	
Planned-order releases		50	100	150		

Component D LT = 1 wk.	1	2	3	4	5	6
Gross requirements			100	200	300	
Scheduled receipts						
Projected on hand						
Net requirements			100	200	300	
Planned-order receipts			100	200	300	
Planned-order releases		100	200	300		

2.   a.   The delay in producing component D will cause a one-week delay in producing subassembly A and the last 75 units of product TT will be delayed one week beyond that time, for a total of two weeks.

Week	4	5	6	7	8
Quantity	25	50			75

    b.

Assembly A LT = 1 wk.	4	5	6	7	8
Gross requirements	50	100			150
Scheduled receipts					
Projected on hand					
Net requirements	50	100			150
Planned-order receipts	50	100			150
Planned-order releases	100		150		

Component B LT = 2 wk.	4	5	6	7	8
Gross requirements	325	50		450	75
Scheduled receipts					
Projected on hand			450	450	
Net requirements	325	50			75
Planned-order receipts	325	50			75
Planned-order releases			75		

Component C LT = 1 wk.	4	5	6	7	8
Gross requirements	100		150		
Scheduled receipts					
Projected on hand					
Net requirements	100		150		
Planned-order receipts	100		150		
Planned-order releases		150			

Component D LT = 1 wk.	4	5	6	7	8
Gross requirements	200		300		
Scheduled receipts					
Projected on hand					
Net requirements	200		300		
Planned-order receipts	200		300		
Planned-order releases		200			

3.   a.   The cumulative usage schedule.

Period	1	2	3	4	5	6
Quantity	60	110	190	260	290	340

    b.   EPP = (Setup Cost)/(Unit Holding Cost) = 500/2 = 250.

c. Calculate cumulative part-periods based on the cumulative quantities.

Period	Lot size	Inventory	Periods carried	Part-periods	Cumulative Part-periods
1	60	0	0	0	0
	110	50	1	50	50
	190	80	2	160	210*
	260	70	3	210	420

*210 is closest to the EPP of 250; produce 190 units.

The 190 units will satisfy the requirements of the first three periods. Repeat the calculation for the next three periods.

Period	Lot size	Inventory	Periods carried	Part-periods	Cumulative Part-periods
4	70	0	0	0	0
	100	30	1	30	30
	150	50	2	100	130

The final entry of 130 does not seem to be close to the EPP of 250. Obtain the requirements for component K for later weeks and continue the calculation

CHAPTER 15
JUST-IN-TIME SYSTEMS

KEY IDEAS

1. Just-in-time is an approach to repetitive manufacturing that emphasizes continual effort to remove inefficiency and waste from the production process. It is the aspect of lean production that is concerned with the flow of material through the system.

2. JIT systems achieve important benefits through the use of small lot sizes, high quality, and a team approach.

3. The main goal of a JIT system is smooth production (i.e., level use of producton resources).

4. An important feature of JIT systems is the use of a pull system rather than a push system to move work through a system. Under a push system, work is moved along as it is completed; under a pull system, downstream operations signal preceding operations when they want/need work. Hence, each operation dictates need to the preceding operation; work proceeds in response to demand of following operations.

5. The building blocks of JIT are product design, process design, organizational elements, and manufacturing planning and control.

6. JIT is different than the traditional approach to manufacturing. Important aspects of this are outlined in Table 15-4 in the textbook.

7. Despite the benefits of JIT, conversion to JIT requires considerable planning. See the discussion of this and possible obstacles in the textbook.

8. JIT can also be applied to services, although the majority of applications have been in manufacturing.

STUDY TIPS

There are many elements in a JIT system. A good way to study this chapter is to make a list of the elements, and then write a few sentences about each, explaining what it is (if it is not obvious from your list) and why it is important for a JIT system to have it.

GLOSSARY

andon: a system of lights used to warn of problems or potential problems in a JIT system.

brainstorming: collective, free-thinking approach to problem solving.

delayed differentiation: used when two or more (typically) assembled products are basically the same except for a relatively few components that can be added near the end of production; the basic module is produced without adding the final components. This permits great flexibility and quick response to demand for specific end items.

just-in-time system: an approach to repetitive manufacturing that emphasizes small lot sizes. minimizing waste, high quality, quick setups, and worker involvement in problem solving.

kanban: a signal that authorizes movement or work on parts or material, often in the form of a kanban card.

multifunctional workers: workers who are trained to handle a variety of production, setup and minor repair tasks.

preventive maintenance: emphasizes keeping equipment in good working order and replacing parts which have a tendency to fail before they actually fail.

pull system: work moves through a system whereby work is moved only when it is requested by the next workstation in line.

push system: each station pushes the work along as it completes its set of tasks.

TRUE/FALSE QUESTIONS

1. JIT is basically a pull system.

2. JIT production systems emphasize a fixed, steady rate of production.

3. JIT lot sizes are small compared to those in more traditional systems.

4. Converting suppliers to JIT is one of the first steps in converting to a JIT system.

5. The kanban approach is simpler than MRP II.

6. A goal of JIT is increased flexibility in the ability to change the production mix.

7. Andon refers to a system of warning lights.

MULTIPLE-CHOICE QUESTIONS

1. Which one of these is not generally associated with JIT?
   a. Low inventories
   b. Preventive maintenance
   c. A push system
   d. Problem solving
   e. A fixed, steady rate of production

2. Which one of these is not usually associated with JIT?
   a. Preventive maintenance
   b. Manufacturing cells.
   c. Multifunctional workers
   d. Large lot sizes.
   e. Quick setups

3. Which one of these is not generally thought of in conjunction with JIT
   a. Reduced space requirements
   b. Waiting lines
   c. Management by consensus
   d. Short lead times
   e. High quality

4. Which of these groups would be least likely to resist conversion to a JIT system?
   a. Workers
   b. Management
   c. Customers
   d. Vendors

5.   Which one is unrelated to problem solving in a JIT system?

    a.   A temporary increase in inventory

    b.   Andon

    c.   Brainstorming

    d.   Worker involvement

    e.   All are related

PROBLEMS

1.   In the course of manufacturing sunglasses, workstation K must attach the lenses to the frame; lenses come from workstation J. These are the nonprescription type of sunglasses which may be bought off of the rack at the drugstore and this problem is concerned only with the lenses, not the frames. Management has scheduled the production of 160 sunglasses per 8-hour shift. Workstation J requires 3.0 minutes to produce a pair of lenses (left and right); once in a while a pair of lenses is defective, and management allows .20 for inefficiencies. The finished lenses are placed in containers of a dozen pairs each. When workstation K opens a container of lenses, it sends the kanban back to station J which takes 15 minutes, it takes 15 minutes for a container to be transported from station J to station K.

    a.   What is the value of D?

    b.   What is the value of T?

    c.   What is the value of X?

    d.   What is the value of C?

    e.   How many kanban cards (or containers) should be used in this system?

2.   (One step beyond) One step in the manufacture of tennis rackets consists of weaving the cross strings into the head of the racket. This task requires a high level of skill and experience, and is slow. In workstation G, six skilled weavers work on tennis rackets; on the average, it takes 45 minutes for one weaver to weave a tennis racket. The head of the racket is produced by a supplier who has been certified; the supplier is located in Portland. OR, while the manufacturer is located in Los Angeles, CA, a distance of about 1,000 miles. Tennis racket heads are shipped by truck from Portland to Los Angeles; each truckload contains six dozen heads and the trip takes two days, i.e., the truck leaves Portland on the morning of the first day (say Monday) and arrives in Los Angeles on the evening of the second day (Tuesday); the racket heads are available for weaving on the morning of the third day (Wednesday). When any weaver opens the shipment, the kanban is sent to the computer room, where an operator faxes the order instantaneously to the supplier's computer; the order will be on the road the next business day. The six weavers work an eight-hour shift with two 15-minute coffee breaks. Production is continuous; with the current popularity of tennis, the firm can sell all of the rackets it can produce, and is in the happy position of having back orders. The weaving jobs are well done, and management allows .05 for inefficiencies and errors.

    a.   What Is the value of D?

    b.   What is the value of T?

    c.   What is the value of X?

    d.   What is the value of C?

    e.   How many kanbans should be in use?

f. Suppose that highway construction forces the trucks to take a detour which delays the arrival in Los Angeles one day. What effect will this have on the number of kanban cards?

g. After consultation with the supplier, It is decided to experiment with larger shipments of tennis racket heads. A larger truck is rented which can carry eight dozen heads. What effect will this have on the number of kanban cards?

h. Suppose one of the weavers retires. An apprentice must be hired and trained. During the training period, the average time required to weave a head is estimated at 60 minutes. What effect will this have on the number of kanban cards?

i. During the trial period, management anticipates that the rate of defective weaving jobs will increase, and the allowance is raised to .20. What effect will this have on the number of kanban cards?

3. The TruTime Corporation produces four styles of wrist watches, described below, with the daily requirements for each style for the month of September.

Style	Description	Requirements
MD	Men's digital watch	24 watches
MA	Men's analog watch	36
WD	Women's digital watch	9
WA	Women's analog watch	60

The setups for models MD and MA are similar. The setups for models WD and WA are similar but are more complicated and lengthy than the other setups.

a. What sequence of models should be used in a production cycle?

b. How many cycles should there be per day?

c. How many of each style should be produced in each cycle?

d. How can the answer to #1-c be improved?

4. Here are the production requirements for the TruTime Corporation (see #3) for the month of October.

Style	Requirements
MD	27 Watches
MA	37
WD	10
WA	55

a. How many cycles are required per day?

b. How many of each style should be produced in each cycle?

CHAPTER 15   JUST-IN-TIME SYSTEMS

True/False

Question	Answer	Glossary/ Key Idea	Textbook ref. page
1	T	4	672
2	T		662
3	T	2	664
4	F		680
5	T		674-675
6	T		662
7	T	G	670

Multiple-Choice

Question	Answer	Glossary/ Key Idea	Textbook ref. page
1	c	4	672
2	d		664
3	b		681
4	c		681
5	e		668,670

SOLUTIONS TO PROBLEMS

1. a. $D = 160/8 = 20$ sunglasses per hour.
    b. $T = 12(3.0) + 15 + 15 = 66$ min. $= 1.1$ hrs.
    c. $X = .20$.
    d. $C = 12$ pairs.
    e. $N = DT(1 + X)/C = 20(1.1)(1.2)/12 = 2.2 \rightarrow 3$ kanban cards.

2. a. $D = 6(7.5$ hrs.$)/(.75$ hrs$) = 60$ woven heads per day.
    b. $T = 1 + 3 = 4$ days.
    c. $X = .05$.
    d. $C = 72$ heads.
    e. $N = DT(1 + X)/C = 60(4)(1.05)/72 = 3.50 \rightarrow 4$ kanban cards.
    f. $N = 4.375 \dashrightarrow 5$.
    g. $N = 2.625 \rightarrow 3$.
    h. $N = 2.625 \rightarrow 3$.
    i. Using the information in 2-h, $N = 3$.

3. a. Combine similar setups. MD-WD-MA-WA would be feasible. (So would MA-WA-MD-WD.)
    b. 3 cycles, since each requirement is divisible by 3.
    c. <u>Cycles</u>

<u>1</u>	<u>2</u>	<u>3</u>	<u>Total</u>
MD(8)	MD(8)	MD(8)	24
WD(3)	WD(3)	WD(3)	9
MA(12)	MA(12)	MA(12)	36
<u>WA(20)</u>	<u>WA(20)</u>	<u>WA(20)</u>	<u>60</u>
43	43	43	

d. Setting up three times for WD may be inefficient; you might schedule all of WD for one cycle.

Cycles

1	2	3	Total
MD(8)	MD(8)	MD(8)	24
WD(9)	WD(0)	WD(0)	9
MA(6)	MA(15)	MA(15)	36
WA(20)	WA(20)	WA(20)	60
43	43	43	129

4. a. 5 cycles, since two requirements are divisible by 5.

b. Try to smooth out production and reduce the number of setups. Here is one way to do it.

Cycles

1	2	3	4	5	Total
MD(10)	MD(10)	MS(7)	MD(0)	MD(0)	27
WD(10)	WD(0)	WD(0)	WD(0)	WD(0)	10
MA(0)	MA(7)	MA(10)	MA(10)	MA(10)	37
WA(7)	WA(10)	WA(10)	WA(14)	WA(14)	55
27	27	27	24	24	129

See if you can devise a smoother schedule. You might also try for fewer setups.

CHAPTER 16
SUPPLY CHAIN MANAGEMENT

KEY IDEAS

1. A supply chain is the flow of information and materials from suppliers through production and distribution to end users. Materials are the physical items (raw materials, purchased parts, fuel, tools, etc.) that are used during the production process. Materials management is concerned with the purchase, movement, and storage of materials, and with the distribution of finished goods.

2. Purchasing is a subset of materials management; it is responsible for obtaining the material inputs for the operating system. Purchasing objectives are to determine (from operations) the quality, quantity and timing requirements; to obtain the best possible price; to maintain good relations with vendors, to maintain sources of supply; and to be knowledgeable on prices, new products and new services.

3. The purchasing function should periodically perform value analysis on parts and materials to reduce costs and/or improve the performance of purchased items. (See Table 16-1 in your textbook for an overview of the value analysis process.)

4. From time to time, the question of whether to make or to buy an item comes up. There is a list of nine factors in the textbook that are usually taken into account.

5. Evaluating sources of supply (vendor analysis) involves looking at price, quality, services provided, location, inventory policies of suppliers, and the degree to which a supplier is willing to be flexible.

6. In recent years, there has been a shift in the way buyers view suppliers; more and more, vendors are being viewed as partners rather than as adversaries. (See Table 16-3 in your textbook for a summary of this.)

7. Bar codes enable companies to monitor goods during production and distribution.

8. JIT II is a philosophy that empowers suppliers to assume responsibilities typically done by a company's own buyers. This may involve planning, order transactions (i.e., ordering), and dealing with problems that relate to the supplier's products.

GLOSSARY

bar code: patterns of lines, spaces, numbers, and symbols attached to labels that can be electronically scanned. They facilitate monitoring items during production and distribution.

centralized purchasing: purchasing is handled by one specialized department.

decentralized purchasing: individual departments or separate locations handle their own purchasing requirements.

distribution requirements planning: is used to plan and coordinate transportation, warehousing, workers, equipment, and financial flows. It is especially useful in multi-echelon warehousing systems.

electronic data interchange (EDI): the direct transmission of inteorganization transactions, computer to computer.

JIT II: empowering suppliers to assume some of the responsibilities of a company's own buyers, such as planning, placing orders, dealing with quality and delivery problems, etc.

logistics: the movement of materials within a production facility and the handling of incoming and outgoing shipments of goods and materials.

materials: physical items used during the production process. Includes not only parts and raw materials, but also tools, fuels, forms, and anything else that supports the production process.

outsourcing: buying goods and services from outside sources instead of making the goods or providing the services inside the organization.

purchasing cycle: the main steps are (1) a requisition is received for a purchase, (2) purchasing selects a supplier, (3) an order is placed, (4) the order is monitored, and (5) the order is received.

supply chain: the flow of materials and information from suppliers through production to the end users.

value analysis: involves examination of the function of purchased parts and materials in an effort to reduce cost and/or improve performance of those items.

vendor analysis: evaluating sources of supply in terms of price, quality, services offered, location, inventory policy, and flexibility.

TRUE/FALSE QUESTIONS

1. A purchasing department focuses exclusively on acquiring raw materials and components for the manufacturing system..

2. The supply chain extends from the supplier to the finished goods.

3. Outsourcing refers to buying goods or services from outside sources.

4. Value analysis involves choosing a source of supply.

5. Negotiation is a win-lose confrontation.

6. Centralized purchasing means that purchasing is handled by one special department.

7. Nearness of supplier can be an important factor in choosing a supplier.

8. In JIT II systems, suppliers may order for their customers.

MULTIPLE-CHOICE QUESTIONS

1. Which one of these is not usually a consideration in outsourcing decisions?
   a. capacity
   b. cost
   c. quality
   d. lead time
   e. all are considerations.

2. Which is not a factor in vendor analysis?
   a. location
   b. quality
   c. price
   d. inventory policy of supplier
   e. all are factors

3. Which statement most closely describes negotiated purchasing?

   a. It is often a win-lose confrontation.

   b. The main goal is to obtain the lowest possible price. currently performs the function in house?

   c. Each negotiation is an isolated transaction.

   d. It is used for special purchasing situations.

4. Which one of these items is not related to EDI?

   a. Supplier audits.

   b. ECR.

   c. Bar codes.

   d. JIT delivery.

   e. Electronic transfer of funds.

5. Which one is often not a benefit of decentralized purchasing?

   a. attention to local needs

   b. quantity discounts

   c. quicker response

   d. nearness to supplier

6. JIT II can be described briefly as:

   a. the replacement for JIT I.

   b. placing the buyer's representatives in the supplier's factory.

   c. empowering suppliers.

   d. replacing one supplier with many suppliers for the same supplies.

   e. the same thing as MRP II.

CHAPTER 16 SUPPLY CHAIN MANAGEMENT

True/False

Question	Answer	Glossary/ Key Idea	Textbook ref. page
1	F	2	695
2	F	G,1	694
3	T		698
4	F	G	697
5	F		699
6	T	G	699
7	T		702
8	T		705

Multiple-Choice

Question	Answer	Glossary/ Key Idea	Textbook ref. page
1	e		698
2	e	5	701
3	d		699
4	a		709
5	b		699
6	c	8	705

CHAPTER 17
SCHEDULING

KEY IDEAS

1.   Operations scheduling involves the timing of specific operations for both workers and machines.

2.   The chief objective of scheduling is to utilize manpower and machines to produce goods and services when they are required and to balance the workload so as to reduce costs, idle time, and excess inventories.

3.   The hierarchy of decisions in production/operations is: capacity planning for long-term decisions on plant size; aggregate or intermediate planning for general use of facilities, personnel, subcontracting and purchased material; and detailed scheduling of manpower and machines.

4.   Material requirements planning (MRP) and capacity requirements planning (CRP) are useful for batch processing with dependent sequential demands. They do not necessarily tell which personnel or machines will work on specific jobs.

5.   Each step of production results in a narrower and better defined set of constraints. Scheduling decisions must take all of these constraints into account.

6.   Flow systems such as processes and high-volume assembly lines are dedicated to single products or services, with possible variations in sizes, models or mixtures. Scheduling flow systems frequently involves line balancing; but disruptions to the system such as fluctuations in demand or machine breakdowns must be allowed for.

7.   Intermediate volume systems have interrupted production schedules. The EOQ models yield lot sizes that minimize setup and inventory costs for a single product with independent demand, but don't always do the job for multiple products.

8.   The assignment model of linear programming does one-to-one matching of operators to machines by an easy-to-use algorithm that assigns employee-machine pairs according to the principle of "least relative cost."

9.   Job shops typically use Gantt charts. Two specific types are load charts and schedule charts. The load chart shows loading and idle times for a group of machines or departments. Schedule charts show the current status of every job, along with planned and actual starting and ending dates.

10.   Job shop scheduling is more complicated than flow systems. Priority rules are used for sequencing in job shops. Different priority rules, first come first served (FCFS), shortest processing time (SPT), due date (DD), slack per operation (S/0), and RUSH, may come up with different sequences. The effectiveness of a rule is measured by average completion time, average lateness, or average number of jobs in the system at any given time.

11.   Priority scheduling rules can be local or global. Local rules take into account information pertaining to a single workstation; global rules take into consideration information pertaining to multiple workstations.

12.   Johnson's rule minimizes throughput (makespan) time for a group of jobs to be processed in the same order at two work centers by a variation of the SPT rule.

13.   Examples of scheduling in service systems are appointments such as in doctors' offices, simple reservations as in restaurants, and computerized scheduling from multiple sources as in airline reservations.

GLOSSARY

assignment method: in situations where there is a one-to-one matching of resources (e.g., workers) available to equipment or facilities (e.g., machines). the assignment method is an efficient alternative for small problems to the simplex method of linear programming for obtaining the optimum (least cost or greatest revenue) one-to-one assignment of resources to equipment or facilities. See also relative cost.

backward scheduling: scheduling by working backwards from the due date(s).

DD (due date): a sequencing rule that gives the highest priority to the job with the earliest due date.

finite loading: jobs are assigned to work centers taking into account the work center capacity and job processing times.

FCFS (first come first served): the sequencing rule that gives the highest priority to the job or customer that arrives at the facility first. FCFS is frequently thought of as being the "fairest" method of assignment for retail or service establishments such as super-markets and automobile service stations, but it cannot be used when there are emergencies, such as in hospitals, and it is frequently less efficient than alternative scheduling systems for job shop production.

forward scheduling: scheduling ahead from some point in time.

Gantt chart: a type of chart designed by Henry L. Gantt, one of the pioneers of scientific management, that shows the progress of a set of jobs over a period of time, and visually displays the difference between planned and actual performance.

high-volume systems: organizations or production systems with standardized equipment and activities that provide highly similar products or services.

horizontal loading: loading the job with the highest priority on all work centers followed by the job with the next highest priority, and so forth.

infinite loading: jobs are assigned to work centers without regard for the capacity of the work center.

intermediate-volume systems: production systems with volume lower than that of a high volume system, but with production quantities greater than those of a job shop.

job shop: an organization with intermittent production activities, and with jobs flowing through the system in batches.

Johnson's rule: an efficient heuristic method for scheduling n jobs through two work centers, where every job goes through both work centers in the same order.

load chart: a form of Gantt chart that shows both the loading and idle times of a set of machines or departments.

loading: assigning jobs to work centers.

makespan: the total time needed to complete a group of jobs.

matching: see assignment method.

relative cost: an aspect of the technique of the assignment method to attain an optimum one-to-one matching of n resources to n facilities. Let us consider an n-by-n matrix with the n rows representing the resources and the n columns the facilities. Out of the n x n potential assignments, representing all the cells of the matrix, the assignment method finds the n assignments, with every resource assigned to a different facility, with the smallest total cost.

reservation system: computerized scheduling systems with multiple numbers of terminals connected on-line to a central computer that maintains master schedule information, and assigns places and times to the customers or users in real time; the best known example of a reservation system is that used by airlines to assign seats on airplanes to customers on specific dates.

schedule chart: a form of Gantt chart used to monitor the progress of jobs through the system.

sequencing: determining job processing order.

SPO (slack per operation): a sequencing and priority rule that gives the highest priority to the job with the smallest ratio of total slack time to the number of operations.

SPT (shortest processing time): a priority rule that gives the highest priority to the job with the least total processing time.

slack: for a job that could be completed before the scheduled due date if it were started immediately and worked on continuously, the slack is the difference in time between the completion date and the scheduled due date.

vertical loading: the finite loading of jobs at a workcenter, one by one, according to some priority rule.

workstation: an area where one person works, usually with special equipment on a specialized job.

TRUE/FALSE QUESTIONS

1. Scheduling is primarily concerned with the timing of operations.

2. Job shop schedule by priority rules is inherently deterministic in nature; the scheduler must plan as if both the order of processing and the amount of time each job would take in each work center were known exactly.

3. Line balancing is a characteristic feature of operations for job shops.

4. Scheduling of work for job shops is usually more complicated than it is for flow systems.

5. The assignment method will solve a wide variety of problems that have to do with flow systems.

6. The assignment problem involves matching of tasks and resources.

7. Load charts, schedule charts and charts showing the arrangement of n jobs through two work centers by Johnson's rule are all forms of Gantt charts.

8. The hierarchy of decisions in operations is, in order:

    (1)   long-term capacity planning

    (2)   aggregate planning

    (3)   material requirements planning

    (4)   capacity requirements planning

    (5)   scheduling

9. If the first come first served rule were used more in industry, it would probably result in more efficient scheduling of jobs.

10. Johnson's rule, the assignment method, and loading and priority rules are all appropriate methods of scheduling for job shops.

11. Priority rules are simple heuristics for determining job processing sequence.

12. Measures of effectiveness for a processing rule include average completion time, average job lateness and average runout time.

13. Different processing rules can often result in different schedules, and all of these can be called optimal in one sense or another.

14. The DD (earliest due date) rule will generally result in better sequences of jobs or assignments than the FCFS rule.

MULTIPLE-CHOICE QUESTIONS

1. Which one of the following is not an appropriate job-shop scheduling rule?
   a. Due date
   b. Assignment method
   c. First come first served
   d. Shortest processing time
   e. Johnson's rule

2. Which one of the following statements is correct?
   a. Flow systems are generally associated with high volumes of production, and every workstation along an assembly line is assigned a specialized task.
   b. Flow systems are associated with job shops.
   c. Machines in a job shop are rarely idle.
   d. Intermittent systems are fundamentally just-in-time, similar to modem Japanese methods of production.
   e. Fixed-position systems are assembly lines in fixed locations, that produce a high volume of merchandise.

3. The term "loading' in the context of scheduling refers to:
   a. the assignment of jobs to processing centers.
   b. using Gantt charts for scheduling.
   c. balancing a production or assembly line.
   d. transporting finished goods to appropriate distribution equipment such as trucks or rail cars.
   e. expanding (horizontally or vertically) workloads.

4. Which one of the following is an optimizing technique?
   a. Shortest processing time
   b. Assignment method
   c. First come first served
   d. Loading
   e. None of these

5. All of the following are possible reasons for using the first come first served rule in service systems except:
   a. It is easy to apply.
   b. It guarantees the shortest throughput time.
   c. It is viewed as "fair" by waiting customers.
   d. No computations are required.
   e. All are possible reasons.

6.   A major disadvantage of the SPT rule is:

    a.   it tends to make long jobs wait.

    b.   it results in high in-process inventories.

    c.   long jobs tend to delay other jobs.

    d.   it does not take processing time into account.

    e.   none of these.

7.   A major disadvantage of the DD rule is:

    a.   it tends to make long jobs wait.

    b.   it results in high in-process inventories.

    c.   long jobs tend to delay other jobs.

    d.   it does not take processing time into account.

    e.   none of these.

8.   Choose the best ending to this statement: Scheduling service systems presents certain problems not generally encountered in manufacturing systems due to:

    a.   the inability to store services.

    b.   the random nature of customer requests for service.

    c.   both a and b.

    d.   the systems tend to operate over a longer day than manufacturing systems.

    e.   both b and d.

9.   Which statement is correct?

    a.   Vertical loading involves infinite loading.

    b.   Horizontal loading involves infinite loading.

    c.   Vertical loading involves finite loading.

    d.   a. and b. are correct.

    e.   b. and c. are correct.

PROBLEMS

1.   Mr. Art Point manufactures drawing pencils in his shop: his product line consists of 2B, 3B, 4B, 5B, and 6B drawing pencils. At the first of the month, he has some inventory of each type of pencil, as shown in the table below. He also has an estimate of the volume of sales of each type of pencil. By running a linear programming problem, he has determined the quantity of each type of pencil to be produced this month.

Type of Pencil	Inventory	Estimated Sales per day	Scheduled Production
2B	2,000	500	12,000
3B	3,000	600	9,000
4B	0	1,200	27,000
5B	3,000	1,000	18,000
6B	6,000	500	5,000

a. What is the runout time for each type of pencil?

b. In what order should the pencils be produced during the month?

c. What assumption about the sales of drawing pencils is made here?

2. Solve problem #1 on an EXCEL spreadsheet.

a. How should the problem be entered on the spreadsheet?

b. How should the formulas be entered?

3. A construction company has a contract to construct an access ramp from a street to an expressway. The principal activities in the project are shown below, along with the scheduled starting date and the estimated number of working days which each step will require.

	Activity	Starting Date	Working days
(1)	Draw blueprints	May 6	10
(2)	Build temporary bypass road	May 13	5
(3)	Build the grade for the access ramp	May 20	15
(4)	Lay the foundation for the pavement	June 3	12
(5)	Lay the concrete pavement	June 17	5
(6)	Paint lines on pavement, etc.	June 24	5
(7)	Remove temporary bypass road	July 1	5

The company works the customary five-day week and observes holidays on Memorial Day (May 27) and on the 4th and 5th of July. Here is a calendar for May, June, and July:

```
        May                        June                       July
S  M  T  W  T  F  S        S  M  T  W  T  F  S        S  M  T  W  T  F  S
         1  2  3  4                          1              1  2  3  4  5  6
 5  6  7  8  9 10 11        2  3  4  5  6  7  8        7  8  9 10 11 12 13
12 13 14 15 16 17 18        9 10 11 12 13 14 15       14 15 16 17 18 19 20
19 20 21 22 23 24 25       16 17 18 19 20 21 22       21 22 23 24 25 26 27
26 27 28 29 30 31          23 24 25 26 27 28 29       28 29 30 31
                           30
```

a. Construct a Gantt Progress Chart as of May 6, showing the schedule of the activities List the activities on the vertical axis and count only working days on the horizontal axis (May 6 = 1).

b. Assume it is June 10. Here Is the history of the project to-date:

Drawing the blueprints started on May 6 and took nine working days.

Constructing the temporary bypass road took six working days, because of heavy rains.

The rains caused a two-day delay in commencing to build the grade, which actually started on May 22, and is incomplete as of June 10.

Laying the foundation for the pavement commenced on June 3. and is incomplete as of June 10.

Prepare the updated Gantt Progress Chart which shows the status of the access ramp on June 10.

4. The Interstate Biology Machines Company leases equipment to hospitals and laboratory for use in medical tests and research on humans and animals. The company has several bureaus in Cities A, B, C and D, which are staffed by technicians who may be sent to customers' establishments in the event of difficulty with the equipment. One day, requests for service have been received from customers in Cities, 1, 2, 3, 4 and 5. The distance each service bureau to each customer, one way, is given in the table below in kilometers.

Bureau	*Customer* 1	2	3	4	5
A	200	50	500	100	60
B	100	200	80	40	600
C	90	200	400	60	200
D	700	100	200	400	90

It is necessary to assign the technicians to the customers so as to minimize the amount of technicians' travel.

a. What is the initial table for solving this problem with the assignment method?
b. What is the final table?
c. Which technician should be assigned to which customers?
d. What is the total round-trip distance which the technicians must travel?
e. Who does without in this schedule?

5. (One step beyond.) Refer to Problem #3.

a. The Service Bureau in City C is not equipped to handle the problem of Customer #1 Incorporate this constraint into the problem.
b. Customer #3 has an emergency; if the equipment is not serviced immediately, the patient may die. Incorporate this constraint into the problem.
c. What is the initial tableau?
d. What is the final tableau?
e. Which technician should be assigned to which customer?
f. What is the total round trip distance which the technicians must travel?
g. Who does without in this schedule?

6.   A number of jobs are waiting to be processed at a work center. The jobs are listed below in the order in which they arrived. For each job, the due date is showing and an estimate of the processing time in workdays. Only one job can be processed at a time, and it is necessary to determine the sequence. Assume it is October 1.

Job Number	Due Date	Processing Time (days)
1	Dec. 10	6
2	Nov. 13	10
3	Oct. 15	8
4	Nov. 18	12
5	Dec. 6	9
6	Oct. 30	7

a.   What is the sequence using the first come first served (FCFS) priority rule?

b.   What is the sequence using the shortest processing time (SPT) rule?

c.   What is the sequence using the due date (DD) priority rule?

d.   What is the difference between these rules and the runout time rule (Problem 1)?

7.   A number of jobs are waiting to be processed through two work centers. Each job must be processed through Center A and Center B, in that order. For each job, the processing time in each work center is given below, in minutes.

Job	Time in Center A	Time in Center B
A	10	12
B	8	15
C	15	9
D	20	11
E	18	10
F	17	13
G	11	14

a.   Use Johnson's rule to determine the sequence in which the jobs should be processe.

b.   Construct a chart showing the sequence of the jobs in each work center, the times the jobs spend waiting, and the times that the work centers are idle.

c.   What is the throughput (makespan) time?

d.   How much time do the jobs spend waiting to be processed?

e.   How much idle time do the work centers have?

CHAPTER 17   SCHEDULING

True/False

Question	Answer	Glossary/ Key Idea	Textbook ref. page
1	T	1	722
2	T	11	734
3	F	6, 9	722
4	T	10	725
5	F	8	729
6	T	G, 8	729
7	T	9	726
8	T	3	722
9	F		736
10	T	10, 12	725-738
11	T	G	734
12	F	10	734
13	F		737-738
14	T		736

Multiple-Choice

Question	Answer	Glossary/ Key Idea	Textbook ref. page
1	b	5	729
2	a	6	722-723
3	a	G	725
4	b	6	729
5	b		736
6	a	2	737
7	d		737
8	c		741
9	a		727

SOLUTIONS TO PROBLEMS

1. a. Runout Time = (Production available + Current Inventory)/Demand Rate.

Type of Pencil	Production	Inventory	Demand	Runout Time (days)
2B	12,000	2,000	500	28
3B	9,000	3,000	600	20
4B	27,000	0	1,200	22.5
5B	18,000	3,000	1,000	21
6B	5,000	6,000	500	22

   b. Produce the pencils in the order of small to large runout times: 3B, 5B, 6B, 4B, 2B.

   c.   It is assumed that there are no priority or rush orders for any of the pencils. A rush order for 4B pencils, for example, would require that 4B pencils be produced first, rather than fourth.

2. a.

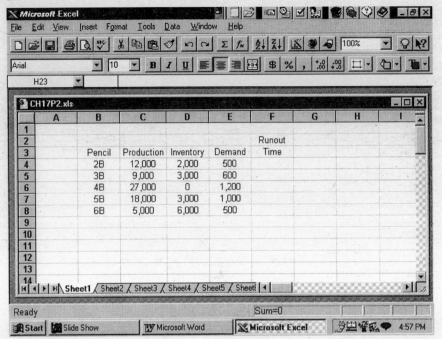

b. In cell F4: =(C4+D4)/E4

    etc.

    Did you get the same answers as in #1-a?

3. List the calendar working days, and count them off, starting with May 6. The count numbers will lie on the x-axis: May 6 = 1; July 12 = 47.

a.

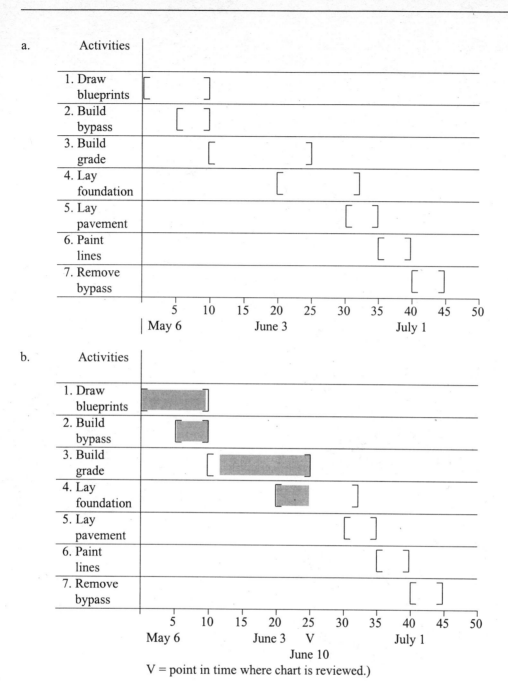

b.

V = point in time where chart is reviewed.)

4. a. Because the table is not square, a dummy Bureau will be required.

Customer

Bureau	1	2	3	4	5
A	200	[50]	500	100	60
B	100	200	80	[40]	600
C	90	300	400	[60]	200
D	700	100	200	400	[90]
Dummy	0	0	0	0	0

b. Subtract the minimum number in each row, marked with brackets above, from every entry in the row. Subtract the minimum number in each column (0) from every entry in the column. The result is:

Customer

Bureau	1		2		3		4		5
A	150	---	0	---	450	---	50	---	10
B	60		160		40		0		560
C	[30]		240		340		0		140
D	610	-- -	10	-- -	110	-- -	310	-- -	0
Dummy	0	---	0	---	0	---	0	---	0

The zeroes in this tableau may be covered with four lines in at least two ways, one of which is show above. The algorithm is not finished. Subtract the minimum unlined number, marked with brackets, from all of the unlined numbers and add it to values at the intersections of the lines. The result is:

Customer

Bureau	1	2	3	4	5
A	150	0	450	80	10
B	30	130	10	0	530
C	0	210	310	0	110
D	610	10	110	340	0
Dummy	0	0	0	30	0

In the above tableau, a minimum of five lines is required to cover all of the zeroes, and the algorithm is finished.

c,d. One assignment of a technician to a customer must be made in each row of the final tableau. Start with rows with only one zero, and check off a row and a column for each assignment.

Assignment	One-way Distance
A-2	50k
B-4	40
C-1	90 (Customer #4 was taken by B)
D-5	90
Dummy-3	0 (The only customer left)
Total	270
Round trip	x 2
Total	540

e. Because the dummy is assigned to Customer #3, Customer #3 will not receive a service call.

5. a. Replace the 90 in cell #C-1 with 1,000.

b. Replace the 80 in cell #B-3 with 0.

c.

		Customer			
Bureau	1	2	3	4	5
A	200	50	500	100	60
B	100	200	0	40	600
C	1000	300	400	60	200
D	700	100	200	400	90
Dummy	0	0	0	0	0

d. Perform the algorithm explained in #4-b. The final tableau is:

		Customer			
Bureau	1	2	3	4	5
A	150	0	450	50	10
B	100	200	0	40	600
C	940	240	340	0	140
D	610	10	110	310	0
Dummy	0	0	0	30	0

e,f.

Assignment	One-way Distance
A-2	50k
B-3	40
C-4	90
D-5	90
Dummy-1	0
Total	280
Round trip	x 2
Total	560

g. Customer #1 does not receive a service call.

6.   a.   The FCFS sequence is the order of arrival: 1, 2, 3, 4, 5, 6.

       b.   The SPT rule is the order of processing times: 1, 6, 3, 5, 2, 4.

       c.   The DD rule is the order of due dates: 3, 6, 2, 4, 5, 1.

       d.   The runout rule should be used in intermediate volume plants, in which there are relatively few large production runs per time period. The FCFS, SPT, and DD rules should be used in job shops in which there are many small orders per time period.

7.   a.   The first few steps in the algorithm are:

          1)   The shortest processing time is 8 minutes for job B in work center A. Schedule B first.

          2)   The next shortest time is 9 minutes for job C in work center B. Schedule C last.

          3)   The next shortest time is 10 minutes for job A in work center A. Schedule A second.

             Proceeding in this manner produces this sequence: B, A, D, F, G, E, C.

       b.

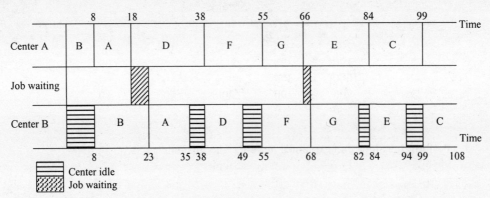

       c.   The throughput time is the length of time from beginning the first job to finishing the last job. It is 108 minutes on the diagram for 6b.

       d.   Jobs A and G have waiting time. The total waiting time is: (23 - 18) + (68 - 66) = 7 minutes.

       e.   Work center B has 5 idle periods. The total idle time is: 8 + (38 - 35) + (55 - 49) + (84 - 82) + (99 – 94) = 24 minutes. It is customary to ignore the idle time of work center A while work center B is finishing up.

CHAPTER 17S
MAINTENANCE

KEY IDEAS

1. Maintaining the production capability of an organization is an important function in any production system. Maintenance includes all activities related to keeping equipment and facilities in proper working order, and making repairs when breakdowns occur.

2. The goal of maintenance is to keep the system in good working order at minimal cost. Decision makers have two basic options for this: breakdown maintenance (deal with breakdowns when they occur) and preventive maintenance (reduce breakdowns through periodic adjustment, inspection, and replacement of worn parts before failure).

3. Preventive maintenance is generally scheduled using some combination of the result of planned inspections that reveal a need for maintenance, according to calendar, and after a set number of operating hours.

4. Predictive maintenance is an attempt to determine when to perform preventive maintenance activities.

5. The major approaches to handling breakdowns include:

    a. the use of standby or backup equipment.

    b. stock of spare parts.

    c. operators who can handle minor repairs.

    d. repair people who can diagnose and correct problems with equipment.

GLOSSARY

breakdown maintenance: deal with breakdowns or other equipment problems when they occur.

maintenance: includes all activities related to keeping facilities and equipment in good working order and making repairs when breakdowns occur.

predictive maintenance: an attempt to determine when to perform preventive maintenance activities to avoid breakdowns.

preventive maintenance: intended to reduce equipment or plant failure by inspecting to discover problems, replacing worn parts before failure, lubricating, cleaning, and adjusting equipment, and so on.

total preventive maintenance: the workers perform preventive maintenance on the machines which they operate. This policy is consistent with JIT systems and lean production.

TRUE/FALSE QUESTIONS

1. Preventive maintenance eliminates breakdowns during operation.

2. Decision makers have two basic maintenance options: breakdown maintenance and predictive maintenance.

3. The age and condition of equipment is an important consideration in how much preventive maintenance is desirable.

4. The optimum level of preventive maintenance occurs when the cost of preventive maintenance equals the cost of breakdown and repair.

5. Predictive maintenance is an attempt to determine when to perform preventive maintenance.

6. Total preventive maintenance is an example of job enlargement.

MULTIPLE-CHOICE QUESTIONS

1. Breakdown programs include all of the following except:
   a. inventories of spare parts.
   b. backup equipment.
   c. periodic inspections.
   d. operators who can perform minor repairs.
   e. repair people.

2. Preventive maintenance is not usually scheduled:
   a. by operating time.
   b. by calendar time.
   c. by planned inspections.
   d. by historical breakdown records.
   e. irregularly, as breakdowns occur.

3. The degree of preventive maintenance that is desirable is influenced by all of the following except:
   a. the age and condition of facilities.
   b. breakdown cost.
   c. salvage value of equipment.
   d. the degree of technology involved.
   e. the cost of preventive maintenance.

CHAPTER 17S   MAINTENANCE

True/False

Question	Answer	Glossary/ Key Idea	Textbook ref. page
1	F	G, 2	759
2	F	2	758
3	T	3	759
4	T		759
5	T	G, 4	760
6	T		761

Multiple-Choice

Question	Answer	Glossary/ Key Idea	Textbook ref. page
1	c	5	761
2	e	3	759
3	c		759

CHAPTER 18
PROJECT MANAGEMENT

KEY IDEAS

1. A project is a set of activities or specialized functions all directed toward achieving a unique objective or goal.

2. A network diagram is a graphic representation of the project and its elements. It consists of directed arrows representing activities or subprojects, each node denoting completion of all preceding activities. The leftmost node is the source representing beginning of the project and the rightmost terminal is the end, denoting completion. Nodes are shown as numbers 1, 2, 3, etc. Arrows are either given alphabetic designations a, *b, c,* etc., or else they are identified by their beginning and ending nodes 1-2, 2-3, etc., numbering makes it easier to identify predecessors and successors.

3. Any connected set of nodes and events headed in the general direction from left to right is called a sequence. A sequence that includes both the start and the end is a path. The path that takes a longer time than any other path is called the critical path and its activities are critical activities. The critical path is the path that determines the length of time for the project. Any hope for shortening project time depends on the ability of the project manager to shorten the time for critical activities. That can sometimes be accomplished by applying more resources to them.

4. Zero-completion-time dummy activities are in A-0-A (activity-on-arrow) diagrams. Dashed arrows are used in certain situations where it is necessary to uniquely identify a path. These are for the most part cases where two activities are parallel, that is, they both begin and end at the same node. Other cases requiring dummies are where two activities have some but not all predecessors in common.

5. The algorithm for finding the critical path involves two passes through the data: first, a forward pass to find the early start (ES) and early finish (EF) times for each activity, and then a backward pass to find the late finish (LF) and late start (LS) times. The critical path is the path for which ES = LS and EF = LF for every member of that path. The slack time is the difference between LS and ES. Thus the activities on the critical path all have zero slack. The critical path is also the path that takes the same amount of time to complete as the project does.

   For the forward pass, assign the time zero to the starting node. This is the ES of every activity emanating from the source; the EF is the time t of completion. The general formula for ES is

   ES = largest early completion *time, EF, of* all immediately *preceding activities*

   The early finish for an activity is EF = ES + t, where t is the activity time. The forward pass computes both ES and EF for every activity.

   The time it takes to get to the final node is the estimated time for the project. This will show up as the LF for all activities ending at the final node.

   The backward pass is reverse of the forward pass. Start the backward pass at the final node at LF time. For every activity ending at the final node, *LS= LF - t.* Then LS becomes the LF for all preceding activities; the formula is

   LF = smallest late completion time, LS, of all immediate successors.

When you are through with the backward pass, all critical activities will show up as having zero slack.

6.   Probabilistic PERT introduces uncertainty into a PERT model. For each activity there are three time estimates:

(1) t_o = optimistic, or shortest estimated completion time

(2) t_m = most likely time

(3) t_p = pessimistic, or longest estimated completion time

The average time , t_e, for completing an activity is a weighted average of t_o, t_m, and t_p .

$$t_e = \frac{t_o + 4t_m + t_p}{6} .$$

The variance of activity completion time is

$$\sigma^2 = \frac{(t_p - t_o)^2}{36} .$$

t_e and σ^2 are respectively the mean and variance of activity completion time under a beta probability distribution.

Assuming there is just a single critical path and there are no parallel critical paths, the expected time for completion of the project is the sum of times t, for the critical path activities. The variance of project completion time is the sum of the variances for critical path activities. The standard deviation of project completion time, σ_{path} , is the square root of the sum of

the variances, σ^2 . The distribution of completion times can be represented by a nor-

mal distribution with mean equal to the sum of expected times, $\sum t_e$, for the activities on the

path, and a standard deviation equal to σ_{path} .

The objective is to find the probability of completing the project in any specified time, t_s .
The way to do so is to determine how far the expected path time is from the specified time in terms

of σ_{path} . Use the following formula to obtain z for that path:

$$z_{path} = \frac{t_s - \sum t_e}{\sigma_{path}} .$$

Look up the probability in the table of areas under the normal curve. For example, if z = 1.96, the probability of completion is 97.5 percent (look up z = 1. 96 in Appendix Table B).

If there are multiple independent paths with probabilistic time estimates, use the approach described in Examples 5 and 6. and Solved Problem 3 in the text.

7. Shortening the time for completion can reduce costs and enhance profitability in several ways:

    (1) Indirect, or supervision, costs are reduced.

    (2) Bonuses are frequently earned for early completion.

    (3) Resources are freed to be used for other projects.

    Under these conditions, it is worthwhile to incur some increases in direct costs to attain the benefits
    of reducing the total time by crashing the project. Give priority to those critical path activities that
    have the lowest cost per day in crashing.

    For each activity, obtain both regular and crash time estimates, in days, and the cost per day of crashing. The number of days available to crash is the difference between regular time and crash time. Rank the critical activities in order of lowest per day crashing cost. Assign funds available for crashing successively to the lowest cost per day until either those funds are all used up or the desired schedule is obtained.

    Crashing can reduce slack time on noncritical activities. Therefore, it frequently happens that as you begin to crash, the slack times for activities on noncritical paths reduce to a point where they become critical too. This results in parallel critical paths. You can continue crashing beyond this point, but only by crashing all parallel paths.

8. PERT has the advantage of forcing managers to organize and quantify the decision-making process. The graphs, tables, and critical path calculations are helpful in showing up how the organization fits together and where to move resources around to achieve the best possible results. For large projects, PERT must be computerized.

TIPS FOR SOLVING PROBLEMS

Computing Algorithm

It can be helpful in working with the computing algorithm to think of nodes with multiple entering or exiting arrows (branches) as being analogous to airports or train stations, and the arrows as arriving or leaving planes or trains.

For instance, in a forward pass (see diagram), think of A and B as arriving trains and C as a leaving train. Train C cannot leave (according to policy) until both A and B have arrived. Consequently, the train that has the latest arrival time (B in this example), establishes the earliest starting time for train C (1 2 in this example). Hence, the rule is: Use the largest EF time of entering arrows (e.g., A = 7, B = 12) for the ES of the leaving arrow.

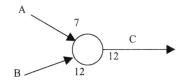

For a backward pass, when LS and LF times are being determined. the most complex case is when a node has multiple leaving arrows (see diagram below). The question is how to determine the LF for the entering arrow (D in this example). The rule is, use the smaller of the LS times (E = 10, F = 18, so use 10) of the leaving arrows. Again, think of trains E and F leaving a train station. But this time, think of the trains as leaving according to a set schedule: E must leave at 10 and F must leave at 18. Therefore, the latest that D can arrive (LF) so that its passengers can make either train, is 10, the earliest of the leaving (LS) times.

Computing Probabilistic Completion Times

1. Always determine the probability of finishing before the specified time (i.e., the area under the normal curve to the left of the specified time), even for problems that call for the probability of crashing after. In the latter case, find P(before) and subtract from 1.00 to find P(after).

2. Compute a z-value for every path in the network. If z is greater than +2.50, treat the probability of that path finishing by the specified time at 100 percent. Use Appendix Table B to obtain normal probabilities.

3. Multiply all path probabilities together to obtain P(crash by specified time). Note that because the normal distribution is continuous, so that the probability of finishing exactly at the time specified is theoretically equal to zero, P(finish before) is equivalent to P(finish by) and to P(finish on or before).

Crashing

Only consider crashing activities that are on the critical path. After each crash, redetermine the critical path(s), and include any new critical activities in the next round of crashing.

GLOSSARY

activity: a task.

A-0-A: activity-on-arrow.

A-0-N: activity-on-node.

arrow: indicates the direction of flow in the precedence diagram.

beta distribution: in PERT with three time estimates for completion of an activity, the distribution form governing the calculation of the means and variances of activity completion times.

CPM (Critical Path Method): PERT and CPM were both developed separately at about the same time in the late 1950s. Both techniques are concerned with integrating and managing a project consisting of a number of different tasks.

crash time: in PERT/COST, the completion-time estimate resulting from crashing it.

crashing: accelerating a project by speeding up those critical path activities which have the lowest ratio of incremental cost to incremental time saved.

critical path: the path in a network diagram that takes the longest time for completion.

critical activity: an activity on the critical path.

deterministic time estimate: a single time estimate for an activity, with no alternative estimates or probability distribution of estimates.

dummy activity: an artificial activity on an A-0-A network diagram, to facilitate distinguishing between two or more activities that both begin and end at the same node.

early finish (EF): for an activity, the early start, plus the time required for completion of the activity.

early start (ES): for an activity, the latest early finish of any predecessor.

event: a node in a precedence diagram, showing both the completion of one or more activities and the start of another task or set of tasks.

Gantt chart: visual aid used for scheduling simple projects.

late finish (LF): for an activity, the earliest late finish of any successor.

late start (LS): for an activity, the late finish minus the time required for completion of the activity.

network: a graph that shows the interconnections between all the elements of a system. See also precedence diagram.

node: see precedence diagram.

normal distribution: in PERT with three time estimates for completion of an activity, the distribution obtained by summing the means and variances of the activity completion times is a normal distribution.

path: an unbroken set of arcs and nodes from the source to the terminal.

PERT (Program Evaluation and Review Technique): see CPM.

precedence diagram: a type of directed network graph used in CPM showing the start of the project at one end and the completion at the other end, with every activity displayed as an arc, and with every node joining two or more arcs showing which activities precede others.

predecessor: for two activities joined at a node, the predecessor is the one that precedes, and the successor is the one that follows.

project: a set of diverse tasks, organized to achieve a single objective.

sequence: the order in which tasks are to be performed.

slack: for an activity, the additional time, over and above completion time, that could be used for the activity, without delaying the project.

standard deviation: the square root of the variance.

successor: see predecessor.

time-cost trade-off: see crashing.

variance: in PERT with three time estimates for completion of an activity, the variance is the square of the difference between optimistic time and pessimistic time, divided by 6. for a project, the variance is the sum of the variances of completion times for all of the activities on the critical path.

work breakdown structure: a hierarchical listing of what must be done during a project.

z-statistic: the random variable of the standard normal distribution, with mean zero and variance one.

TRUE/FALSE QUESTIONS

1. Because a Gantt chart is a scheduling technique, it should not be used for project management.

2. The early start of an activity is the latest early finish of any immediately preceding activity.

3. The late finish of an activity is the earliest late start of any immediately preceding activity.

4. There can be two or more parallel critical paths, all having exactly the same completion time.

5. The term "work breakdown structure" refers to a failure in the work structure.

6. The estimated means and variances of project completion times are respectively, the sum of the means and variances for the beta distributions of the activities on the critical path.

7. One use of a dummy activity is when two activities would otherwise have the same starting and ending nodes.

8. In crashing it may be necessary to shorten noncritical activities in order to accelerate the project.

9. Activity A has an ES of 8, an EF of 12, an LS of 13, and an LF of 17; the slack time is 4.

10. If two paths are tied for the longest duration, both would be considered to be critical paths.

11. The activity-on-node method of representing a network diagram makes it possible to draw the diagram without any dummy activities.

12. The activities on the critical path have the smallest slack.

13. In PERT, if the scheduled project completion time and sum of the average completion times for critical path activities are the same, the probability of completing the project on schedule is estimated at 50 percent, assuming no other paths are near-critical.

MULTIPLE-CHOICE QUESTIONS

For the background information on the first group of three questions, refer to the table that follows.

Activity	Immediate follower	Estimated time
A	E	6
B	F	5
C	D, G	8
D	F	4
E	end	5
F	end	10
G	end	10

1. The critical path is:
   a. B, F. b. C, D, F. c.   C, G. d. A, E.

2. The time for the critical path is:
   a. 20 days.
   b. 11 days.
   c. 18 days..
   d. 19 days.
   e. none of the above.

3. The path with the greatest slack time is:
    a. A,E. b. B,F.   c. C,D,F.   d. C,G.

4. A major limitation of Gantt charts in project management is that they do not:
    a. indicate the major activities involved.
    b. show activity times.
    c. show the timing of activities.
    d. show precedence relationships.
    e. give a visual portrayal.

5. Which is not a feature of PERT/CPM?
    a. An estimate of how long a project will take.
    b. A graphical display of project activities.
    c. An indication of critical activities.
    d. An indication of slack time.
    e. All are features.

6. Which of these may require the use of a dummy activity?
    a. Gantt chart.
    b. Activity-on-arrow network.
    c. Activity-on-node network.
    d. Both b and c.
    e. None of these.

7. Using the computing algorithm, activity slack can be computed as:
    a. LF – LS.   b. LS – LF.   c. LS – ES.   d. LF – EF.   e. c or d.

8. The standard deviation of a path is computed as:
    a. the sum of the standard deviations of all activities on the path.
    b. the square root of the sum of the standard deviations of all activities on the path.
    c. the sum of the variances of all activities on the path.
    d. the square root of the sum of the variances of all activities on the path.
    e. none of these.

9. An important assumption in PERT calculations is:
    a. activity times are normally distributed.
    b. activity times are independent.
    c. a computer will be available to do the calculations.
    d. a and b.
    e. a and c.

PROBLEMS

1. A project consists of 10 activities, lettered A through J, as shown in the accompanying precedence diagram, with the activities on the arrows. For each activity, the deterministic time estimate in weeks is shown in the following table.

Activity	Time	Activity	Time
A	2	F	3
B	4	G	4
C	3	H	4
D	5	I	3
E	6	J	1

    a. List all of the paths through the network.

    b. What is the duration of each of the paths?

    c. What is the critical path?

    d. What is the second-most critical path?

    e. What is the slack tine for each activity?

    f. Calculate the ES, EF, LS and LF times for the network.

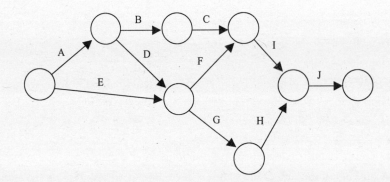

2. A project consists of 11 activities, lettered A through K, below. For each activity, the preceding activity is given, and a deterministic estimate of the length of time required to complete it in weeks..

Activity	Time	Preceding Activity	Activity	Time	Preceding Activity
A	1 week	-	G	4 weeks	E
B	3	A	H	6	F
C	2	A	I	2	G
D	4	C	J	1	H,I
E	2	-	K	1	B,D,J
F	3	E			

    a. Draw the precedence network for this project, with the activities on the arrows.

    b. List all of the paths through the network.

    c. What is the duration of each of the paths?

d. What is the critical path?

e. What is the slack time for each activity?

f. The materials required to accomplish activity F have been delayed for two weeks by a strike at the supplier's plant. What effect will this have on the length of time required to complete the project?

g. An equipment breakdown has delayed activity B for one week. What effect will this have on the length of time required to complete the project?

3. A project consists of 8 activities, lettered A through H. below. For each activity, the preceding activity is given, and a probabilistic estimate of the time required to complete it. Times are in days.

Activity	Preceding Activity	Optimistic Time	Most Likely Time	Pessimistic Time
A	--	2 days	4 days	6 days
B	A	3	6	9
C	A	2	5	11
D	--	2	10	12
E	C,	4	8	15
F	B,E	2	4	12
G	D	3	4	11
H	F,G	1	1	1

a. Determine the expected time for each activity.

b. Determine the variance for each activity

c. Draw the PERT network for this project, with the activities on the arrows.

d. List all of the paths through the network.

e. What is the duration of each path?

f. What is the variance of each path?

g. What is the critical path?

h. What is the second-most critical path?

i. Activity D was delayed three days by an earthquake in the area. What effect does this have on the length of time required to complete the project?

4. Refer to Problem 3 and the original critical path before the earthquake.

a. What is the mean of the probability distribution for the completion time?

b. What is the standard deviation of the probability distribution for the completion time?

c. What is the probability of finishing the project within 24 days?

d. What is the probability of finishing the project within 22 days?

e. What is the probability that the project will take longer than 28 days?

5.   After the earthquake, in Problem 3-i., management faced the problem of how to make up the lost time, and how much it would cost. Estimates of crash times and costs for each activity are given below.

Activity	Crash Time	Cost per Day
A	Not possible	-
B	3 days	$200 per day
C	not possible	-
D	not possible*	-
E	5 days	$300 per day
F	2 days	$500 per day
G	not possible	-
H	not possible	-

*(because of the earthquake)

a.   Which activity should be crashed?

b.   How many days should it be crashed?

c.   How much will it cost?

6.   Construct the PERT network for Problem 3 with the activities on the nodes.

7.   (One step beyond) Use the time estimates and the network for Problem 2 for solving this problem. Today is Monday, May 1, and work on the project is just beginning. The project is scheduled to be finished on Friday, August 11. Use this information to calculate the ES, EF, LS, and LF.

CHAPTER 18   PROJECT MANAGEMENT

True/False

Question	Answer	Glossary/ Key Idea	Textbook ref. page
1	F		770
2	T	5	778
3	F	5	778-779
4	T	7	790
5	F	G	770
6	T	6	782
7	T	G	774
8	F	G,3	789
9	F	5	780
10	T		790
11	T		787
12	T	5	780
13	T		784

Multiple-Choice

Question	Answer	Glossary/ Key Idea	Textbook ref. page
1	b	3	775-776
2	e	3	775-776
3	a		775-776
4	d		771
5	e		771
6	b		774
7	e	5	780
8	d	6	782
9	b		784

SOLUTIONS TO PROBLEMS

1. a, b.

Path	Duration (weeks)
A-B-C-I-J	$2 + 4 + 3 + 3 + 1 = 13$
A-D-F-I-J	$2 + 5 + 3 + 3 + 1 = 14$
A-D-G-H-J	$2 + 5 + 4 + 4 + 1 = 16$
E-F-I-J	$6 + 3 + 3 + 1 = 13$
E-G-H-J	$6 + 4 + 4 + 1 = 15$

c. The critical path is #3.

d. The second-most critical path is #5.

e. The slack is the difference between the duration of the critical path and the duration of each alternative path. When an activity appears on more than one path, the slack is the smallest difference.

Activity	Path	Slack (wk.)
A	3	0
B	1	3
C	1	3
D	3	0
E	5	1
F	2	2
G	3	0
H	3	0
I	2	2
J	3	0

f.

Activity	ES	EF	LS	LF	Slack (wk.)
A	0	2	0	2	0
B	2	6	5	9	3
C	6	9	9	12	3
D	2	7	2	7	0
E	0	6	1	7	1
F	7	10	9	12	2
G	7	11	7	11	0
H	11	15	1	15	0
I	10	13	2	15	2
J	15	16	5	16	0

2.   a.

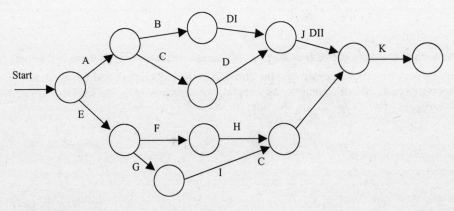

DI = a dummy activity
DII = a dummy activity
It is possible to draw this network without dummy activities

b,c.

Path	Duration (weeks)
A-B-DI-DII-K	$1 + 3 + 0 + 0 + 1 = 5$
A-C-D-DII-K	$1 + 2 + 4 + 0 + 1 = 8$
E-F-H-J-K	$2 + 3 + 6 + 1 + 1 = 13$
E-G-I-J-K	$2 + 4 + 2 + 1 + 1 = 10$

d. The critical path is #3, with a duration of 13 weeks.

e.

Activity	Path	Slack (wk.)
A	2	5
B	1	8
C	2	5
D	2	5
DI	1	8
DII	2	5
E	3	0
F	3	0
G	4	3
H	3	0
I	4	3
J	3	0
K	3	0

f. It will delay the completion of the project by 2 weeks.

g. It will have no effect on the completion of the project.

3. a,b. For activity A: $t_e = \dfrac{t_o = 4t_m + t_p}{6} = \dfrac{2 + 4 * 4 + 6}{6} = 4$ days.

Repeat for each activity.

For activity A: $\sigma^2 = \dfrac{(t_p - t_o)^2}{36} = \dfrac{(6-2)^2}{36} = .4444$.

Repeat for each activity.

Activity	Expected time (days)	Variance
A	4	0.4444
B	6	1.0000
C	5.5	2.2500
D	9	2.7778
E	8.5	3.3611
F	5	2.7778
G	5	1.7778
H	1	0

c.

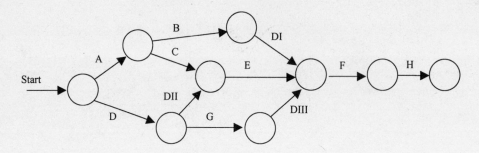

d,e. There are four paths through the network.

Path	Duration (days)
A-B-DI-F-H	$4 + 6 + 0 + 5 + 1 = 16$
A-C-E-F-H	$4 + 5.5 + 8.5 + 5 + 1 = 24$
D-DII-E-F-H	$9 + 0 + 8.5 + 5 + 1 = 23.5$
D-G-DIII-H	$9 + 5 + 0 + 1 = 15$

f. The variance for each path is obtained by adding the variances of the activities on the path. For Path #1) Variance = .4444 + 1.0000 + 0 + 2.7778 + 0 = 4.2222. Repeat for each path.

Path	Variance
1)	4.2222
2)	8.8333
3)	8.9167
4)	4.5556

g. The critical path is #2, with a duration , $\sum t_e = 24$ days.

h. The second-most critical path is #3, with a duration of 23.5 days.

i. The duration along the path, D - DII - E - F - H, is increased to 26.5 days. Because this total is larger than 24 days, this constitutes a new critical path.

4. a. The mean is the longest duration, or 24 days.

b. $\sigma_{path} = \sqrt{8.8333} = 2.9721$.

c. Find the value of z in order to read the table of the areas of the standardized normal curve:

$$z = \frac{t_s - \sum t_e}{\sigma_{path}} = \frac{24 - 24}{2.9721} = 0$$

$P(z \le 0) = 0.50$.

d. $z = \dfrac{t_s - \sum t_e}{\sigma_{path}} = \dfrac{22 - 24}{2.9721} = -0.67$

$P(z \le -0.67) = 0.2514$.

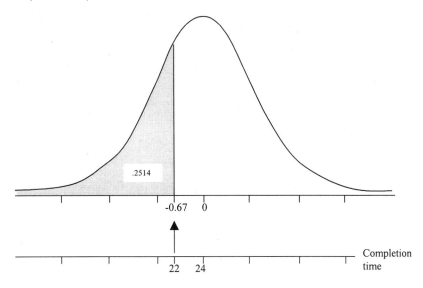

e. $z = \dfrac{t_s - \sum t_e}{\sigma_{path}} = \dfrac{28 - 24}{2.9721} = 1.35$

$P(z \ge 1.35) = 0.0885$.

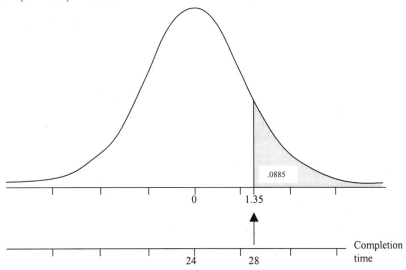

5. a. Activity E should be crashed because it is on the critical path and crashing it would be less expensive than crashing activity F.

    b. Activity E should be crashed for 3 days to make up for the earthquake.

    c. The expense will be: 3 days x $200 = $600.

6.

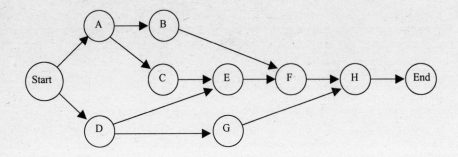

7. From Monday, May 1 to Friday, August 11 is 15 work weeks; set the last LS equal to 15.

Activity	ES	EF	LS	LF	Slack (wk.)
A	0	1	7	8	7
B	1	4	1	14	10
C	1	3	8	10	7
D	3	7	0	14	7
DI	4	4	4	14	10
DII	7	7	4	14	7
E	0	2	2	4	2
F	2	5	4	7	2
G	2	6	7	11	5
H	5	11	7	13	2
I	6	18	11	13	5
J	11	12	13	14	2
K	12	13	14	15	2

CHAPTER 19
WAITING LINES

KEY IDEAS

1.   Waiting lines are an important consideration in capacity planning. Waiting lines tie up additional resources (waiting space, time, etc.); they decrease the level of customer service: and they require additional capacity to reduce them.

2.   Waiting lines occur whenever demand for service exceeds capacity (supply). Even in systems that are underloaded, waiting lines tend to form if arrival and service patterns are highly variable because the variability creates temporary imbalances of supply and demand.

3.   All of the waiting line models presented in the chapter (except the constant service time model) assume, or require, that the arrival rate can be described by a Poisson distribution and that the service time can be described by a negative exponential distribution. Equivalently, we can say that the arrival and service rates must be Poisson, and the interarrival time and the service time must be exponential. In practice, one would check for this using a statistical Chi Square test: for problems provided here and in the textbook, assume that these distributions hold. Note that if these assumptions are not met, alternate approaches (e.g., intuition, simulation, other models) should be considered.

4.   Much can be learned about the behavior of waiting lines by modeling them. A wide variety of models are presented in the text, different models pertain to different system characteristics.

5.   A major distinction in waiting line models relates to whether the number of potential arrivals to the system is limited (finite) or unlimited (infinite). Perhaps the classic example of a finite source system is the machine, repairperson problem, wherein the server or servers handle calls for repairs on a small, fixed number of machines. Note that the definition of terms in Table 17-6 in the text follows this somewhat (e.g., average number running). Other examples of finite source systems include passengers on a plane who might request assistance or information from a steward or stewardess, a sales rep who handles a small set of customers, and a telephone operator who places outgoing calls for residents of a small hotel. Examples of infinite-source systems are plentiful: service stations, banks, post offices, restaurants, theaters, supermarkets, libraries, stop signs, and telephone switchboards.

6.   Once a situation has been modeled and the relevant data gathered (e.g., an-arrival rate, service time, number of servers, etc.), formulas and/or tables can be used to obtain information about the system such as the expected number waiting for service, the expected waiting time, the maximum line length, system utilization, and so on. This information can be used to compare various system alternatives (e.g., one server versus two servers, different equipment possibilities, and so on) with respect to cost and impact on waiting times, etc.

7.   The goal in queuing analysis is to develop a system in which the sum of capacity costs and waiting costs is minimized. Sometimes this goal may be taken in an absolute sense or the goal may be to minimize total costs given a minimum level of customer service specified by management.

8.   Most of the models described in the chapter assume arrivals are processed on a first-come, first-served basis (FCFS). Many examples of FCFS exist. Sometimes, however, customers are processed on a priority basis rather than FCFS. That is, late arriving customers may be processed ahead of those already waiting. A hospital emergency room is an example; seriously ill or injured persons are attended to while less seriously ill persons wait. A key difference in the multiple priority model compared to other models is computation of average waiting times, and average number waiting, for each of the classes or categories of waiting customers.

STUDY TIPS

Much of the material is highly mathematical. Do not to let this overwhelm you. Note that many of the problems can be solved using tables rather than formulas, and that many of the formulas do not involve extensive computation.

The chapter presents two kinds of queuing models, one for infinite source (unrestricted entry) systems, and another for finite source systems. There are four infinite source models and one finite source model. Instead of trying to absorb the entire chapter at once (or even a major portion of it), begin with the general discussion of waiting lines, and then focus on a few infinite source models (e.g., single channel and single channel with constant service, which represent the first two infinite source models), leaving other models to another time. This can be reinforced by attempting some problems at the end of the chapter which relate to the models you have focused on. Moreover, if you have done a good job in studying a particular model, you should be able to ascertain whether or not a given problem can be solved using the model.

TIPS FOR SOLVING PROBLEMS

1.   A key element of infinite source models is the number of channels. Generally, there is one channel for every server. The exception would be if the servers work in teams; then there is one channel for every team.

2.   Key measures for infinite source problems are the arrival and service rates. The formulas and tables require rates, although times may be given, necessitating a conversion to a rate. Moreover, arrival and service rates must be in the same units (e.g., both in customers per hour, both in customers per minute). Consider these examples for arrivals:

   a.   10 units per hour. This is okay, it is a rate.

   b.   Customers arrive at an average of one every 20 seconds. This gives the time between arrivals. To find the arrival rate, use the information to determine the number of customers, say, per minute. Thus,

   $$\frac{60 \text{ seconds/minute}}{20 \text{ seconds}} = 3 \text{ customers per minute.}$$

   c.   The interarrival time is 90 seconds. Again, we have the time between arrivals. Dividing this into 60 seconds per minute, we get .667 customers per minute. Multiplying this by 60 minutes will give us the rate per hour: .667/minute x 60 minutes/hour = 40 customers per hour.

   Now consider these examples relating to service:

   a.   Three customers per hour. This is okay, it is expressed as a rate.

   b.   Four customers can be served in an hour. Thus, the service rate is 4 customers/hour.

    c.   Service time is 15 minutes. This means that four customers can be served in an hour:

$$\frac{60 \text{ minutess/hour}}{15 \text{ minutes/customer}} = 4 \text{ customers per hour.}$$

    d.   The service time is 12 minutes. The service rate is 1/12 per minute. Multiplying by 60 gives us the hourly rate: 60 (1/12) = 5 customers/hour.

3.   When a problem refers to the average number waiting in line, check to see if it pertains to all arrivals, or just those that actually wait, since customers that arrive when the service facility is idle would not have to wait, thereby lowering the average waiting time of all arrivals. Use the formula or table for W_s if the average for all customers is required; and use W_q if the average waiting time only for those that wait is required. Note that in a heavily loaded system, most customers will have to wait, in which case the two averages, W_s and W_q will be approximately equal. More generally, W_q will be greater than W_s.

GLOSSARY

channels: "avenues" for service (e.g., a bank with one teller is a single-channel system, a bank with more than one teller is a multiple-channel system). The terms "server" and "channel" are synonymous.

customer: a unit an-arriving for service (e.g., a person, an order, an item in need of repair). finite population source: a system that has a limited number of potential customers.

finite population source: a system that has a limited number of potential customers.

infinite population source: a system that has a potential number of customers that is very large relative to the capacity of the system.

multiple-channel system: a system with more than one possible avenue of customer service (e.g., a bakery counter with more than one server).

multiple-priority model: a waiting line model that has more than one category of customers; arriving customers are assigned to a category and then processed according to priority category rather than first-come, first-served.

queue: a waiting line.

queue discipline: the order in which customers are processed or served. First-come, first served is service in order of arrival.

server: attendant, machine, etc., that handles customer service or processing.

service time: processing time: the time a customer is in the system minus time spent waiting in line for service.

steady-state conditions: a system operating under stable conditions (i.e.. arrival and service patterns are not changing over time).

system: consists of customers waiting in line plus those being served.

system utilization: the proportion of time a service facility is busy with customer processing.

waiting time in line: the usually nonproductive time customers wait before being served or processed.

waiting time in the system: time in line plus processing time.

TRUE/FALSE QUESTIONS

1. A waiting line tends to form when service demand exceeds capacity.

2. Queuing systems tend to be overloaded and highly variable.

3. A finite source model is appropriate when the potential number of arrivals is relatively small.

4. Service time is the reciprocal of service rate.

5. If the average time between customer arrivals is five minutes, the arrival rate is twenty per hour.

6. The terms "server" and "channel" are used interchangeably to mean the number of possible service routes available to customers.

7. As system utilization increases, the expected number of customers waiting for service increases.

8. For infinite source systems, the average number of customers being served is equal to the arrival rate divided by the service rate.

9. In a finite-source system, the arrival rate is dependent on the number waiting for service.

MULTIPLE-CHOICE QUESTIONS

1. A three-step repair service with one server at each step would be an example of a:
   a. multiple-phase, multiple-channel system.
   b. single-phase, multiple-channel system.
   c. multiple-phase, single-channel system.
   d. none of these.

2. A system with an arrival rate of two per hour, a service time of 20 minutes, and one server, would have a utilization of.
   a. 10%
   b. 33%
   c. 40%
   d. 67%
   e. none of these

3. The term "queue discipline" refers to:
   a. customers waiting in a single line for service.
   b. processing order.
   c. the willingness of customers to wait in line.
   d. well-behaved customers.

4. As the system utilization increases, the average number waiting:
   a. doesn't change.
   b. increases.
   c. decreases.
   d. impossible to say.

5. Waiting lines tend to form in underloaded systems because:
    a. capacity always exceeds demand.
    b. capacity sometimes exceeds demand.
    c. demand always exceeds supply.
    d. demand sometimes exceeds supply.
    e. none of these.

6. Which of these would not increase system utilization?
    a. a decrease in the number of servers
    b. a decrease in the service rate
    c. a decrease in the arrival rate
    d. an increase in the arrival rate

7. For an infinite-source system with an arrival rate of 6 per hour (Poisson) and service time of 6 minutes per customer (exponential), the average number being served is:
    a. .10
    b. .60
    c. 1.0
    d. none of these

8. Which one of these would illustrate a finite-source system?
    a. Supermarket
    b. Bakery
    c. Drug store
    d. One-lane bridge
    e. None of these

PROBLEMS

1. A bank has a drive-in window, which is open from 10 a.m. to 3 p.m. on business days. Customers drive up at a mean rate of 12 per hour, according to a Poisson distribution. The teller requires a mean of 2.4 minutes to serve each customer. service times have a negative exponential distribution.
    a. How many channels are there?
    b. Do the customers come from a finite source or from an infinite source?
    c. Which queue model is appropriate here?
    d. What is the value of λ ?
    e. What is the interpretation of λ ?
    f. What is the value of μ ?
    g. What is the interpretation of μ ?
    h. What is the system utilization, ρ ? Is this a feasible system?
    i. What is the proportion of idle time?
    j. What is the mean number of customers being served?
    k. What is the expected number of customers waiting for service?

l. What is the expected duration of the wait?

m. What is the mean number of customers in the system?

n. What is the mean time that a customer spends in the system?

o. What is the probability that the system will be idle?

p. What is the probability that there will be one car in the system?

q. What is the probability that there will be three cars in the system?

2. In a factory, the parts to be copper-plated must be immersed in an electrolytic solution so that copper ions will be deposited on the part. The company has one electrolytic bath, in which each part is submerged for 20 minutes. Parts to be copper-plated arrive at a mean rate of 20 per 8-hour shift, according to a Poisson distribution.

a. How many channels are there?

b. Do the parts come from a finite source or from an infinite source?

c. Which queue model is appropriate here?

d. What is the value of λ?

e. What is the interpretation of λ?

f. What is the value of μ?

g. What is the interpretation of μ?

h. What is the system utilization, ρ? Is this a feasible system?

1. What is the proportion of idle time?

j. What is the expected number of parts waiting for copper-plating?

k. What is the expected duration of the wait?

1. What is the mean number of parts in the system?

m. What is the mean time that a part spends in the system?

3. A bank has an array of five drive-in windows, some or all of which may be open from 10 a.m. to 3 p.m. on normal business days. At each window, the teller requires a mean of 2.4 minutes to serve each customer; service times have a negative exponential distribution. Customers arrive at a mean rate of 65 per hour, according to a Poisson distribution. (Use Table 19-4)

a. Do the customers come from a finite source or from an infinite source?

b. What is the value of λ?

c. What is the interpretation of λ?

d. What is the value of μ?

e. What is the interpretation of μ?

f. What is the minimum number of drive-in windows which should be open to have an underloaded system?

g. What is the expected number of customers waiting for service with three drive-in windows open?

h. What is the expected duration of the wait?

i. What is the expected duration of the wait if all three open windows are busy.?

j. What is the probability that the system will be idle?

k. What is the probability that an arrival will have to wait for service?

4.   Rework Problem 3 with five drive-in windows open.

   a.   What is the expected number of customers waiting for service?

   b.   What is the expected duration of the wait?

   c.   What is the expected duration of the wait if all five windows are busy?

   d.   What is the probability that the system will be idle?

   e.   What is the probability that an arrival will have to wait for service?

5.   The bus company in a small city has a fleet of 10 buses and a single mechanic to service the buses as needed. Buses break down or require periodic maintenance at a mean rate of one every other day, seven days a week. The mechanic works five days per week (40 hours), and the mean time required to service one bus is four hours, with a negative exponential distribution. Buses which break down on Saturday or Sunday are parked until the mechanic can attend to them in the following week.

   a.   How many channels are there?

   b.   Should the bus arrivals be treated as coming from a finite source or from an infinite source?

   c.   Which waiting line model is appropriate here?

   d.   What is the number of potential customers, N?

   e.   What is the value of the mean service time, T?

   f.   What is the value of the mean time between service calls, U?

   g.   What is the value of the service factor, X?

   h.   What is the value of the efficiency factor, F?

   i.   What is the expected number of buses running, J?

   j.   What is the mean number of buses being serviced, H?

   k.   What is the mean number of buses waiting for the mechanic, L?

   1.   Check to see that $N = J + L + H$.

6.   A typing pool for a large corporation consists of six typists, each of whom can type at the rate of 12 pages per hour, on the average, with a Poisson distribution. The pool receives various kinds of typing jobs from a very large number of executives and managers. The jobs are classified into four priority levels as they arrive. Each level is shown below, with the mean of its particular arrival rate. Typing jobs arrive according to Poisson distributions:

   first priority: correspondence with customers (to be typed first); $\lambda_1 = 9$ pages per hr.

   second priority: correspondence with suppliers; $\lambda_2 = 8$ pages per hr.

   third priority: correspondence with federal, state, and local governments (other than that dealing with sales); $\lambda_3 = 6$ pages per hr.

   fourth priority: internal memoranda and communications and miscellaneous correspondence; $\lambda_4 = 31$ pages per hr.

   a.   Which set of waiting line formulas should be used here?

   b.   What is s?

   c.   What is the value of λ ?

   d.   What is $1/\lambda$?

   e.   What is the value of μ ?

   f.   What is $1/\mu$?

g. What is the system utilization, ρ?

h. On the average, how many pages are being typed at any one time?

i. Determine the value of L_q?

j. Determine the value of A.

k. Determine these values:

   B_0

   B_1

   B_2

   B_3

   B_4

l. Determine these values:

   W_1

   W_2

   W_3

   W_4

m. Find the average time in the system for pages in each priority class.

n. Find the average number of pages in the queue for each priority class.

o. Discuss the results of the above analysis.

CHAPTER 19   WAITING LINES

True/False

Question	Answer	Glossary/ Key Idea	Textbook ref. page
1	T	2	813
2	F	2	813
3	T	3	833
4	T		820,839
5	F		816
6	T	G	815
7	T		819
8	T		820
9	T		833

Multiple-Choice

Question	Answer	Glossary/ Key Idea	Textbook ref. page
1	c		815-817
2	d		821-822
3	b	G	816
4	b		819
5	d	2	813
6	c		819
7	b		820
8	e	G,5	815

SOLUTIONS TO PROBLEMS

1. a. $M = 1$ channel.

b. An infinite source.

c. Single channel, single phase, Poisson arrivals, negative exponential service times.

d. $\lambda = 12$ cars per hour.

e. λ is the mean number of customers who demand service every hour.

f. $1/\mu = 2.4$ minutes and $\mu = 60/2.4 = 25$ cars per hour.

g. μ is the mean number of cars which the teller can handle in one hour.

h. $\rho = \lambda/M\mu = 12/(1*25) = 0.48$, which is less than 1. The system is feasible.

i. The proportion of idle time $= 1 - \rho = 1 = 0.48 = 0.52$.

j. $r = \lambda/\mu = 12/25 = 0.48$ customers.

k. $L_q = \dfrac{\lambda^2}{\mu(\mu-\lambda)} = \dfrac{12^2}{25(25-12)} = 0.44$ cars in the queue.

l. $W_q = L_q/\lambda = 0.44/12 = 0.0367$ hrs. or 2.20 min.

m. $L_s = L_q + r = 0.44 + 0.48 = 0.92$ cars.

n. $W_s = W_q + \dfrac{1}{\mu} = 2.20 + 2.40 = 4.60$ min.

o. $p(0 \text{ cars}) = 1 - (\lambda/\mu) = 1 - 0.48 = 0.52$.

p. $p(1 \text{ car}) = p(0)*(\lambda/\mu)^1 = 0.52(0.48) = 0.2496$.

q. $p(3 \text{ cars}) = p(0)*(\lambda/\mu)^3 = 0.52(0.48)^3 = .0575$.

2. a. $M = 1$ channel.

    b. An infinite population.

    c. Single channel, single phase, Poisson arrivals, constant service times.

    d. $\lambda = 16$ parts per shift or 2 per hour.

    e. λ is the mean number of parts which arrive per time period.

    f. $\dfrac{1}{\mu} = 20$ min. and $\mu = \dfrac{8*60}{20} = 24$ parts per shift.

    g. μ is the maximum number of pieces which can be electro-plated per shift. (Compare this with 1-g.)

    h. $\rho = \dfrac{\lambda}{M\mu} = \dfrac{16}{1*24} = 0.6667$. The electrolytic bath is in use 67% of the time and system is feasible.

    i. The proportion of idle time $= 1 - \rho = 1 - 0.6667 = 0.3333$.

    j. $r = \lambda/\mu = 16/24 = 0.6667$.

    k. $L_q = \dfrac{\lambda^2}{2\mu(\mu - \lambda)} = \dfrac{16^2}{2*24(24-16)} = 0.6667$ parts.

    l. $W_q = L_q/\lambda = 0.6667/16 = 0.0417$ .of an 8-hour shift, or $.0417(8) = .3333$ hrs. or 20 minutes.

    m. $L_s = L_q + r = 0.6667 + 0.6667 = 1.3334$ parts.

    n. $W_s = W_q + \dfrac{1}{\mu} = 20 + 20 = 40$ min.

3. a. An infinite source.

    b. $\lambda = 65$ customers per hr.

    c. λ is the mean number of customers who demand service at the array of drive-in windows per hour.

    d. At each window, $\dfrac{1}{\mu} = 2.4$ min. and $\mu = 25$ customers per hr.

    e. μ is the mean number of customers which any one teller can handle in one hour.

    f. ρ must be less than 1; hence $\rho = \dfrac{\lambda}{M\mu} = \dfrac{65}{25M}$ and M must be at least 3.

    g. Use Table #19-4 in your textbook. $\lambda/\mu = 65/25 = 2.6$ and $L_q = 4.933$ cars.

    h. $W_q = \dfrac{L_q}{\lambda} = \dfrac{4.933}{65} = .0759$ hrs. $= 4.55$ min.

    i. $W_a = \dfrac{1}{M\mu - \lambda} = \dfrac{1}{3*25 - 65} = 0.10$ hrs. $= 6$ min.

    j. Use table 19-4; $p(0) = .035$.

k. $P_w = \dfrac{W_q}{W_a} = \dfrac{4.55}{6} = 0.76$.

4.   a. Use Table 19-4; $\dfrac{\lambda}{\mu} = \dfrac{65}{25} = 2.6$ and $L_q = 0.161$ cars.

    b. $W_q = \dfrac{L_q}{\lambda} = \dfrac{0.161}{65} = 0.0025$ hrs. = 8.9 sec.

    c. $W_a = \dfrac{1}{M\mu - \lambda} = \dfrac{1}{5*25 - 65} = 0.0167$ hrs. = 60.1 sec.

    d. Use Table 19-4; p(0) = .072.

    e. $P_w = \dfrac{W_q}{W_a} = \dfrac{8.9}{60.1} = 0.1481$.

5.   a. M = 1 channel, namely the mechanic.

    b. The customers come from the finite fleet of 10 buses.

    c. The finite source model.

    d. N = 10 buses.

    e. T = 4 hrs.

    f. Presumably the buses run 24 hours a day, 7 days a week. U = 168 hrs./3.5 breakdowns = 48 hrs. between breakdowns.

    g. X = T/(T + U) = 4/(4 + 48) = .077.

    h. Use table 19-7 in your textbook. For X = .077 and M = 1, F ≈ .973.

    i. J = N(F)(1 – X) = 10(.973)(1 - .077) = 8.98 buses.

    j. H = F(N)(X) = .973(10)(.077) = .75 buses.

    k. L = N(1 – F) = 10(1 – .973) = .27 buses.

    l. Check: N = J + L + K = 8.98 + .75 + .27 = 10 buses.

6.   a. The multiple-channel, multiple-priority model.

    b. s = 6 typists.

    c. $\lambda = \sum_{k=1}^{4} \lambda_k = 9 + 8 + 6 + 31 = 54$ pages per hr.

    d. $\dfrac{1}{\lambda} = \dfrac{1}{54} = 0.0185$ hrs = 66.67 sec.

    e. $\mu = 12$ pages per hr.

    f. $\dfrac{1}{\mu} = \dfrac{1}{12}$ hrs. = 5 min.

    g. $\rho = \dfrac{\lambda}{s\mu} = \dfrac{54}{6*12} = 0.75$.

    h. $r = \dfrac{\lambda}{\mu} = \dfrac{54}{12} = 4.5$ pages.

i. $L_q = 1.265$ customers (from Table 19-4).

j. $A = \dfrac{\lambda}{(1-\rho)L_q} = \dfrac{54}{(1-0.75)1.265} = 170.75$.

k. $B_0 = 1$.

$$B_1 = 1 - \frac{\lambda_1}{s\mu} = 1 = \frac{9}{72} = 0.8750$$

$$B_2 = 1 - \frac{\lambda_1}{s\mu} - \frac{\lambda_2}{s\mu} = 1 - \frac{9}{72} = \frac{8}{72} = 0.7639$$

$$B_3 = 1 - \frac{\lambda_1}{s\mu} - \frac{\lambda_2}{s\mu} - \frac{\lambda_3}{s\mu} = 1 - \frac{9}{72} - \frac{8}{72} - \frac{6}{72} = .6806$$

$$B_4 = 1 - \frac{\lambda_1}{s\mu} - \frac{\lambda_2}{s\mu} - \frac{\lambda_3}{s\mu} - \frac{\lambda_4}{s\mu} = 1 - \frac{9}{72} - \frac{8}{72} - \frac{6}{72} - \frac{31}{72} = 0.2500$$

l. $W_1 = \dfrac{1}{AB_0 B_1} = \dfrac{1}{170.75(1)(0.8750)} = 0.0067$ hrs. = 24 sec.

$W_2 = \dfrac{1}{AB_1 B_2} = \dfrac{1}{170.75(.8750)(0.7639)} = 0.0088$ hrs. = 32 sec.

$W_3 = \dfrac{1}{AB_2 B_3} = \dfrac{1}{170.75(0.7639)(0.6806)} = 0.0113$ hrs. = 40 sec.

$W_4 = \dfrac{1}{AB_3 B_4} = \dfrac{1}{170.75(0.6806)(0.2500)} = 0.0344$ hrs. = 2.1 min.

m.

Priority Class	Average Time in System
1	$W = W_1 + 1/\mu = 0.400 + 5 = 5.400$ min.
2	$W = W_2 + 1/\mu = 0.525 + 5 = 5.525$ min.
3	$W = W_3 + 1/\mu = 0.675 + 5 = 5.675$ min.
4	$W = W_4 + 1/\mu = 2.064 + 5 = 7.064$ min.

n.

Priority Class	Average Pages in Queue
1	$L_1 = \lambda_1 W_1 = 9(.0067) \approx 0.06$ pages
2	$L_2 = \lambda_2 W_2 = 8(.0088) \approx 0.07$ pages
3	$L_3 = \lambda_3 W_3 = 6(.0113) \approx 0.07$ pages
4	$L_4 = \lambda_4 W_4 = 31(.0113) \approx 1.07$ pages.

o. This system looks feasible; $\rho \leq 1$ and the jobs in each priority class are typed within a reasonable time, on the average.

CHAPTER 19S
SIMULATION

KEY IDEAS

1. Simulation is a tool managers can use to describe the behavior of a system under specified conditions. A major feature of simulation is the ability to answer "what if" questions by describing how a system will behave given certain changes.

2. Simulation is especially useful in situations that are too complex to be analyzed mathematically.

3. Monte Carlo simulations involve the use of random numbers to incorporate randomness in models of system behavior.

4. Simulations that use random numbers must be run a sufficient number of times to enable a decision maker to separate the "real" aspects of behavior from the random aspects.

5. In developing simulation models, it is important to thoroughly test the models to assure that their results are consistent with reality.

6. Simulation applications are found throughout production and operations management. Examples include product design, facilities layout, aggregate planning, scheduling, and project management.

7. The advantages of simulation include:

    a. It is useful when situations are too complex for analytical models.

    b. It can be used to answer "what if" questions for a variety of conditions.

    c. Time is compressed; simulations of a year's experience can be run in a matter of seconds.

    d. Simulations can serve as training exercises for managers and others.

8. Among the limitations of simulation are:

    a. It is descriptive, it does not provide an optimal solution to a problem.

    b. The construction of large-scale simulations can be very costly and time consuming.

    c. Monte Carlo simulation is only appropriate when randomness is a factor.

9. When a random event can be described by a theoretical distribution, simulation models should incorporate that; empirical distributions can be used for situations not adequately described by a theoretical distribution.

TIPS FOR SOLVING PROBLEMS

A frequently asked question is: "How can I tell which distribution type (normal, Poisson, etc.) to use in solving a simulation problem?"

The answer is that (1) if a theoretical distribution such as the uniform, normal Poisson, or exponential is appropriate, this will be specified in the problem, (2) if an empirical distribution is called for, the frequencies will be given in the problem (see, for instance, Example 19S - 1 in the textbook). In a few instances, the distribution will be given in a more subtle way, such as: "The four outcomes are equally likely." The implication is that each of the four outcomes has a probability of 1/4, or .25.

Another question that often comes up is: "Which random number table should I use?" Use Table 19S-1 for all problems except when a distribution is normal. In the normal case, use Table 19S-2.

Finally, the question of how to obtain the simulated values. Here is a summary of the methods used:

Distribution Type	Get Simulated Values by
Empirical	matching RN with cumulative empirical ranges.
Poisson	matching RN with cumulative probabilities using Appendix Table C.
Uniform	a + .RN(b - a), where a is the lower end and b is the upper end of a uniform distribution.
Exponential	$-1*\ln(.RN)/\lambda$
Normal	mean + RN*(standard deviation).

GLOSSARY

experiment: a simulation run or trial.

Monte Carlo method: a type of simulation involving the use of random numbers to incorporate randomness in models of system behavior.

random: chance; having no discernible pattern.

random number table: a table of numbers which, if read systematically, will not exhibit discernible pattern.

simulation: a descriptive technique used to portray the behavior of a system.

validation: step in the process of model development intended to assure that the model will produce meaningful (realistic) results.

TRUE/FALSE QUESTIONS

1. Managers can use simulation to obtain optimal answers for a wide range of problems.

2. Monte Carlo simulations are deterministic.

3. In many real-life applications, computers are used to conduct simulations.

4. Simulation is a descriptive tool.

5. Simulation is especially useful for situations too complex to be analyzed using mathematical models.

6. When using a random number table, it is important to avoid always starting to read numbers in the same spot.

7. A normal distribution is a theoretical distribution.

8. Monte Carlo simulations produce approximate results rather than exact results.

9. Simulation is often the first choice of decision makers instead of analytic models.

MULTIPLE-CHOICE QUESTIONS

1. Which of the following would not generally be listed as a reason for the popularity of simulation as a managerial tool?

    a. Ability to provide optimal solutions

    b. Useful as a training device

    c. Ability to conduct experiments

    d. Extensive software packages are available

    e. All are reasons for its popularity

2. Given this frequency distribution, the random number, 22, would be interpreted as a demand of:

Demand	Frequency
0	38
1	22
2	22
3	18

    a. 0   b. 1   c. 2   d. 1 or 2   e. 3

3. "Random" means:

    a. normal.

    b. empirical.

    c. exponential.

    d. Poisson.

    e. Chance.

4. The main reason that a large number of runs of a simulation would be made is:

    a. It is a form of sampling, and large samples give more accurate results than small samples.

    b. Computers are usually used, and they can easily handle large runs.

    c. It is part of the scientific approach.

    d. Large run sizes are more apt to provide optimal answers.

    e. None of these.

5. Which one of the following would not be a probable reason for choosing simulation as a decision-making tool?

    a. An intuitive approach doesn't seem applicable and the situation is too complex for a mathematical model.

    b. There is a limited time in which to obtain results.

    c. Good results have been obtained in the past using simulation.

    d. Users are able to understand the model.

    e. All of these are probable reasons for choosing simulations.

PROBLEMS

1. The Orange Octagon Discount Department Store sells snowblowers during the winter months. Snowblowers cost $175.00 each and sell for $395.00. The manager knows that the volume of sales is not large, as indicated by the following data on the number of snowblowers that were sold in each week during the past two selling seasons, which contained 20 weeks each: 0, 1, 3, 1, 2, 0, 3, 4, 2, 1, 4, 2, 0, 2, 0, 0, 2, 0, 1. 3, 1, 1, 1, 3, 3, 2, 2, 0, 4, 1, 1, 0, 2, 2, 0, 1, 3, 1, 3 snowblowers. The manager has decided to start the season with four snowblowers on hand. Only snowblowers on hand at the beginning of the week can be sold. Additional snowblowers can be ordered from the supplier, with a two-week lead time, and the manager plans to order two of them whenever the quantity on hand falls to two or less at the end of the week. Use the random numbers that follow to simulate this policy for 10 weeks: 491, 631, 139, 502, 006, 856, 904, 91, 821, 757.

   a. What is the empirical probability distribution for the weekly sales of snowblowers?

   b. What random numbers go with each value of the random variable?

   c. Construct a table in the style of Example 19S-2b(2) in your textbook, showing the history of the inventory of snowblowers for the 10-week period.

   d. How many snowblowers were sold? How much gross margin was made?

   e. How many sales were lost? What was the dollar amount of the loss?

   f. What is your evaluation of the policy?

2. The number of ambulance calls can be represented by a Poisson distribution with a mean of four per day. Obtain the Poisson distribution from Table C in the Appendix of your textbook and use the following random numbers to simulate six days of ambulance calls: 005, 820, 471, 187, 177, 341.

   a. Which random numbers go with each value of the random variable?

   b. Construct a table in the style of Solved Problem I in your textbook to show the history of the six days.

3. The daily sales of unleaded gasoline at the self-serve pump can be represented by a normal curve with a mean of 300 gallons and a standard deviation of 30 gallons. Use row 8, columns 1, 2, 3, 4, in Table 19S-2 in your textbook to simulate four days of gasoline sales.

4. (One step beyond) Use an EXCEL spreadsheet to simulate ten days of gasoline sales for the self-serve pump in problem #3. This will require the use of EXCEL's Analysis ToolPak VBA. To see if it is installed in your system, click on TOOLS and look for Data Analysis at the bottom of the list. If it is there, you are ready to proceed. If not, click on Add-Ins and select Analysis ToolPak VBA. Data Analysis should now appear in your TOOLS menu.

   a. How should the problem be entered on the spreadsheet?

   b. What are the daily sales?

5. The length of time which a customer spends pumping gasoline at the self-serve pump can be represented by a negative exponential distribution with a mean of 2 minutes. Use these four random numbers to simulate four customers pumping gasoline: 84275, 07523, 33362, 64270.

   a. What is the value of λ?

   b. What are the four times?

6. (One step beyond) The plant manager knows that in the production of fluorescent light tubes, 6 percent will turn out to be defective; the remainder will be satisfactory. Use rows 10-12 in Table 19S-1 in your textbook to simulate the production of 36 fluorescent light tubes.

    a. Which random numbers go with each type of fluorescent tube?

    b. What is the sequence of satisfactory (S) and defective (D) tubes.

    c. What percent of the 36 tubes are defective?

    d. Is the plant manager mistaken in the 6% figure?

CHAPTER 19S   SIMULATION

True/False

Question	Answer	Glossary/ Key Idea	Textbook ref. page
1	F	8	846
2	F	G, 3	848
3	T		856
4	T	G, 1,8	846
5	T	2	846
6	T		849
7	T		853
8	T		858
9	F	8	857

Multiple-Choice

Question	Answer	Glossary/ Key Idea	Textbook ref. page
1	a	8	846
2	a		849-850
3	e		848
4	a	4	850-851
5	b	8	846

SOLUTIONS TO PROBLEMS

1.   a, b.

x	f	p	Cumulative Probability	Random Numbers
0	9	.225	.225	001-225
1	12	.300	.525	226-525
2	9	.225	.750	526 750
3	7	.175	.925	751-925
4	3	.075	1.000	926-1000
Totals	40	1.000		

c.

Week	Random Number	Demand	Sales	Quantity Ordered	Quantity Received
1	491	1*	1	0	0
2	631	2	2	2	0
3	139	0	0	2**	0
4	502	1	1	2	2
5	006	0	0	0	2
6	856	3	3	0	2
7	904	3	3	2	0
8	091	0	0	2	0
9	821	3	0***	0	2
10	757	3	2	2	2
Totals		16	12		

*491 comes between 226 and 525 and designates X = 1.

**Since the inventory contains 1 snowblower at the end of the third week.

***Because the beginning inventory is 0.

Week	Beginning Inventory	Sales	Receipts	Ending Inventory
1	4	1	0	3
2	3	2	0	1
3	1	0	0	1
4	1	1	2	2
5	2	0	2	4
6	4	3	2	3
7	3	3	0	0
8	0	0	0	0
9	0	0	2	2
10	2	2	2	2

d. The total of the sales column is 12 snowblowers. The gross margin = 12(395 - 175) = $2,640.

e. The difference between the total of the demand column and the total of the sales column is 4 snowblowers. The gross margin lost = 4(395 - 175) = $880.

f. While 10 weeks is a very small sample, a tentative hypothesis is that more snowblowers could be sold if the order quantity were increased.

2.   a.

Number of Calls	Cumulative Probability	Random Number Range
0	.018	001 018
1	.092	019 - 092
2	.238	093 - 238
3	.433	239 - 433
4	.629	434 - 629
5	.785	630 - 785
6	.889	786 - 889
7	.949	890 - 949
8	.979	950 - 979
9	.992	980 - 992
10	.997	993 - 997
11	.999	998 - 999
12	1.000	1,000

b.

Day	Random Number	Number of Calls
1	005	0*
2	820	6
3	471	4
4	187	2
5	177	2
6	341	3

*005 comes between 001 and 018 and designates X = 0.

3.

Day	Random Number	Sales
1	2.40	372.00*
2	0.38	311.40
3	−0.15	295.50
4	−1.04	268.80

*Sales = Mean + (R.N.)(standard deviation) = 300 + (2.40)(30) = 372.00 gal.

4.   a.   Click on TOOLS; DATA ANALYSIS; RANDOM NUMBER GENERATOR. Number of Variables = 1; Number of Random Numbers = 10; Distribution = Normal; Mean = 300; Standard Deviation = 30; Random Seed = 1776*; Output Range = C3:C12.

b.

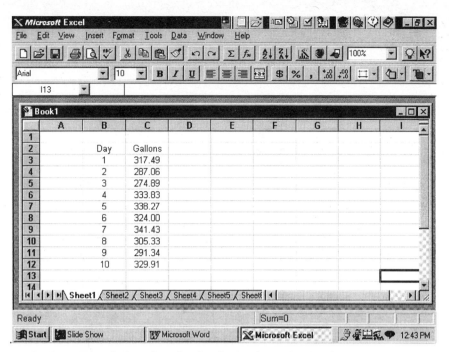

*NOTE: The choice of a value for the Seed Number is arbitrary. Experiment with some other seeds, such as your birthday in the form of 62175, perhaps.

5. a. The service time: $1/\lambda = 2$ minutes, and $\lambda = .50$.

    b. $p(T) = \exp(-0.5t)$, and $t = -(1/\lambda)(\ln(.RN))$.

    c.

Week	Random Number	ln(.RN)	Pumping Time (min.)*
1	.84275	−0.1711	0.3422
2	.07523	−2.5872	5.1744
3	.33362	−1.0978	2.1958
4	.64270	−0.4421	0.8842

*Pumping Time $= -2 \cdot \ln(.RN)$

6. a.

Type of Tube	Random Number Range
Satisfactory	01-94
Defective	95-100

    b. Reading Table 19S-1 horizontally: S S S S S S S S S S S S S S S S S S S S S S S S S S S D S S S S S S S S S S S.

    c. $p = 1/36 = 2.78\%$.

d.   Not necessarily; the 6% defective tubes will occur over the long run but not for any very short period. (For the statistician: the standard error of the sample percent, if the true percent of defective tubes is, in fact, 6% is 3.96% and it is easy to draw a sample with p = 2.78% from a population with 6% defective items.)